A PASSIONATE PRODIGALITY

By the same author

BECKFORD: a biography
A BIBLIOGRAPHY OF THE WORKS OF WILLIAM BECKFORD
THE THIRD REPUBLIC OF FRANCE
CULTURE AND SURVIVAL
THE DREYFUS CASE: a reassessment

After the attack at La Boisselle, 9 July 1916

GUY CHAPMAN

A Passionate Prodigality

FRAGMENTS OF AUTOBIOGRAPHY

'... to drink of the ashes of dead relations, a passionate prodigality. He that hath the ashes of his friend, hath an everlasting treasure.'

URN BURIAL

BUCHAN & ENRIGHT, PUBLISHERS
London

First published in 1933 by Ivor Nicholson & Watson Ltd
Second edition published in 1965 by MacGibbon & Kee Ltd

This edition first published in 1985 by
Buchan & Enright, Publishers, Limited
53 Fleet Street, London EC4Y 1BE

British Library Cataloguing in Publication Data

Chapman Guy
A passionate prodigality. — (Echoes of war)
1. World War, 1914–1918 — Campaigns — Western
2 World War, 1914–1918 — Personal narratives, British
I. Title II. Series
940.4'144'0924 D544
ISBN 0-907675-42-5

Printed in Great Britain by
Redwood Burn Limited, Trowbridge, Wiltshire and
bound by Pegasus Bookbinding, Melksham, Wiltshire

TO THE MEMORY OF

CERTAIN ✠ SOLDIERS

WHO HAVE NOW BECOME A SMALL

QUANTITY OF CHRISTIAN DUST THIS

FAINT REANIMATION

AND FOR

R. A. SMITH

CONTENTS

All the characters in this narrative are or were actual persons: in a few cases, for obvious reasons, names have been changed.

A PASSIONATE PRODIGALITY

PART ONE

THE AMATEURS

'In such a condition there is . . . no account of time ; no Arts ; no Letters ; . . . and the life of man, solitary, poor, nasty, brutish and short.'

LEVIATHAN

I

'... *mere militia ... which are to be looked upon only as temporary excrescences bred out of the distemper of the State.*'

BLACKSTONE'S COMMENTARIES

FOR a long time I used to think of myself as part of a battalion, and not as an individual. During all that time the war, the forms and colours of that experience, posssessed a part of my senses. My life was involved with the lives of other men, a few living, some dead.

It is only now that I can separate myself from them. For that and other reasons this is more strictly the account of a company and begins in July, 1915, when a battalion of the New Army set out for France.

I was loath to go. I had no romantic illusions. I was not eager, or even resigned to self-sacrifice, and my heart gave back no answering throb to the thought of England. In fact, I was very much afraid; and again, afraid of being afraid, anxious lest I should show it. Nevertheless, I concluded that it was easiest to meet a fate already beginning to overawe, as an integral figure in the battalion I had been born into.

As yet it had little but familiarity to commend it. When (after three months in the Inns of Court and a strenuous course at the Staff College) I joined it on the eve of 1915, I was shocked by my first contact with the New Army. It was not so much the circumstances; the dull little south coast watering-place in winter; the derelict palazzo, the head-quarters, facing on one side the tumbling grey sea and on the other an unkempt field; it was not the men in shabby blue clothes and forage caps with their equipment girt about them with bits of string: it was the obvious incapacity and amateurishness of the whole outfit which depressed. The 13th had been broken off from a swarm of men at the depot some three months earlier, and from then left almost completely to its own devices. It never had more than three regular officers, and those very senior and very retired, two from the Indian Army and not one from the regiment. In consequence it learned nothing of the traditions of its name—few could have told you anything of Alma or Albuera—and knew nothing of its four regular battalions. Below these seniors lay a heterogeneous mass of majors, captains and subalterns from every walk of life; colonial policemen, solicitors, ex-irregulars, planters, ex-rankers, and in three cases pure *chevaliers d'industrie*. Many displayed only too patently their intention of getting through the war as quietly, comfortably, and as profitably as they could manage. They effectively discouraged the juniors from demonstrations of excessive zeal, and by sheer negation tried to stifle our hunger for information. They failed, but nevertheless, the miasma of petty jealousy, bickering and foolish intrigue, which surrounded them, was the cause of much melancholy and profanity in us juniors. In the ranks there were a few time-expired N.C.O.s, among whom one was found giving the fire-commands of forty years before, 'Ready—present—fire.' The ten months' training, which the battalion went through before it reached France, was therefore a compound of enthusiasm and empiricism on the part of the junior subalterns and the other ranks. Even now I am amazed at the zeal which induced some of us after dinner to push matches representing platoons about the table, uttering words of command in hoarse whispers, or on Sunday mornings climb the frosty, wind-cropped downs to practise map-reading and marching by the compass. We had no one to explain things to us. We had to get our text-books by heart before we could impart a crumb of information to our platoons. We seized on and devoured every fragment of practical experience which came our way, gobbled whole the advice contained in those little buff pamphlets entitled *Notes from the Front*, advice, alas! out of date before it was published. We listened hopefully to the lectures of general officers who seemed happier talking of Jubbulpore than of Ypres. We pondered the jargon of experts, each convinced that his peculiar weapon, machine gun, rifle, bayonet, or bomb, was the one designed to bring the war to a satisfactory conclusion. We were inclined to resist their pedantry, suspecting that in truth they knew little more than ourselves; and we—we knew nothing. We were in fact amateurs, and though we should stoutly have denied it, in our hearts amateurs we knew ourselves to be, pathetically anxious to achieve the status of the professional. The testing of the results of all these pains and ardours now lay elsewhere.

* * *

The bugle blew the 'Fall in', and the companies clustered on the edge of the camp poured themselves into the mould of a battalion. I told off my sections and stood at ease, noticing with an uneasy eye that the sergeant of the platoon in front was hiccoughing gently and swaying on his feet. The colonel gave the word and the battalion moved off. The band brayed *The British Grenadiers*. The sun shone its bravest. A group of ladies in summer frocks waved handkerchiefs. We had started for France.

The train carried us slowly through the south of England, hopeful by following branch lines to be inconspicuous. But the men hung their newly shaved heads out of windows, waved, roared, shrieked, yelled, sang, and defeated official precaution. In the corner of my compartment, an elderly major slept. He knew all about departures, and was thankful for the opportunity of a few hours' peace. The rest of us chattered away about our anticipations. We were all very young and girded impatiently at the slowness of the train. At one point I saw the house of an elderly friend and hoped I might survive to drink his port again. The train seemed abominably dilatory. Our first juvenile excitement waned as we began to suffer that other juvenile softness, hunger. Darkness came down. We had now been six hours on our way and fell to debating whether after all we were to embark. Then a quiet voice said, 'Folkestone'.

The boat lay at the lower pier. We clattered down the iron steps and thrust our way on board. In spite of protests, the junior subaltern—myself—was detailed for duty somewhere in the bottom of the ship. I seated myself on a flight of steps and trusted that I should not be sick. The men lay tightly pressed together, rows of green cigars, and a great odour of sweaty, dusty humanity clotted between the decks. A jerky movement was imposed upon our smooth passage. I began to feel qualms. There was a bar in this part of the ship, much frequented by a party of Highlanders returning from leave. As they came down the stairs, each man jolted against me, and at each jolt, my nausea increased. At last, I rose and kicked out the subaltern who was due to relieve me. I climbed wretchedly into the bows. Two destroyers flirted playfully round and about us, making signals at intervals. Someone began to talk of submarines. I didn't care. I looked down into the sea and was very ill.

In my misery, I hardly noticed our entrance into harbour, and was nearly the last to leave the boat. As I staggered on to the quay, burdened with a pack weighing 53 lbs., a rifle, a revolver, field-glasses, a prismatic compass, 120 rounds of rifle ammunition and 24 of revolver, my newly nailed boots shot from under me and I clattered on the pavé. 'Nah then,' roared a voice from the darkness. 'Come on you—always late, blast yer!' I was far too shattered to answer the R.S.M. I tottered up and ran painfully down the quay.

So on the 31st July, 1915, we landed in France. It was one o'clock of the morning. As we swung over the bridge, the band broke into the Marseillaise. Windows were flung up and night-capped heads thrust forth. They were very angry. A stray dog or so joined us; and a small boy attached himself to me, offering the services of his sister—jig-a-jig. I cuffed his head. We began to climb a hill, which rapidly became the side of a house. The band gasped and broke down. A man fainted and was dragged to the side of the road. The pace dwindled to a crawl. As we reached the top, panting, the column of the Grande Armée, rising darkly against the sky, sneered at us from its veteran experience. At the camp, the men tumbled gladly into their tents, and we, after a rapid inspection of our own, elected for the open air. In ten minutes, we were asleep.

We woke in broad sunlight. Women were walking between our prostrate bodies, offering apples. I bought some; they were very sour. Below us, Boulogne preened itself, and the sea was all golden dimples. As soon as I had finished breakfast, the adjutant seized me and bade me go in search of a station called Pont de Briques. I was inclined to grumble until I heard the Colonel declaring that it was a fair day for a route march round Boulogne. I fled thankfully. Chestnut avenues shaded me, and at Pont de Briques I found not only a station but commendable beer. During the afternoon subalterns were permitted one hour in Boulogne in batches of four. We bathed, and later sought the bar of the Folkestone, where we gazed round-eyed at the resplendent figures, rich as Spanish galleons, of the Base Commandant's staff. One specimen, an A.D.C. clad in golden breeches and golden puttees, carrying in his arms a Pekinese, particularly took my fancy. 'See what comes of being good,' I murmured to myself.

Night was falling as we marched down the hill. We waited an hour at Pont de Briques, and then, as if by a miracle, a train clattered in bearing our transport, which had come by way of Havre, the second-in-command, and the quartermaster. We made our first acquaintance with HOMMES 40, CHEVAUX-EN-LONG 8. 'Where are we going?' we asked; but no one could answer us. Captain Burns, the T.O. (a Cockney Fluellen, if ever such existed, a solemn man with a very private sense of humour; on occasions it permitted him to grin and twinkle below and above his heavy cavalry moustache) reproved our excited conjectures. 'You'll find out quite soon enough,' he muttered, 'too soon, may be.'

At length, it may have been some three hours later—those hours spent in sauntering along French railways contract with the space of years—our train came to a considered halt. We fell in on the platform. A damp board, spelled out by torchlight from end to end, proclaimed this place as Watten—empty information since we had no maps. I was given a bicycle and told to follow the brigade billeting officer. We rode in silence down silent roads, colourless, wreathed in mist. At last at the entrance to a village, he dismounted. 'This is Nortleulinghem. You've got the whole village. Put your men where you like; —and don't wake the *maire*': a supererogatory piece of advice. I should not dare to wake anything so august. Too shy to question him as to where Nortleulinghem might be by the map, I saluted and he faded into the mist.

I walked to the crossroads and in the waking dawn looked up and down. Everywhere there was silence; not even a cock crowed. Faint misgivings as to whether I was or was not in the war zone beset me. It was better to be on the safe side. Unbuttoning my holster and loosening my revolver, I strode into Nortleulinghem and began to explore. A charming village with well-built houses and barns. Trees heavy with fruit bowed over walls. A field of corn on the hill-side looked almost ripe for cutting. A lean cat came out, yawned and was friendly. A dog woke into passionate yelps. I chalked signs and numbers on doors. Still not a gun fired, not a rifle. Where was this fabled war?

At last there was the sound of marching feet and the battalion came in sight. I reported to the adjutant, and then asked diffidently, 'Where exactly is Nortleulinghem, sir?' 'Where?' he echoed. 'Oh, about ten minutes behind St. Omer.' I withdrew confusedly.

Four days passed rapidly in Nortleulinghem, days on which we drew oddments of equipment, learned to put on our gas-masks, started to censor letters. The battle atmosphere began to pervade us. Captain Burns stalked the village, upbraiding subalterns he found wanting. ''Ere,' he would say, 'where's your revolver? Suppose a body of Oolans was to come down that hill, where'ud you be? Don't answer me back. Go and put it on.'

On the fifth morning we resumed our march. I had carefully mislaid my rifle.

II

'Wolcum, Innocentes, everichone.'

It was a night of august splendour. I lay back and contemplated those flaming stars which trooped in droves across the sky as if all heaven were in migration.

The battalion had marched all day, and late that afternoon had come down by-lanes—for our divisional artillery filled all the roads with the clatter and dust of their wheels—to this village, Campagne by Arques. There were no billets, only a few rooms for senior officers. My company bivouacked beneath some slender apple trees in a meadow behind headquarters, its officers in the middle. The men had washed, fed, and had their feet inspected; and having explored the village and found nothing, had retired to sleep under the little bivvies they had built, two by two or four by four, out of their ground-sheets. The long dewy grass was soft and threw up its gentle scent; and the men lay smoking the butts of their fags, as they listened to the dying fall of 'Lights Out'.

We had been six days in France and were slowly moving up the line to go through a period of instruction at the hands of more experienced troops. We needed it. The 13th were as raw as any other battalion in the New Armies.

But in this lush grass, staring at those wheeling stars, with the consciousness of two hundred other souls of the company lying round me, no better and no worse than myself, there came a thrill of intense happiness that I was one of this favoured group of adventurers, whatever our destiny might be. And while I savoured that mood, there was carried from the distance the sound of tramping feet and the voice of men singing:

O je veux quand je meurs qu'on m'enterre
O je veux quand je meurs qu'on m'enterre
Dans le cave,
oui-oui-oui,
Dans le cave,
oui-oui-oui,
Dans le cave où le vin est bon;
Dans le cave,
oui-oui-oui,
Dans le cave,
oui-oui-oui,
Dans le cave où le vin est bon.

A French labour company was marching back to billets; and as the deep chorus of that old song died away to a rhythmical *oui-oui-oui* . . . *oui-oui-oui*, I fell asleep.

* * *

The heat on the next morning was a hammer-blow of the August sun; and there was no wind. Beneath a burning sky, molten as a looking-glass, I set out with a troupe of orderlies to explore the billeting accommodation at a place named St. Sylvestre. On army bicycles, heavy as chariots, we slogged along the road to Hazebrouck, falling or being pitched off at short intervals. Under the myriad heels, hoofs, and wheels which had crossed it during the last year, the pavé had lost all trace of evenness, and lay jagged and furrowed, while the earth at each side ran up and down like billows in a seascape.

St. Sylvestre was a straggling village on the Cassel-Bailleul road. A long straight funnel of poplars enclosed the road northwards; and crowning the narrowing lines of trees, hung the orchards and roofs of Cassel, towers for some fast-pricking Gawaine to adventure.

As at Campagne, billets were scarce, six small homesteads. There were few barns, and the owners, for the most part women, were cold and uncivil. Perhaps my barbarous French was the cause, for one angular hag looked blankly at me when I asked if the men could sleep in her fields.

'Dans les champs?' she replied. 'Pas compris.'

'Mais les champs, les prés . . . voila!' I waved an arm towards the pasture.

'A-ah, les champs!' she broke out, rhyming the word with tarn.

I went back with my guides to the crossroads to meet the brigade. The air had grown heavier, and the sun blazed on remorselessly. At length the head of the column appeared. We could see it sagging as it toiled wearily up the hill. Four hundred yards short of us, the whistle blew, and the leading battalion slid over in a heap at the side of the road, like a hoarding tossed down by the wind.

At last the 13th came up. When I look back, it is always a battalion marching which I see. As I watched it marching into billets, the men, their jackets soiled with the dust of the road, their faces scarlet beneath the layer of grime through which the sweat had streaked furrows, their shoulders bent and narrowed under the strain of the ungainly packs burdened with all the little extras by which kind friends and mothers had tried to lighten the moment of farewell; the young platoon commanders anxious, and though as laden as their men, energetically passing up and down the ranks, exhorting and encouraging, sometimes bearing two, even three rifles of those they found faltering; the robuster sergeants, also bearing an extra rifle, grimly determined that at least their little lot should not fail, giving the step in voices hoarse with reiteration, with parching, with reproof; I was overwhelmed by the simplicity of all these men, with the comely innocence which in spite of the obscenity and profanity breaking from harsh throats, was borne above them like a banner.

As they staggered in that afternoon, someone passing asked: 'Good billets?' I shook my head. My gesture was quickly understood. Voices from the ranks took up a cry which I was often to hear again: 'What? No billets? Oh, lucky old Firteenf.' And then from No. 16 platoon: 'What abaht pore old sixteen! Pore old ragged arse of the battalion.'

We remained two days at St. Sylvestre, gloomy days. It rained, and in the intervals we tried our sodden platoons' tempers with such trivialities as kit inspections and musketry. Then we moved a square nearer the line. Bailleul, ancient fief of the Holy Roman Empire, still mounted by its lovely rosy belfry, was now as anglicized as ever a French town may be. We dined well, almost luxuriously, in the salle-à-manger of some small hotel, served by a dark and flashing-eyed woman; and later I slept gratefully between sheets in a nunnery. Bailleul remains in my mind chiefly by the recollection of a group of officers standing in the square while children played round them with an ancient football. Once the ball brushed the Colonel's legs, whereon Captain Burns stepped forward and, addressing himself to the delinquents, said very slowly: ' 'Ere, you boys, sortez that ball.'

Bailleul was a flown memory. On the following afternoon I was despatched on my inevitable courier's progress to find accommodation in Armentières. Two companies and a skeleton headquarters were to go up to build part of a support line. Armentières, as I rode in, seemed a depressing city, shabby, unkempt, reddish in colour. Every now and then a noise as of distant thunder made me wonder. Guns, I concluded. I had been given the wrong rendezvous. After a long hunt I beat up the man who was to allot the billets, and left him with several addresses in my hand and the warning 'not to hang about in the square'. By the time I had identified the various lodgings, I was caught up by a messenger, who told me that half the battalion was halted in the

Place. On panic feet, I ran down the street and found the companies sprawled in the very spot I had been warned against. Major Ardagh treated my urgency with a fatherly smile, as the men shifted into their gear. No alarm, no excursion, as I was to learn later, would ever move that thin little wisp from a whole-hearted contempt for warnings of inexperienced disaster. He had only joined us a few days before we embarked, a frail figure, and a thin face faded by African sun to parchment, faded like his jacket, which bore faded ribbons.

The two companies lay indignantly in a concrete-floored warehouse of the most chastening type, while the company officers were presented with a large mansion from which all the furniture except one bed and one table had been removed. A luxurious bathroom was discovered on the third floor; Sidney Adler tried it at once. The few gallons of rusty water would have dissuaded the most fanatic of bath fiends. We dragged our valises into the conservatory, which seemed to offer the least adamantine floor, and got down to it.

Only four officers were required on the following day, and I was left behind. They returned in the evening excited and talkative. *They had been shelled.* It was a matter of surprise and importance. Those of us who had been left behind were filled with jealousy, and plied these veterans with questions. What did it sound like? Did it make a large explosion, a large hole? Had they heard the gun-fire? However, the next day answered our curiosity and excitement.

In a morning still opaque with mist, we crossed the river frontier into Belgium. I speculated vaguely whether this was the very bank up which Milady had shinned to escape the executioner of Lille. We passed through untidy suburbs; here and there a smashed house. I was surprised that the others were still inhabited. Presently we broke up into platoons and again into sections. We passed up a tree-lined road and entered a shallow trench through a field of standing corn. On the further side we came out into an orchard with a farmhouse and a low breastwork at its edge. The men already knew their tasks and started filling and piling sandbags. Spencer, Leader, and I squatted on the berm of a trench. Suddenly, out of nowhere, came a whisper, an insistent, ominous sound, growing rapidly in urgency. There was no need of warning. I slid into the trench. So did the others. Our first shell burst some hundred yards beyond us in a cornfield and did no damage. Leader laughed. I detested him and detested the shell. More shells followed, falling in haphazard fashion about our work. When one more accurate than the rest fell just outside the breastwork, the men cheered. After eight or nine, the battery ceased fire. We began to conceive a contempt for German gunnery, though a small voice within me refused to silence its sinister prophecies, which were confirmed next morning, when a man bolting across the road was hit and horribly mutilated.

So daily we digged and wired round this farmhouse, which in spite of its unfailing ration of shells, was still occupied by the farmer and his family. On the last day, a thunderstorm drove us to refuge in the kitchen. At the same time, the now familiar battery opened fire. In between the roars of the thunder, we could hear the swish and explosion of the shells. The woman of the house showed no sign of fear, though she sent two brats down to the cellar, but with an impassive face busied herself about the fire, now and then hushing a baby, born, I must suppose, to the clatter of musketry up yonder at Ploegsteert.

During the off days, we killed time as best we could, gaining our first experience of the greatest bane of the life of a soldier, boredom, *cafard*, or whatever you call it. Perhaps we subalterns found it most irksome. Our seniors, or some of them, found their medicine in bars or other amusements: but we were less habited to these wayside pleasures. Our edges were still too keen and undulled for us to blunt them in this fashion. Idling in the mess on an afternoon, Sidney Adler, the most irresponsible of our group, suddenly remarked: 'X is with that woman again. He is a dirty dog. And he had that thing in our billet at Bailleul. And he's only been married a few weeks.' 'Too bad,' we nodded in agreement. We felt that X was letting the battalion down. A qualm of distrust invaded us. We had known all about X, Y, and Z's amours in England; they didn't matter. But over here. . . .

The digging tour ended. We were joined by the remainder of the battalion and housed in what must have been a girls' boarding school: hundreds of small neat bedsteads crowded the upper floors. The house was high, but in this flat country not tall enough to top the buildings eastwards and we could only see a barrier of roofs and chimneys. Occasionally a shell fell in the neighbourhood with the peculiar viciousness the echo of streets lends to the intensity of the down-sweeping sound.

From here we were despatched with our platoons to do 24-hour periods of instruction in the line. Our own 9th battalion, which had preceded us to France two months earlier, were the veterans told off to teach us the job. On my first evening towards sunset, a negligent figure with a rifle, a cotton bandolier and a gas-mask greeted me at the corner of a factory where a new suburb was just growing. The fields on either side bore the look of those wan meadows you see on the outkirts of London, stretched ready to be stifled by the jerry-builder's hutches; or was I wrong, had houses already stood here and paid the penalty for venturing so close to the war? There was no time to find the answer; for our guide led us round the corner of the blind and staring factory and descended into a ditch between high walls. This communication trench, I discovered later, was not generally used; but in consideration of our inexperience, we were permitted its joys. It was just wide enough to accommodate a man with a full pack, and about seven feet deep, so that one's vision was limited to a patch of darkening sky and the shoulders of the man in front. Its floor was covered with a foot of tensely glutinous mud. We drove slowly through this morass, wrenching out each foot before putting it down again. Darkness fell. After what seemed half a night, the guide stopped and said: 'There's a road 'ere. See and 'urry over it. There's a machine gun on it. See? One at a time.' We tore ourselves singly from the mud and bundled on to the road, diving towards a dark opening in the other bank. The machine gun threw a few desultory shots past us. The bullets cracked sharply overhead. We tumbled into another trench and went on. This one was narrow, too, but shallower and duck-boarded. We moved more quickly. We could see lights rising and falling in front of us, and the noises interpreted themselves as rifles and machine guns firing. Suddenly someone said: 'Hullo,' and Smith, my company commander, loomed up. In a flush of Very-light, I caught an amused grin on his lean ascetic face.

'Is this the front line?' I asked. 'That's it.' He pointed to a dark wall. Someone else bustled out of the darkness. 'What platoon are you? No. 2. Send your men up to the right, two by two. Your platoon sergeant? He'll go with mine.'

The men moved on, and someone guided me to a clean and pleasant summer-house with boarded walls, decorated with Kirchner drawings and portraits of English beauties torn from the *Tatler*. 'We'll find you a dugout later,' said the company commander. 'Drop your pack and come round.'

The trench was not a trench at all. The bottom may have been two feet below ground level. An enormous breastwork rose in the darkness some ten or more feet high. All about us there was an air of bustle. Men came and went bearing mysterious burdens. Men were lifting filled sandbags on to the parapet and beating them into the wall with shovels.

Bullets cracked in the darkness. Flares from the German side, thrown further than usual, illuminated a shoulder, a cheekbone, a straining thigh. Every now and then a figure would appear on the skyline and drop skilfully on to the firestep. 'Be careful coming in over the top,' said my guide. 'One of my blighters sat on a bayonet the other night. Care to see the wire?'

I followed him gingerly over the edge of the wall, and slid clumsily down a ramp of greasy sandbags. A small party was working swiftly over a tangle of some dark stuff. Two of my own were being inducted into the ceremony of wiring. ' 'Old it tight, chum,' growled one figure. He proceeded to smite a heavy baulk of timber with a gigantic maul, the head of which had been cunningly muffled in sandbags. The noise seemed enough to waken the German army, but there was no answering excitement from the dull hummock across the way. One of our machine guns broke into Aristophanic chorus over our heads, which roused an acquaintance opposite. But the party in the wire went on with its work unmoved. 'He's shooting at our parapet,' said my guide, in a loud voice. 'We're quite all right down here.'

As the night passed, the labour grew less and less tumultuous. Men came in over the parapet, settled down in the corners of firebays and dropped asleep. A sentry in each embrasure, with one of the 13th, watched raptly over the top. Here and there a man boiled up a can of tea over a tiny fire skilfully dug in the side of a traverse. This domesticity seemed completely fantastic.

About two o'clock I was shown a doorway. 'You can sleep in there. The roof's quite good.' I found myself in a tiny cell, six foot by four. A stump of candle burned in a niche carved out of the clay wall. Half the space was occupied by a bed of wire stretched on poles. I lay down and blew out the light. Mysterious rustlings became audible, grew louder; there was a scamper of little feet. Rats, I guessed and shuddered. I relit my stump. The rustling abruptly ceased, and I dozed off. . . . I came back to the surface with a jerk. I could hear something scrabbling beside my ear. I turned my head and caught a glimpse of what looked like a small pink monkey, clambering up the wall. With a spasm of disgust, I threw myself off the bed and bolted into the mess, where I sat shuddering and retching until the subaltern on duty pushed his head in and called 'Stand-to'. I was not yet hardened to rats.

I felt my way behind him into the darkness. Over the breastwork, the blackness was fading. The desultory shooting of the early hours of the night had died away to an occasional shot. On the duckboards there was the sound of feet stamping to restore the circulation and put to flight the dawn chill that strikes a man who has slept in his clothes. As the light hardened, I looked over the parapet. What I had expected, I do not know; certainly not this derelict dump which lay between us and the inert sandbag wall two hundred yards away, the German line, guarded by its leaf-brown belt of patched and rusty wire; not the diseased stumpy trees in the orchard behind; not the tumbled-down gape-roofed house over there on the left, nor the unkempt skyline, growing stronger every moment as the sun rose.

'We'd better get down,' said my companion. 'Their snipers will start soon. You can't show your head in daylight.' 'Stand down,' he passed along the line. In five minutes, little fires of dry chips were brisking up along the trench. In alternate bays, men pitched their eyes to periscopes. Looking through one, you could see patches of smoke rising from the line opposite. The war lapsed and men broke their fast.

The morning passed quietly. A rare rifle shot echoed. A few shells passed overhead travelling to the back areas. Parties came and went with wood, wire, and sandbags. The sanitary men bent over their malodorous task. Presently Blake came along. His battered clown's face was that of a man who has discovered an awful joy. 'Seen ——? It's the funniest sight in France. He's as nervous as a cat and speaks in a hoarse whisper for fear the enemy will overhear him. The men can't make him out.'

The afternoon passed even more quietly than the morning. At dark, Walter Spencer arrived with No. 4 and we dragged ourselves back through the mud to Houplines. Two nights later we returned. We arrived in what to some veteran of Albuera might have seemed a battle. As we reached the front line a deafening noise broke out. From both sides machine guns racketed, rifle-fire crashed. Bullets cracked overhead or came spinning past with a sharp whine. The men were crowded on the fire-step, blazing off S.A.A. as if victory dwelt in their exertions. There was a certain air of levity about the performance, a bank holiday spirit. The men were cheering and cheering: it was very like a football match. After two minutes, it died down, and we were left in an empty world, in which, so sudden was the stoppage, the only movement seemed to be the Boche machine-gun bullets racing overhead.

'We're just giving them two minutes' rapid,' it was explained. 'a kind of celebration for the gun-boats they've lost off Riga.'

The next days passed exactly as the first. We learned trench routine; and so far as my company was concerned, not one shell was aimed at the acre of barren earth on which we squatted. We bade our instructors good-bye and marched for the last time down the Houplines road. Orders came for us to rendezvous at Bailleul. The next morning we set out, our term of finishing school over, nominally trained soldiers. I tried to reckon up what we had learned. It was very little. We could put up wire, keep ourselves clean. We knew something about ration parties and other fatigues, and we had learned to build sandbags into a wall which looked strong, a seductive art, too seductive, as we were soon to learn. I think that most of us had been disappointed. We had keyed ourselves to such a pitch of expectation that the reality proved a trifle flat. For my own part, I was vastly relieved.

III

'Fontaneto fontem dicunt, villam quoque rustici,
ubi strages et ruina Francorum de sanguine;
orrent campi, orrent silvae, orrent ipse paludes.'

ANGILBERT

At one o'clock in the morning two days later, I stiffly climbed down from the train at a place named Doullens. It was not marked on any map which I possessed. I reported to the Staff-Captain and mounted my clumsy bicycle. We pulled out on to a moonlit road and began to climb a long steep hill. On and on we went along a wide road, bordered with poplars. At length we turned off and came to a village, Grenas. We were led into a tall gaunt building, and told to sleep. By now I was growing excited. At the corner where we had turned off the main road to this place, the other finger of the signpost had indicated Arras. Ghosts of Cyrano and the Duke of Marlborough flitted dimly through my memory, but offered no help. The British Army was tucked away miles to the north. Were we about to join the French?

Grenas was a sordid wretch. It possessed only two houses, occupied by the headquarters of the two battalions sent here. After a brief inspection of the few barns and odd rooms available, officers and men preferred to bivouac. 'Château de puce,' 'Hôtel des punaises,' were not the worst comments freely inscribed on the walls by the poilus who had preceded us. Our decision was mocked. The sky opened and for six days we crept to and fro, sodden and curst.

On the seventh, we moved ten miles eastwards to St. Amand. As I halted my billeting party in Pas, a group of French soldiers gathered round us. One plump poilu, who knew London, tried to impress his friends with his linguistic culture, but 'Regent Street?' 'Oui, oui, près de Laystaire

Squar,' seemed the limit of the conversation. One more night. . . .

'Here, you, go and find the road to Bienvillers. There's a map.' I picked up *Lens 11*, which (along with *Hazebrouck 5a*) was to be my constant bedfellow for another three years, and set out. After I had gone a mile and examined my map, I knew I was on the right road and came back. During the afternoon we got our orders. Two companies were to take over billets from the French in Bienvillers, two at a hamlet called Hannescamps. We set out in the gathering darkness, myself at the head of the column. From the east there came no sound, not the echo of a shot, nor the dull explosion of a gun, a trick of this rolling country where one valley seizes on a sound and will not share it with its neighbour. Since singing and talking had been forbidden, there was nothing to be heard but the dogged tramp of feet. Mist rose as the gloom deepened, and in front of us no genial flares rose and fell to prove that man was still alive. The colonel rode uneasily beside me. It seemed a long march. On my calculation we should have covered the distance in an hour. Yet at the first halt there was still no outline of our destination. An awful thought rose in me that my reading of the map had been at fault, and that we were on the wrong road. I did not confide this horrifying speculation to the adjutant, but when the whistle blew, scuttled on ahead. Thank heaven, a dark mass lay in the valley just over the next rise. I boldly reported it as Bienvillers, and slunk back to my platoon. Slowly we penetrated the streets, Even the thick darkness failed to conceal the fact that this was a war-soiled village. Against the sky, skeleton roofs and pierced walls heaved up.

A few lights glimmered through sacks masking glassless windows. Busy shadows dipped and mopped behind them. We shuffled to a halt. The word was passed for officers. 'Get your platoons into those barns,' said Smith; 'no man is to go beyond the barrier up the road in daylight.'

We turned into the courtyard of a farm. Some battered barns, wooden frames supporting daub and wattle walls, offered shelter. The men clattered in and we rejoined Smith. 'That's company headquarters over there; but we can't get in till the French commandant goes. He's in bed now.' We roamed disconsolately about the courtyard. The men had settled down. A chilly moon rose over a group of tall elms, and peered at us through the mist. It grew colder and colder. At last, worn out, we crept into the entrance of the house, and laying our heads on our packs, fell asleep on the tiles. I have a recollection of a light suddenly flooding on us at some time and of a tall figure stumbling with many ejaculations over our bodies. I take it to have been the French commandant. When, cold and stiff, I woke, faint light was peeping through the doorway. I rose and stretched into the air. On the other side two of the batmen were busy over a blazing fire, the fuel a derelict pigstye which they had broken down. Frost, Smith's man, gave me his bull-terrier grin as I held my shivering hands to the blaze. 'We'll have some tea in five minutes, as soon as the captain comes back. D'you think you could get us some eggs, sir? They won't sell us any. They don't seem to understand us in these parts.'

As I came out of the farm, some of the relieved French troops were plodding slowly down the muddy road. They were cuirassiers, little men, bow-legged like dismounted toy cavalry. They wore rusty breastplates, and their tall brass helmets were covered by a khaki cap, below which the horsehair plumes dangled.

This end of the village was smashed and deserted, but up a by-road I spied a small house with chickens running about it. A middle-aged woman answered my knock. She was very willing to sell her eggs and gave me two dozen in a basket for a couple of francs.

'Vous êtes encore tranquille ici, Madame?' I asked.

'Mais oui, Monsieur. Mais c'est triste. Alors, la guerre est triste, n'est ce pas?'

'Pas de peur avec les Boches si près de Bienvillers?'

'Aha, les Boches!' She made a derisive grimace. 'Coupez les gorges, tous, tous.'

I had made the conventional speeches, received the conventional replies, and was able to retire.

We took over trenches that night. The French in the front line had been relieved by one of our rifle battalions; but a new defence scheme—as yet we had not probed the myth of defence schemes—called for two of our companies on the left of the brigade sector. On the way through Hannescamps, a ghost of a village, Leader strolled up. 'What kind of things did you relieve?' he asked; 'I had to take over the barriers from a lot of Moroccans—at least, I think they were Moroccans—great, big black bastards you couldn't see in the dark, except when they showed their teeth—didn't speak any language I could recognize. I collected a chair and sat by the barrier. They kept crowding round me, chattering and grinning in my face. Frightened me to death. Well, so long.' Leader drifted away into the darkness, and we went on our way. It was a weary progress. A light drizzle made the road and the bottom of the communication trench greasy. Every now and then a man burdened with his awkwardly poised equipment would slip and stagger. The French *boyau* was very deep and wide, far deeper than those up in the north. It ran beside the road to Monchy-au-Bois, a village in German hands, and above our heads swayed the slim trunks of the poplar trees sighing for their fate. The night was strangely silent. Only now and again a shot cracked. It was so quiet that one reached the front line without being aware of it.

The platoon shuffled into the narrow labyrinth. The present occupiers stood on the firestep, and as each man of my platoon came opposite to a rifleman, the latter stretched down and passed further along the trench, while the fusilier took his place. The outgoers then passed into a trench about ten feet behind the fire-trench, and so back and down the *boyau*. As soon as the relief was complete, and the order to stand down passed along, one sentry was left in each bay: the rest of the platoon dumped their packs in the shelters and dugouts.

At this period of the war, machine guns were still the ark of the covenant to an infantry battalion: but while the regulars were equipped with Vickers guns, the New Army had been given nothing but the lately invented Lewis gun, mounted on the heavy Vickers tripod, and only four of these. As it was impossible for these four guns to cover the battalion front, the fire-trenches had to be manned by the whole strength of the company throughout the night. At first each bay held three men, two up watching, and one sleeping. At the end of two hours, one of the watchers was relieved by the sleeper, while the other watched for another two hours.

The first night passed, and with the first greyness of dawn, our heads were eagerly peeping over the parapet to see what lay round and in front of us. Gradually an outline was blocked in against the paling sky, the outline of hills dominating our trenches. A thick wood became visible, filling the centre of the background, and further to the right other clumps of trees, certain evidences of villages, washed themselves in against the morning. We had only one map, a print from some obsolete French sheet, but from it we were able to identify Essarts, and round behind our right shoulders, a mound crested with a grove of feathery trees which we guessed to be Gommecourt. Presently details began to grow into the picture. White lines appeared in the foreground; the enemy parapet, sketched in chalk. It ran down the valley to our right and disappeared behind a bank of willows: '*oseraie*' said the map. To our front, 250 yards away, it hid itself behind a dusky haze of tangled wire, thick as a blackberry patch. To our left the ground rose; and the road to Monchy, sliding athwart our trench, masked the northward prospect. We could just see the tops of trees and the hint of a skeleton house in a valley. Behind our left shoulders, a broken sullen tower, Monchy mill, glared at us malevolently through the trees bordering the road. At the corner of the trench rose superbly one of those obelisks of ferro-concrete called *poteaux* with which the roads of Artois were adorned.

The sun crept up, and as we jigged up and down on the firestep an enemy machine gun from the right came clop-clopping, slowly shot by shot along the parapet. 'Time for breakfast,' said Smith. 'Stand down.'

I take it that every subaltern remembers his first platoon and his first fire-trench with the same vividness with which one recalls one's first pantomime, Dan Leno as the Widow Twanky, and one's first tanning. By September, 1915, many of the troops in France had assumed that air of performance which grows on caretakers left in charge of some unwanted, unwieldy barrack of a house. As yet we knew nothing of the great preparations in the north, three weeks later to be tested in the battle of Loos. We set about exploring our line, and discussing its possibilities. These trenches were quite foreign to our Flanders-trained eyes. For one thing, they were in, not on, the ground: and while the parapet was non-existent, an enormous mound of earth, christened by some scholar at G.H.Q. a parados, rose behind our heads. Then, instead of being traversed by great bulkheads of sandbags, there was no protection at all at the sides of the bays. An occasional fascine stood, like a stone vase in some noble parterre, to give decoration to a dull alley. The French preferred, to speak heraldically, the fesse dancetté to the English crenellé: their bays ran to angles. Most disconcerting, perhaps, was the sanitary accommodation, built, I concluded, for more robust races. A large pit, covered by a few boards, had been dug in—yes, actually in—a firebay. 'FEUILLES' read a laconic notice board; but the nose had compassed the exact translation of those leaves ten yards before one reached it. To cover this noisome plague breeder was No. 2's first task, undertaken with alacrity by the occupants of the adjoining posts.

On the other hand, we admired the splendour of the commodious *abris* which our predecessors had constructed, big recesses hewed out of the chalk, covered by layers of solid logs, such as were not available to the British up north. The French never scrupled to despoil a countryside to build an arbour, though they resented it in their allies and charged them thumping prices. We admired less when we discovered active relics of our predecessors in the shape of vermin of every kind.

The next weeks fade into the monotony of trench life, a subfusc tapestry brightened only by moments of excitement or comedy. We were too young and too busy to feel any resentment over useless toil. A serious little group we of No. 1 Company: I think the spirit of Terence Blake sat heavily upon us all. Smith, our company commander, when released from the efficacy of Blake's nervous spirit, developed a delicious dry carelessness, and an irreverence for rule of thumb, which caused senior officers to eye him with suspicion, until they discovered his immense capacity in action. Yes, Terence was a little indigestible: he took his war more seriously than the great K himself. I can see now his spare angular figure, the sunken cheeks and curious broken nose, the ugly mouth that opened like a clown's (he had a grateful talent for buffooning in the moments he could spare from the army), an arm extended, hand clenched, thumb jutting upward, as he harangued his platoon in a harsh voice on the art and craft of soldiering. He was a brave man, but he possessed an imaginative nervousness, and unconsciously communicated it to his fellows. In my perplexities, therefore (for perplexed I frequently was in this mutable existence), I clung more readily to Smith, the true type of natural soldier. He had been born in Ceylon. At the age of eight, he had run away from home to wander for a week in the jungle. Sent to school in England, he had run away at sixteen to enlist in the Royal Sussex and to fight through the South African War. Sane, cool, and monosyllabic, he would when the occasion demanded take enormous risks and, with an uncanny sensibility, carry them off. He was one of those rare individuals who seem to require the stimulus of danger to raise them to the highest pitch.

Besides these, there were three juniors, Georgi, Walter Spencer, and myself. Georgi, a science student, was given to fits of abstraction, when he would sit with his clean spade-like jaw flung up and sideways, gazing into the air, working out, we suggested, abstruse chemical formulae. Later when he became bombing officer, he would suddenly say at lunch à propos of nothing at all: 'They were bursting beautifully this morning.' We did not, I fear, pay sufficient tribute to this praiseworthy absorption. Walter, a red-headed elderly child, just down from Oxford, had a sardonic humour, which would encourage me during those miserable winter hours when soaking to the chest we waded up and down the line. We deplored the levity with which No. 3, our relief company, treated the war. The hours of rest between tea and evening stand-to were spent in debating the relative methods of securing traverses, of siting sump-pits, of revetting fire-bays, of rapid wiring. Most of the conversation was purely theoretical. The Third Army, to which we belonged, had but yesterday come to birth. Of supplies it was as naked as any other newborn child. Even sandbags were scarce, and an order was promulgated that they were not to be used for personal requirements. This order became more stringent when some admirable ladies in England formed a sandbag club for our benefit, and their first contribution began to arrive. For these sandbags were obviously too good to be put to such humdrum uses as parapets or traverses. Beautifully stitched—hand-stitched—of materials which Patou would not disdain to handle; of colours which the doting Joseph might have dyed for Benjamin, they were too splendid to have mere clay thrust into them. To be sure, some barbarians in No. 4 Company did roof a dugout with their share, a stately pyramid which lay conspicuously above the surrounding country. But the other companies found better use. A really charming black pair kept my boots from soiling my blanket when I slept; another of silken magenta pillowed my head, while a nattier blue affair held my washing tackle. Batty-Smith, our machine-gun officer, who shared my dugout, had a preference for green in varying tinges. We blessed our unknown benefactresses.

As for timber, wire, duckboards, angle irons, extra shovels, picks, mauls, they were worth their weight in the not over clean paper money which we drew from a rare field cashier. Primed, then, with the most modern theory of the angle of incidence, I would go into committee with my sergeant, Brown, a short, thick, brown-moustached man of florid complexion, wearing the benignant air of a cricket professional. Together we would go to THE TRAVERSE, and like a brace of Michael Angelos considering the marble block for the outlines of a David, ponder the base of earth and bags on which should rise a monument to No. 2's skill. That traverse would become our incubus. It would be handed over with suppressed pride and explicit directions to No. 10 when they relieved us. 'All right, old dear,' Sidney Adler would say; 'we'll get on with it.' But Sidney had his theories too: and his successor had his, while the fourth occupant had a little private plan of his own for constructing firebays in a sap, and neglected our masterpiece. When we returned after six days in support and twelve in reserve, the pile of wet sandbags bulged in unsuspected places, was swollen in the middle, lurched a trifle in gait, and generally presented a debauched spectacle. Swearing full-blooded oaths, we tore it down and rebuilt it on a more solid foundation. But alas! when at length I came to bid it farewell, it was sinking fast. Frost and rain had finished it. Somehow it still held together, but not of itself. Girt with stakes, expanded metal, rabbit wire, and corrugated iron, it lurched, a dissipated charwoman, half out of the stays we careful corsetiers had furnished to it.

In these architectural memories, I forget that we are at war and that a few hundred yards away from us there is an enemy as eager for our death as we for his. These days were before the Canadians had set the costly and depressing fashion of raiding the other side. Patrols went out as soon as the dusk had blackened to night. Our friends over the way rarely came past their own wire. The French and Germans in these parts had taken matters very amicably. We were told by the Leicestershires on our left, that the French Territorial battalion, who marched with them, only kept two sentries in the line, and that once a week they fired their rifles in the air to see whether they still worked.

If he was invisible, yet the enemy did not permit us any liberties. One morning Smith, Blake and I lay in a tangle of weeds on the parados trying to distinguish some object in the opposite trenches through a screen of rough grass. When we had finished, Blake and I slid carefully into the trench: but Smith, more leisurely, rose to his feet and stood balanced against the sky. As he jumped, there was a sharp crack. He picked himself up from the bottom of the trench, and broke into a laugh. 'Look at that,' he said, pulling at his breeches. On the cloth inside his thigh ran the mark of the burn which the bullet had made as it grazed his leg.

The German gunners left us alone for three days, but when they woke up, we made the unpleasant discovery that Blake's and my own line could be quite accurately enfiladed. Still, our first six days ended without our blood being shed, and satisfied that we had not as yet disgraced ourselves, we made our way contentedly down the long communication trench, now frivolously christened Lulu Lane. We took over support points in Hannescamps and hoped to loaf. This was a delusion. Not only were we all required on daily digging parties to rebuild the support lines which our conscienceless allies had allowed to fall in; we were also sent every other night into close support of the front line. Here we dug from dark to midnight and then huddled down on the firestep to shiver and doze till dawn.

Still there was leisure to explore Hannescamps, a deserted skeleton through whose ribs coarse weeds and grass were already pushing their way. Here one discovered the eternal difference between the French and English. The Frenchman will take infinite pains and spare no labour to make himself safe and comfortable; the English prefer indolent discomfort and to chance their arm. Hannescamps had been badly battered. Perhaps two roofs of the thirty-odd houses still pretended to offer a shelter from the wind and rain. Of those nearest to the line only a few broken walls stood. Rank grasses were pursuing their march over what had been brick floors. On this side of the main street the French had built from the stone debris a high wall some five hundred yards in length, perhaps ten feet high, to protect passers-by from stealthy assassination by the bullets which came flying over the ridge half a mile away and, helped by the fall of the ground, whined through the orchards like evil insects. It was a wise precaution, but such was our perversity, that before we left this Arcadia, we had torn down most of it for other purposes; and the rest had lapsed into ruin.

The British had already begun to take over the village. The crossroads were placarded as Piccadilly Circus (we were a completely London brigade), and the ruins of the large farm at the corner naturally became Leicester Square. The machine gunners with prompt wit had named their dark hovel 'The Two Inch Tap'.[1] Exploration led one into the wilderness of a civilization overcome. Here behind Leicester Square lay a secluded garden. The lawn was draggled and

[1] Before the war, a machine gunner was trained to tap the butt of his gun with sufficient strength to move it two inches, which deflected the muzzle so that at, I think, 200 yards, there was an unbroken arc of fire.

mossy, but pink roses nodded and scented the air, while the peacock, so cunningly carved from a box bush, still flaunted a defiant shell-burnt tail. He at least had no doubts of the outcome of the war; but when I passed that way in the spring of 1918, nature, a kindlier wrecker, had sprouted him to a mere shrub.

As one pushed deeper into the outlying parts of this tangled maze, there was always something to arrest the eye: a stentorian Michelin advertisement, miraculously preserved, a grey rat creeping under a fallen log, a bird shouting nonsense from a dilapidated apple-tree, slugs fat and horribly red. On the plaster of this broken wall is drawn in pencil with supreme genius a mêlée of legs and buttocks, a pornographic satire; yet with so much spirit has the pattern been wrought that we catch our breath in admiration for this unknown, perhaps dead, Gavarni.

There is a secret magic about these waste lands. While you wander through the corrupted overgrown orchard, there is always someone at your back. You turn. It is nothing but the creak of a branch, broken with the same wanton merriment with which a shell breaks a human limb and leaves it hanging by the frail tension of the skin. In all these destroyed places at the fringe of the line, places to be manned only in case of attack, such as the keeps on the road from Pont Fixe to Chocolate Menier Corner, the suburbs of Arras, Voormezeele, Calonne and this place Hannescamps, there is always the apprehension of ghosts; not those of the men who have died there, but of something older, something less perishable, the spirit of the place itself which watches the inquisitive idler with eyes half fearful, as if to ask, 'Will you too profane me?' But if you turn to surprise the watcher, there is nothing except the fog filtering between the trees and the smell of rank vegetation. You stand still, half hoping to surprise the wounded guardian, but while you wait—your involuntary summons about to be answered—the spell is shattered. An infernal woodpecker, the machine gun in the distance, taps; bullets slap against the crumbling wall; and the spirit which you hoped to incarnate has shrivelled and is gone.

We took what shelter we could find. The accommodation was scanty, but most of the cellars had been converted into living rooms; and here and there a recess hollowed in a bank had been fashioned into an *abri* with plank sides and a timbered and clodded roof, warm and pleasant, but infested with rats, which ran across one in the dark and plucked boldly at one's blankets.

If I dwell too long among these forgotten ruins, I crave forgiveness. This broken village and its defences was the school where this battalion grew to manhood, and though we passed through many worse as well as easier periods, it is by Hannescamps that the originals swear. To have been at Hannescamps made you free of the battalion. A late comer, however gallant, however loved, had to earn his right to that primitive integrity before he was admitted to the brotherhood. Years later when I was asked to do something, I forget what, and shyly protested my unworthiness in the face of better men, I was reproached with, 'Ah! but you was at Hannescamps.' And for those words, I summon as powerfully as my poor words will command, the ghost of that devastated hamlet once more to fill a skyline.

IV

'The pedestrian is unquestionably the most independent of travellers, and to him alone the beautiful scenery of some of the more remote districts is accessible. A couple of flannel shirts, a pair of worsted stockings, slippers, the articles of toilet and a stout umbrella will generally be found sufficient.'

KARL BAEDEKER, NORTHERN FRANCE

OUR first twelve days are over. Our relief is marching in; and we are despatched by platoons to an unknown village some six miles away. There is some dispute over the pronunciation of its name. The machine-gun officer, directing the sergeant of the reserve teams told him to go to 'Oom-bare-con'. The sergeant slapped the butt of his rifle; but, a hundred yards further on, asked in a puzzled voice: 'Where did he say?' Whereupon from the back of the section rose the irreverent voice of Pte. Archbold. 'He said Oom-bare-con; but you, poor ignorant perisher, probably call it Humber-camps.' So let us stick to the English manner.

Humbercamps was typical of all the villages on these Artois downs, stone houses clustered round a tiny *place*, a grove of Norman poplars, a school, an odorous *abreuvoir*; its outskirts hazy with orchards. In fact, a dull little village, tucked away from the main Doullens–Arras road, which edged the ridge. Our company occupied one corner of the village, a farm and the house of the secretary to the *mairie*. Although three of us occupied half his small house, I believe he and his wife liked having us; we produced a tang of excitement in their life. A stream of back-chat of a primitive nature flowed between Smith and Madame, a short lusty woman, invariably scarlet under the weight of some domestic burden. I was often called in to translate. There was a wretched cross-bred terrier chained up across the garden. 'Ask her why it's always barking,' said Smith. I translated.

'Ah! parcequ'il a un ver solitaire.' 'She says he's got a solitary worm,' I produced, 'but what a solitary worm is, God only knows.' 'Why, a tape worm, of course; you'd bark if you had one.'

Reserve did not spell rest. We were overwhelmed with working parties. One day was spent in the support lines at Hannescamps or Bienvillers, eight hours' digging, ten miles' marching; the next on a strong-point four miles westward. Once when through a mistake in orders the battalion paraded at 5.30 instead of 6.30 a.m., the four companies fixed themselves beneath the adjutant's window, and for an hour by the clock sang him *Michigan*. In the intervals there were the inevitable kit inspections (these always afflicted me with a sense of trespass on the liberty of the individual), foot inspections, gas-mask inspections, guards, minor fatigues—'subaltern and 40 o.r. to unload lorries at railhead.' There were parties to cut brushwood beyond Pas, which frequently ended in the laying waste of some promising copse and a quarrel with the sappers, or the injury of a soldier who had been trimming the branches of a tree while his comrades were at work on the trunk. At Pas, too, were the Divisional baths; once a week we were sent in fatigue dress to the brasserie, where the men pranced in enormous vats and the officers lowered themselves cautiously into narrow tanks filled with a boiling fluid of suspicious colouring. There were drafts to be fetched from railhead, usually arriving at dusk, dead beat: their guide was lucky if he did not lose a man or two on his way back. These and all the hundred other little details of corporate life beset the battalion. As they marched home in the waning light, the working parties sang:

We are but little soldiers weak;
We only get five francs a week.
The more we do, the more we may,
It makes no diff'rence to our pay.

Then one morning as the company busied itself about a strong-point at the corner of the village, we heard the voice of our colonel, a throaty tenor, shouting: 'Smith! Smith! Blake! Blake! All officers! At orderly room at once.' He came cantering past, his long feet sticking out until, as someone remarked, 'his mare must fancy she's back in the milk-cart.' We flung down our tools wearily and cursed as we struggled into our jackets. We were used to these demonstrations which invariably followed a call of the C.O. at brigade H.Q.: for he loved tittle-tattle and its dissemination. This time, however, it was worth our hearing; for he was primed with orders for us to prepare to join in the general advance eastward as soon as the French on our left had broken the enemy's front system. On 24th September, we dumped our valises at the quartermaster's stores, and were warned to be ready to move out at two hours' notice. That afternoon our newly appointed adjutant, Cuthbertson, once leading lady of the Footlights, took me with him on a reconnaissance of the most covered tracks to the French front line. We worked our way down shallow valleys until we came to Berles-au-Bois. As we came out from the edge of the village, we looked across to the northern corner of the dark Bois d'Adinfer. We could see the German trenches roughly scrawled in chalk across the grey downland. From them ascended column on column of variegated smoke. Red, black, yellow, and brown, they never ceased to climb skyward. As quickly as one thinned another took its place. From the valley below us came an incessant pommelling of the air, a rumbling, bruising sound, flooding the sky. This was the artillery preparation of which we had heard tell. It looked as if nothing could live through it; yet it had been going on for six days. Snug in Humbercamps we had not heard a murmur, thanks to the trick of the hills. I gazed across the valley, fascinated, with an ever-increasing apprehension. While we lingered, a fat and spectacled commandant of French heavies came panting up the hill. After ceremonious gestures, he unburdened himself. Was he now at Ransart? We assured him no: Ransart was at present in the hands of the enemy; after tomorrow, no doubt. . . . But —he produced a map—it could not be, could not possibly be so. He swung the map about like a puzzled child, wrapped it round him, unsheathed himself, and, planting a pudgy finger on a fold, announced: 'Mais, c'est ici, Ransart.' We did our best, but in the end we had to leave him disconsolate and unconvinced on the hill-top. I hope nothing happened to him. There were craters, recently made, of ominous significance at that corner.

At the foot of the hill, dug into the chalk, we came upon the French batteries at work. The teams, stripped to the waist, toiled unresting over their spitting, clapping guns. In the road, a country cart had broken down and a group of men in horizon blue were helping the driver, an old peasant in corduroys, to free the wheels.

As we walked back Cuth remarked that everyone seemed a damned sight too optimistic for anything to happen. I inquired what our objective was, and he said that we were expected to reach the Douai-Valenciennes line in rather less time than we could march the distance.

For three nights more, we all slept fully dressed on our floors, our packs ready, expecting each hour to bring us the summons. Magniloquent news of the battle up north at Loos was published several times. We had not yet learned to discount all these communications. But of the French attack we heard nothing. We still hoped, and when two days later the battalion paraded, it was still half believed we were marching on Douai. The belief only vanished into thin air as our march led us once more to the foot of Lulu Lane. Later we were told that the Turcos had attacked and carried the front line, but had lost it; and that though they repeated the exploit twice more, they were so badly cut up that a fourth attempt had been countermanded.

During our first period in the trenches above Hannescamps, it had been nearly impossible to send out patrols. The French had wired themselves in so tightly that we had to cut ourselves out again. It had been a long job. I lay on my back for six hours one night snipping a path through these snarled tendrils. Their scent was not briar. The kex crackling under my weight was foully greasy, and the grass full of meat cans and other refuse thrown there by the French. During that tour the guns had been quiet. A few shells had fallen about the trench without doing any harm. To add to the peaceful atmosphere we had caught the brassy strains of a band playing in a village we could just see over the hill, Bucquoy. But by now the enemy had woken up to the fact that a change of tenants had taken place and were resenting it with spontaneous and explosive anger. During our next tours, I learned to distinguish the whizz-bang, the four-two and the five-nine, but to have no preference. The German machine guns hailed the dawn, slowly traversing our parapet, breaking now and then into a chattering frenzy. One morning an expert away on the right saluted the *poteau* at the end of my trench with belt after belt of fire, spraying its slim column from tip to base. We gathered below it, laughing at the display, until we found that ricochets were bouncing among us and that chips of concrete wildly scattered could sting more fiercely than wasps.

Early one morning between stand-down and breakfast, as I stood warming myself in the autumn sunlight, I heard a shot which intuitively I knew had neither hit the parapet nor fled away to Hannescamps. I went round the traverse to the next platoon and found Foakes, our big-drummer, a big ruddy boy, and another stretcher bearer busy over a dun cocoon. It was the body of an elderly man named Cruise. A bullet had pierced the top of his skull as he stood on sentry in a little sap-head. Blood and some white stuff disfigured the earth. I flinched at the rattling, moaning sound, made by a man hit in the brain, which bubbled from his lips as they carried him away. He died an hour or so later, and was buried by Father Leeson, our Catholic padre, in Humbercamps. This was our first death in the company.

It may have been the evening of that morning that Georgi, patrolling with a party of ten, ran into a body of Germans. We, working on the parapet and wire, heard bombs exploding and cowered. Presently the patrol crawled in, but five were missing. Search parties went out; they could find nothing. Four of the missing were from Blake's platoon, one, Brand from mine. This Brand, a melancholy dyspeptic creature, with stiff black hair and a bristle moustache, had once lived in Graz, and, it was said, had been despatched over the frontier by a suspicious Austrian police. On this legend had been constructed another; that Brand was neither more nor less than a German spy; and here naturally was the confirmation. ' 'E's gorn over to join 'is friends,' said a voice darkly. This theory was knocked on the head about four o'clock in the morning, when a sentry showed me a dark figure running up and down in front of our wire in the very action of the pacing wolves in the Zoo. I went out and found the miserable Brand, yet more miserable and completely exhausted. After the scuffle, he had lost his patrol, and then promptly lost all sense of direction. Twice he had crawled on to the German wire, and discovered his mistake. At last, he had run into the trees on the road spanning No-Man's-Land, the most conspicuous landmark in the district, and put his back to a trunk for another couple of hours before setting a course again. 'But why didn't you come down the road?' I asked. 'Road?' he repeated blankly; 'I never knew there was a road.' Such impenetrability should have disposed of the spy theory for good: but once more during that morning, I heard a voice say scornfully: ' 'E was with 'is friends all the time.' Fortunately a bout of fever shortly afterwards swept this menace to the base and out of our existence for ever.

Just before dawn, a second missing man, the dark willing

Crossley, came in over the parapet of the company on the right. But of the other three no trace had been found when the last search party returned in the greying light. These three were all Irish and Catholics. During the afternoon, I heard a sudden burst of contention along the trench, and Blake's voice saying, 'I won't let you, Father; you'll wreck tonight's search party.' I strolled down the trench and found him in hot argument with Father Leeson. The padre was a curious figure in these surroundings, a thin awkward man with a face of a kind middle-aged spinster; one could almost see the grey corkscrew curls falling below a lace cap as he peered forward through his short-sighted eyes. We loved him, this lined Catholic priest, and refrained from mocking his anxiety as he bestrode his evil, ewe-necked screw, a very Rosinante. Now he was flushed by the excitement of pointing out to Blake that these three members of his flock might be dying out there without absolution; and that so far as he was concerned, his first duty was to them: the matter of our defences was outside his sphere. He even invoked his rights over Blake's own Catholic soul. 'Go and get Smith,' said Blake to me. But before I could move, the padre had clambered over the parapet and was stooping gingerly through the gap in the wire. We waited dumbly for shots to come; but the air remained still. The padre disappeared into a little hollow. Still there was silence. The tension lessened; time crept on. At last we saw the flat cap and the black triangle dodging back through the wire. The padre slid over the parapet in perfect tranquillity, told us he had found nothing, laughed gently at Blake's sulky face, and disappeared down Lulu Lane. The search party that night also found nothing; but later a letter from Germany told us that at least two of the three were safe 'for the duration'.

My own first patrol remains in my mind as four hours conscientiously wasted. With ten braves I set out on an attempt to capture an alleged sniper. Of course, there was no sniper; in two or three weeks our knowledge would have grown so far that we knew there couldn't be one. My ten and I tagged heavily to and fro on our bellies for a long time. At one moment looking over my shoulder I was horrified at catching sight of a huge blood-red object floating over the Bois d'Adinfer, only to realize after several prolonged minutes of acute terror that I was looking, not at a new device of Hunnish barbarity, but merely the last quarter of the September moon. Then the enemy started shelling the front line, so I lay doggo until he had finished. When I at last brought my wet, dirty and sleepy party home, I was greeted by Smith with a round cursing for spending half the night out.

Our rewards from patrols were small. The Germans rarely came out, and never approached our lines. In fact the only reward for so much pains and energy was the finding of an ancient *Gazette des Ardennes* with the phrases, 'Ivangorod est prise,' 'Varsovie est prise,' pencilled in an unformed hand, evidence of a mutual information bureau set up by our allies and our enemies.

The Boche was equally invisible by daylight. In front of us his trenches fell back into dead ground. Sometimes in the valley on the right, a grey shadow would stand for a few seconds, and then slide from sight, like a water-rat into his hole. At these we fired; but claims to have scored were not usually upheld. Once we heard him. On a morning when light filtered through a bleached world, and a blanket of mist was spread upon the ground so that our eyes could only pierce to the edge of our own wire, the whole company seized the opportunity to repair the damages of shell fire. We worked furiously with muffled mauls and all the coils of wire we could beg. Presently we realized that the enemy was doing as we were; dull thuds and the chink and wrench of wire came from his side. We might perhaps have opened fire, but that suddenly there came out of the blankness the sound of a young voice. It was raised in some Dorian-moded folksong. High and high it rose, echoing and filling the mist, pure, too pure for this draggled hill-side. We stopped our work to listen. No one would have dared break the fragile echo. As we listened, the fog shifted a little, swayed and began to melt. We collected our tools and bundled back to our trench. The singing voice drew further off, as if it was only an emanation of the drifting void. The sun came out and the familiar field of dirty grass with its hedges of wire and pickets rose to view, empty of life.

My dugout, a hole ten feet deep into the red soil, roofed with five layers of logs, was shared by our machine-gun officer, Batty-Smith. He was the youngest of us all and by far the most cheerful. The dismalest prognostication, the most horrific of rumours drew from him shouts of laughter. We used to lie on our bunks in that afternoon hour of rest before stand-to, and Batty, his smooth cheeks quivering with mirth, would sometimes read an absurd letter from a brother, a prisoner in a strafe camp in Germany, which conveyed under a painstaking code that our enemy (disguised as Uncle Eugene) had not long to live. I envied Batty his job, which allowed him to rove at will from one end to the other of the battalion line, instead of being pinned, as I was, to a hundred yards of decaying trench, which collapsed a little more each time a shell fell near it. That week it nearly crumbled altogether. At present Georgi's and my platoons were not in touch along the front line, but only through a cut across the road, ten yards back. We were ordered to span the arc with a new fire-trench. We had made a lot of progress and most rashly had thrown up several mounds of white and brown earth. One morning, while I was inspecting the rifles of the sentries on duty, I was startled, not to say alarmed, by three whizz-bangs bursting as it seemed all round my head. Immediately afterwards the biggest explosion I had yet seen threw great chunks of Lulu Lane into the air. Half a minute later there came a humming. I looked up and saw a monstrous minenwerfer shell tumbling out of the air into the latrine. That was a dud. By the time the enemy had got the range accurately, we were hurrying to and fro with confused gestures. As I ran, I heard one coming very close, caught a glimpse of it out of the tail of my eye, and at that moment slipped. I picked myself up, but before I could reach my full height, the minnie burst. A furious hot whirlwind rushed down, seized me and flung me violently back against the earth. I lay half-stunned while a rain of earth and offal pattered down on me, followed by something which whizzed viciously and stuck quivering in the trench wall; it was a piece of jagged steel eighteen inches long. Scared out of my ten wits, I jumped up and ran frantically to company headquarters. 'Artillery, for God's sake. . . .' I blurted out to Smith. He grinned and that pulled me together. 'I've rung through,' he said; 'come and look.' The minnie stopped and we heard an English shell pass overhead. 'Dud,' I said. A second burst in our wire. A third—'Dud,' said Smith. We waited a minute. 'Any more?' He cocked his head to listen. 'No; that's the lot.'

'We can't help you,' the F.O.O. explained later in the day. 'Every bloody shell is going up to Loos. Our teams have been taking our spare stuff there for the last week. We haven't got any shells. Three a day is our allowance, and you've had it this morning.'

I was not to experience that minnie a second time. During the afternoon, I was ordered to report at battalion headquarters to take over the job of spare machine-gun officer, *vice* Batty-Smith deposed.

On our last taking over of trenches, the machine gunners had been inspected by Batty on parade before starting. Two old sweats, Packer and Palmer, had maintained under inspection the stony face of innocence which a life of army crime lends a man. How was nineteen-year-old Batty to know that both had been drinking freely of the carefully laced *vin blanc*, a speciality of the army area? This was only revealed during the first halt, when Private Packer, burning with a sense of alcoholic injury, accused L.-Cpl. Palmer of trying to trip him up, and smote him on the ear. Upon which L.-Cpl. Palmer, no whit behindhand, struck back. In the middle of the riot that followed, the brigade major suddenly appeared, placed all the combatants under arrest (several other spirits had joined the mêlée), and reported the whole affair to our headquarters. The colonel, in a gust of apprehension that he would fall into disfavour with the brigadier, dealt out Field Punishment right and left, and concluded by depriving Batty of his command. So on this afternoon, Batty took over my platoon and I retired to Hannescamps. A few days later I was despatched to the Machine Gun School at Wisques to learn the technicalities of my new trade.

Before I went away, I visited the platoon again. They had received a second visitation from the minenwerfer, in pairs this time. There had been no casualties, but the trench and the wire hardly existed, and all the tools had been smashed. Two boys, Kingsford and Lipscomb, had been entombed in a sap-head. Another lad, but three days joined, had been blown out of the trench into the wire, and had come running in, undamaged, save that his smoke helmet had been dexterously snatched from its satchel. 'And,' said Batty, 'we've dug up the dud. It's nine inches across the base and thirty-three long. I'm going to dig its guts out, an' take it home for an umbrella stand.'

V

'I really believe all the oddities of the three kingdoms and Germany are met in this army. I could almost wish your Lordship would crown us, though wishing you here is no compliment, for never poor devils lived harder or earned their pay more than we all do.'

LORD PEMBROKE (FROM THE BRITISH ARMY IN HESSE) *to* LORD CHARLEMONT, 1760

THEY used to tell us, 'Get to know your men.' It was hammered in at training schools, in O.T.C.'s. 'Know your men, young man,' the pundits would say, 'and they'll follow you anywhere. Why, I remember . . .' Let us draw a decent veil over these glorious perorations, but stay a moment to inquire whether the general thesis may be held. I have an old platoon roll before me; three pages of names, numbers, trades, next-of-kin, religions, rifle numbers, and so forth. Faces come back out of the past to answer to these barren details, the face of this man dead, of that vanished for ever, Here and there rise memories of their habits, their nicknames, the look of one as he spoke to you, the attitude of another shivering in the night air, as he leaned over the parapet, watching with tired bloodshot eyes those posts which moved and swam as you gazed. Husky voices re-echo endless talks held over braziers: 'Was you ever at 'atfield? Ah, that's a fine 'ouse.' 'Naoh, I don't know that side of the county.' 'P'raps you worked at Shardeloes?' The faces of the speakers have disappeared. Only the shabby outlines and the voices remain, and the names of those stately palaces. Did I know you? I censored your letters, casually, hurriedly avoiding your personal messages, your poignant hopes: 'when we've finished with Fritz,' 'roll on, leaf.' Alas! some of you have finished with Fritz many years back, and your 'leaf' rolled over and over, tumbled by high explosive. Did any of us know you? ever pierce your disguise of goose-turd green, penetrate your young skin and look through you to learn the secret which is the essential spirit, the talisman against the worst that fate can offer? No. That was yours. As you would have said: 'Gawd knows; but 'E won't split on a pal.' So you still remain a line of bowed heads, of humped shoulders, sitting wearily in the rain by a roadside, waiting, hoping, waiting—but unknown.

A week at Wisques, a week of pouring rain, crammed technicalities, and dinners at St. Omer. On our way back, we tried to board the Doullens train, but the R.T.O. would have none of that. 'You don't go direct,' he said firmly, like the professor in *Sylvie and Bruno*; 'you go the *other* way.' The other way brought us to Calais, and at night to Abbeville. We did not complain. The bath was hot, the dinner was good, the beds soft at the Hôtel de France. Lucile bewitched four more hearts. These circumnavigations of France were a beguilement, until the back areas became too crowded. Two days later our little party rejoined the brigade.

The battalion was in Humbercamps, preparing for the line in proper November weather. Mist rose early in the evenings, leaving its breath on the floors of trenches. We went once more into the familiar sector, 69–74B. One night in the thickening fog we heard far away a tinkling sound. It came nearer, filled the valley and began to climb our hill. 'Gas alarm.' We drew on our smoke helmets, when someone, not over politely, observed: that the wind, such as it was, was blowing from the wrong quarter. This good sense did not overtake all. Capt. Burns, riding alone through Hannescamps after delivering the rations, heard the warning jangle. Tearing his helmet from its satchel, he cowled himself with the eyepieces to the rear. Then, putting spurs to his horse, he galloped furiously through Bienvillers back to St. Amand. He flung his reins to his groom and staggered, shaken and white-faced, into the mess. The quartermaster, startled by his old friend's haggard stare, cried:

'My dear fellow, what's the matter?'

'Gas, Fairburn, gas! As I rode through Bienvillers, the men were dying like flies by the roadside.'

Fairburn had been pouring him out a tot of whisky. He stopped in his beneficent action.

'But . . . but, I had a call through half an hour ago to say it was a false alarm.'

The tale was good. By breakfast it was in the front line, and that furious ride passed into legend.

We laughed, because it is always pleasant when one of our seniors makes a fool of himself, or again because by now even cheap laughter was a thing to lay store by. The big minnies had departed as secretly as they had come; they were spoken of a couple of miles away at Gommecourt: but in their place we were being harried by minor monsters which threw an object shaped like a large blacking bottle. Georgi, now our bombing officer, attempted to terrorize this new offence with an instrument known as a West's Spring Gun, based on Caesar's catapults at the siege of Argusium. It was supposed to hurl a hand grenade with much force and accuracy into the enemy's lines. In practice, it was more apt to shoot the missile straight up into the air to return on the marksman's head, supposing he still possessed one; for the machine was also calculated to decapitate the engineer if he was clumsy enough to stand in front of its whirling arm. Since the spring was not strong enough to carry the distance, the staff, chagrined by its failure, passed rapidly over 1800 years and produced (from the Invalides Museum, it was said) some ancient pieces of ordnance, warranted to be trench mortars. These pieces had no doubt performed admirable service in their day at Ulm and Borodino. They were introduced into our trenches with much ceremony. Their commander enlarged on the danger to anyone in the front line while he was at work, and at his request, the garrison evacuated its position for fifty yards on either side. After an interval of painful anxiety, there was a faint detonation, and a small object was observed to lollop into the middle of the debatable land where it exploded feebly. After a long interval, a second produced a similar result. After the fourth, quick-eared soldiers declared they could hear roars of laughter coming from the German trenches. The T.M. officer then packed up, and the garrison returned. Five minutes later we received several bursts of 4.2's and minnies in rebuke of such presumption.

Nor was this vented on the front line alone; our peaceful rusticity at Hannescamps was invaded by sudden bursts of hate. One afternoon as we were sitting in the Leicester Lounge (you know; at the corner of Leicester Square), we were jolted by four terrific explosions almost over our heads. A moment later, the door opened and Major Ardagh slipped in. 'By Jove,' he said, 'by Jove, they nearly got me; by Jove, they did.' We did not pay the second-in-command the attention he usually received, for we were listening to more explosions and guessing that the guns were traversing the length of the street. A voice outside began to shout 'Stretcher bearers.' We bundled out. Just above Piccadilly Circus, a salvo had burst among a working party of the Loyals. Blood and limbs seemed to be strewn about the road. Mangled bodies lay silent or groaning. A memory of a coster's barrow spilt among the traffic and splashes of fruit on the pavement shot into my mind. Arthur Bliss, very white and resolute, was holding a man's arm which fountained blood, while its owner strove to control the screams his torn body wanted to utter. Stretcher bearers came and the road was cleared, but there were purple stains of blood floating on the yellow puddles and in the creases of the mud. We went back very solemnly to the mess. Even the most secluded spots were beginning to wear a menacing air. The arching brick of the Lounge looked less impervious, as we censored letters, played Canfield, and listened to Harry Tate on soldiering.

I was liking my new job. The machine gunners considered themselves the élite of the battalion. They lived apart from the companies, and except in emergency were excused fatigues. In trenches they were responsible only for their immediate surroundings. They were not permitted to shoot from their battle positions, and there was a constant digging of strafe emplacements, a grisly task, from which the genteeler members flinched, since the French had buried a number of their dead in the parapet and parados. It was, however, easy to find volunteers. The two stalwarts who had caused Batty's downfall, Packer and Palmer, showed no squeamishness. At nightfall they would start digging in the charnel spot. Presently I would find them in the midst of a true *Stinkschwamm*, busy as vultures.

'I've fahnd 'is trahsers,' one would say.

'Anything?'

A moment of grim and malodorous fumbling, while the spade forced an entrance. Then the sound of spitting and a disgusted voice:

'Tuppence . . . tuppence! Can yer beat it?'

Only once did these heroes budge. I admit the stench was unusually overpowering; but, with the best will in the world, you can't get the price of a drink out of a dead horse.

Palmer was the true type of old soldier, a small face tanned by Indian and African suns, a neat moustache, a back as straight as a poplar's trunk, fierce in liquor, blasphemous of speech, with an eye as cold as a gravestone to an officer, and a knowledge of K.R. wide enough to reduce any New Army subaltern to pulp. Beside him, Packer was merely a giant. But all these men were ingenious in devilry, and innocent as pie, even Happy Day, ex-sailor, nominally the No. 1 of a team, but because of the quality of his cooking, invariably left at the Two Inch Tap. Here, a heavy recincarnation of Apollo, he would sing and twang an appreciated lyre—or was it an accordion? There was also a gipsy, a practised poacher and robber of hen roosts. I have been told it was a pleasure to watch the artistry with which he could wring the necks of fowls with never a betraying squawk, while Packer and Palmer held the owner of the roosts in fascinating talk. So bemused were the victims, that not a word of this practice ever grazed my ears.

What's that you say? Report at the orderly room? What for? Leave? *LEAVE*? Run down Lulu Lane. Never mind those two shells bursting on the road. They can't touch you now. The bus, the orderly room says, passes the crossroads in St. Amand at 1 a.m. Report to quartermaster's stores. And so I padded over the soiled track to St. Amand to enjoy life for seven days with no lurking shadows to dismay.

The quartermaster and transport officer shared an enormous mansion, approached through a towering stone gateway, and with the midden discreetly concealed. Here were made welcome all passengers to and from the battalion. Tour host was Lieutenant and Quartermaster W. L. Fairburn, and when I name that name: '*Sonnez, clairons; chantez coucous!*' Only the frenzy of Cyrano can do justice to that matchless figure.

Born in the army, bred in the army, bombardier in the Eagle troop, Quartermaster-sergeant of A Battery, Royal Horse Artillery, the Chestnut Troop, the right of the line and the pride of the army, Master Gunner of Ordnance, wearing the cocked hat of blameless efficiency, you were fully entitled to cock your cap, stroke your plump cheek and trim moustache, to swing lightly into the saddle, neatly touching old Bob with the spur so that he gave a couple of bucks to let you display your firm seat. Your look of puzzled anxiety as we told you our painful stories, the 'H'm, we must see. Tell you what, old chap . . .', a smile and an upward look . . . 'Have a drink,' have won you a hundred hearts. And then your songs! Songs of the old army: 'A boy came into a chandler's shop,' 'The Beano,' 'Little pigs make the best of pork' (sung with appropriate gestures).

And your tales! Of the quartermaster at Umballa who gave the elephant an enema from the fire-engine; of the whist-drive at Devizes; of the bazaar fight at Delhi, yourself armed solely with a goose; why the Scottish Rifles cannot lie in the next lines to the Cavalry; these can never wither. Or the old legends of battery histories. 'And he turned his guns about and galloped back through the French escort. . . . As he came into the English lines, the Duke of Wellington called, "Well done, gallant Ramsey!" And the next morning put him under arrest for disobeying orders.' Was it Salamanca? I forget. But I hear your voice growing deeper as you recite these passages—and perhaps your mind turns back to those Christmas Days when the major read aloud these tales from the battery's records. Kindliest and best of mortals, these words offer but a grain of the tribute I would pay you.

So having eaten your dinner and drunk your whisky (very hard to come by in these parts) I waited under a high noon at the crossroads, enraptured. A hard frost had set in and I was glad to creep into the fug behind the matchboarded windows of the bus. We jolted desperately away, and at last tumbled out at Doullens. The train was due at 3 a.m. It arrived at 6, and a searching wind throughout those hours did not drive a single candidate from the platform. I climbed shivering on board and was given a kind welcome by four senior officers who made cocoa on Tommy's cookers. Six hours later, we stopped at a bridge with one house in sight. 'Hurry, young fellow,' said one of my neighbours, 'this way for the omelettes!' A crowd of officers was already sprinting for the lonely house, where a mother and two daughters were turning out golden omelettes at a speed unequalled in any restaurant. After half an hour the engine whistled and the train proceeded on its way as slowly and as statelily as a triumph. It was thirteen hours to Le Havre, but who cared? We hurried on to the *Queen Elizabeth*, which had abandoned its normal Harwich–Hook passage in favour of the narrow seas. Next morning we were gliding in sunlight up Southampton Water. England was an intoxication. The houses seemed of unparalleled cleanliness, the train offered cushions of down; the dull fields and hedges of Hampshire, the autumn beeches assumed a new radiance; the bacon and eggs from the buffet at Basingstoke were ambrosial, Waterloo Station a palace. A little above myself I hailed a taxi. London had not yet reached the pitch of exasperated egoism, which it later touched. London was Elysium and seven days there were seven days won.

The break was all too short. It was in no mood of confidence that I dozed through the long hours on the way back to Doullens.

The weather had already broken before I went on leave. Rain had made our bare trenches a quag, and earth, unsupported by revetments, was beginning to slide to the bottom. We hailed the first frost which momentarily arrested our ruin, and frantically demanded some generosity in the matter of R.E. stores, sandbags, rabbit wire, expanded metal, frames, duckboards. Our prayers were hardly heard, and by now nothing could stave off our ruin. Lulu Lane became a vast conduit into which the trenches emptied their top waters. At the western end it was ten feet deep, lipping the berm. Saps filled up and had to be abandoned. I was not sorry to see the West Spring Gun vanish. The cookhouse disappeared. Dugouts filled up and collapsed. The few duckboards floated away, uncovering sump-pits into which the uncharted wanderer fell, his oaths stifled by a brownish stinking fluid. All too late came the issue of long gum boots, held as trench stores. There were only sufficient for the front line. Mobs of cursing men, burdened with the paraphernalia of the army, exchanged boots, in the dark, pinned in by the walls of the trenches. Fortunate the man who did not emerge from the hurly-burly with two left boots. In spite of frenzied work, the floods began to gain on us. The pumps broke down. At the beginning of December, the front line was relieved every four-and-twenty hours. The garrison, cold, hungry, and exhausted, trailed back to Hannescamps to grouse and rub their water-blanched feet with whale-oil. Then the front line garrison was reduced by half, and the cellars in the support village filled to the stairway. The front line melted and slid. It became impossible to move along it. Bent double, we reached isolated groups by newly discovered routes over the top, entailing lengthy detours. At night we walked from post to post along the coast-line.

The enemy was more happily situated than ourselves, for his trenches drained into a road under a bank. He did not cease to harry us. The minnies opposite lobbed at our ruins, and the batteries on the hill at Essarts and La Brayelle farm mocked us with shattering gifts. One morning, as I was lying in the rude hut which sheltered Leader and myself, I was awakened by a savage howl. Before I could move there was a thud, and the walls shook, followed by a rush of falling earth, blacking out the light and closing the door. Somehow I pushed my way through the thin slit, and gingerly stepping over the dud, a handsome scarlet cylinder with an evil-looking brass nose-cap, marked Dopp Kz, waded at my best pace through the scummy flood to company headquarters, where I was received with shouts of laughter.

This diluvial period brought us very low. The men came to wear a strained look, which the issue of rum, carried in the dark from post to post, only momentarily relieved. We began to have fever and sickness, and even the continual rubbing of feet did not resist trench foot. This disease was so simple to get and so hard to cure. A fall into water, followed by twenty-four hours in trenches, would bring it on. And there was an increase in the dead and wounded. Some had already gone. Sidney Adler, shot across the stomach on the wire, wrote proudly from England that he now possessed three navels. Our bombing officer had been crushed, buried, deafened, and nerve-shattered for ever by a minnie falling on him in London Road. Georgi, who had succeeded him, departed to join the euphemistically named Chemical Warfare companies. And now Anthony, the commander of No. 3, was shot through the body by a stray bullet, as he watched his company pass the Hannescamps barrier in the dawn, and died on his way to C.C.S. A genial, ruddy, easy-going man, with two African campaigns to his credit, well liked. Many of his company hereafter carried his photograph as a kind of amulet. Tempers were getting frayed. Blake returned much perturbed from another company. He had inquired at a dark doorway where the company commander might be found, to which a voice from the dark replied: 'If I knoo, I'd shoot the barstard.' I fear some of us sympathized with the aggrieved unknown. We moved with sullen, sluggish, sodden minds, not improved by the constant and ever-increasing number of returns and reports demanded by higher formations. All kinds of gadgets were added each week to our equipment, sometimes for experiment, usually for keeps, a novelty gas-mask, wire cutters, wire shears, wire breakers, hedging gloves, not to speak of the fur coats; by now a small man must have carried nearly his own weight in clothes and equipment. Last of all came the new steel helmet, the battle bowler, handed out sparingly to be kept as trench stores. These early fruits were doled out first to the snipers; and, as fate would have it, Gerrard, a charming intelligent boy in No. 3, was at once killed. A fragment of shell tore through the steel and pinned his brain. Thereafter the helmet was condemned with one voice. No man would wear one, except under the direct orders and observation of an officer, and the trench store was gradually put to other uses. They were found to make admirable washing basins, were not to be despised as cookpots, and could be put to all kinds of uses not contemplated by their designer, often of a nature not to be recorded.

One night shortly before Christmas we heard some shouting on our left flank where the British line ran up into a salient. The sounds carried clearly on the cold air. 'Hallo, Tommee,' cried a German voice, 'are you soon going home on leave?' 'Next week,' the Englishman shouted. 'Are you going to London?' was the next question. 'Yes.' 'Then call at two-two-four Tottenham Court Road and give my love to Miss Sarah Jones.' 'I'll go all right and I'll jolly well. . . .' The fate of the lady was eclipsed in a roar of laughter from our side and the angry splutter of a machine gun from across the way.

Christmas drifted up gloomily. Though we had come back to reserve, it was not gay. The staff, perhaps threatened by fire-eaters in London, had forbidden all fraternization, and to ensure their orders being carried out, commanded slow bombardment during the 25th. It seemed an act of churlish discourtesy to recognize the day in this fashion. Jimmy Lammin and I commented freely on the nature of this performance as we sat in our damp Armstrong hut. As we listened to the dull explosions of guns, we reflected bitterly that shells were being wasted on this whim, shells which could not be spared to us when our trenches were being knocked about.

That week two South African officers joined us, Sykes and Tebbutt Whitehead; the latter was an experienced machine-gun officer. To my disgust, I, with my poor empirical knowledge, was transferred to No. 3 company. The newcomer had fought against Maritz, had been taken prisoner, when half the column he was with 'verted to Germany, and had spent months in the heart of South-West Africa. He had also been twelth man in a Test-match team. As, on New Year's night, I led No. 10 platoon in single file through the creeping mud up the Monchy road, I dwelled with loathing on his large placid face, little thinking how much I should come to like it in later years. The floods had not abated, nor the mud lessened. But already it seemed as though the days were lengthening. It was earlier in the morning that I warmed the milk and added the rum for Leader and myself to drink at stand-to. Rumours of a move began to circulate. In mid-January, I was sent a few miles north to billet the battalion in Bailleulmont, a clean village, inhabited by a battalion of French territorials. A middle-aged *adjutant* of philosophic turn of mind did the honours and snuffed loudly at the admirable cookery in each *popote*. On the next night we marched out. One sentence in orders —'The battalion will hand over steel helmets to the Royal Warwickshire Regiment, and be re-equipped with new helmets at Bailleulmont'—added a fillip to our departure.

VI

'My dear Spencer, I should define tragedy as a theory killed by a fact.'
HUXLEY

THERE is an old soldiers' byword which runs: 'They gives yer cheese to bind yer: and they gives yer jallap to loosen yer: there ain't nothing that they can't do to yer in the Army.'

I did not accompany the battalion to Bailleulmont. Perhaps as a consolation for my disappointment over the machine guns, headquarters decided to follow the adage and attempt to transform me into a spare transport officer. I was despatched to Havre for a three weeks' course of riding, driving, and veterinary work. I was anything but an accomplished horseman, and jogging over to railhead beside Captain Burns, disclosed my tremors. 'You'll be all right,' the T.O. grunted; 'keep your elbows into your sides and your heels down, and' (with infinite contempt) '*they'll* not see any difference.' All the same, I think they must have.

The Base Horse Transport Depot allotted to me a gigantic strawberry roan to ride, feed and groom. It was a nice beast and carted me about the parade ground in a comfortable and knowledgeable fashion, though its habit of giving me an occasional nip while I groomed its legs led me to love it less than I might otherwise have done. However, for me, the course terminated after ten days. The weather on the hills above the Creusot works was bleak and raw; snow fell: and one morning as we rode out, I was suddenly seized by furious pains in the ribs. With a feeble yelp, I gathered myself into a ball and rolled from the saddle. When I rose, I was sickle-shaped; but I got no sympathy from the riding master, who cursed me for a fool to come on parade in that state. I crawled away, an agonizing question mark, and Tortoni saw me no more. Twice a day I dragged my body a mile to the M.O., where a rough-handed orderly rubbed me with unguents until I was sore. I was fit just in time to return to the battalion. As we waited on the platform, we heard the news of the opening of the Verdun offensive.

We left Havre at midnight. In my carriage sat a sober old subaltern in the Sherwoods, named Hoare, and a solid cheerful Canadian, Hessey. I woke at intervals through the night and peered shivering into the darkness to try to find out how far we had got. By seven in the morning we had come seventy miles and reached Rouen, to be told we should not go on until four o'clock. We stepped out gaily on to the bright, cold quais. After breakfast, and a wash and shave in the public baths, Hoare and I loitered round the cathedral. Hoare's battalion had been twice badly cut up in the past year, and he talked very melancholy of death. Presently we found Hessey drinking cocktails in the Angleterre, and after we had had one or two ourselves, we began to be more cheerful. Then in consideration of the fact that we would be back in the line in a day, we had a long and very good lunch. I began to feel extremely cheerful, and was willing to be led anywhere. Hessey took us to an underground bar, where there was a billiard table. He and Hoare began to knock the balls about, while I sat at the zinc and talked to the barmaid in execrable French. At last Hoare said we must go. Hessey at once announced that he was very drunk and begged me to look after him. I promised to do so, but as soon as we got out into the bright sunlight, I realized that I had drunk far too much myself. Hoare, however, wore his usual solemn immovable face, and we put him in the middle. Hessey insisted on taking off his hat to every wounded poilu he met, and threatened to kick a large bearded sous-lieutenant for having more medals than he had. Hoare dragged him away and we reached the train in a whirling and argumentative bunch. I jumped into the first carriage and went off to sleep. I was wakened by someone pulling my hair. The train was clattering and rocking along at a fine pace, I looked up, and there was Hessey leaning in through the window. 'Must say good-bye, old man,' he shouted over the din; 'couldn't bear not to say good-bye.' I told him either to come inside or go back to his own carriage, but he would not do so until he had shaken me warmly by the hand. Then I watched him swaying and clambering along the footboard until at last he disappeared suddenly into the train. I dropped off to sleep again. When we had been sixteen hours on the journey and covered eighty miles, we came to Abbeville. Here we were given another half day to wait, which we wasted in the usual cathedral, barbers' shops and heavy lunch. That night I started once more. It took another twenty-four hours to reach the battalion.

There was an aspect of cheerfulness in Bailleulmont. Perhaps it was due to the departure on account of infirmities of certain elderly officers of caustic tongue and uncertain temper; perhaps it was due to the bright spring weather: but probably chiefly to a well-authenticated story of a spell of rest, a holiday such as we had not known in our seven months in France. So even the death of poor old Captain Goodman, sniped while walking in the open to avoid the slushy trenches, did not damp our spirits. On the day after my return, I had the as yet unusual experience of relieving trenches in broad daylight. I felt as self-conscious as an amateur on a first night as I led No. 10, broken up into little blobs at a hundred yards' distance, along a ridge in the full view of an uninterested German audience. But it did not matter. Nothing happened in this sector. It was so quiet that the French, to do honour to their allies, had abandoned their broken-down winter abodes and had dug a complete new spring accommodation some fifteen yards in advance. I imagine this to be a unique occurrence in the history of the war; but it was a less hazardous enterprise than may be thought, since the lines were here some 1200 yards apart. Between them lay a green valley, in which partridges were nesting, sometimes coming to roost on the wire, to be picked off by experts and retrieved in daylight. The French declared that it had been a pleasant friendly war. One officer even boasted that he had visited the enemy in the village of Ransart, a tree-clustered hamlet in the German front line.

During the time we spent here, the only incident of note was of domestic character. One Sunday morning, five minutes before lunch, our mess cook stabbed the mess waiter, the alleged reason of the assault being that the victim had called his mate a bastard. This affair of honour seemed almost eighteenth century: one remembered the victor of Wynendael and John Churchill. The court probably took the same view; for the aggressor got off with fourteen days' F.P. No. 1, carried out in the mess kitchen.

Our relief was not a rumour. On a fair March morning, I rode into Barly, a village a dozen miles behind Doullens, and after a brief interview with the *maire*, chose the best-looking house for my own company. My early scruples in the matter of billets had long been blunted by the constant upbraidings of the dissatisfied, and I abandoned them at the sight of beds.

Four weeks were spent in this tranquil valley, hardly disturbed by the irksomeness of platoon and company training. Even the morning run became a pleasure, as our physical natures recovered from the cramping of trenches, even route marches a jaunt. The grotesque bombing practices, lustily carried out, turned to a tournament pursued with cheers and laughter: rapid wiring became a game conscientiously played. At the end of a fortnight, we were shown to the great. Both Sir Douglas Haig and Lord Kitchener expressed a desire to see the division. Both exhibitions afforded spectacles not allowed for in the regulations.

Amberton, our company commander, was on leave, and

in his absence Leader rode Ginger, a charming chestnut mare with a turn of speed, as, some half-hour before the C.-in-C. was due, we marched up the slope of the hill-side on which we were to be inspected. The battalion formed up in mass and the officers dismounted. Platoon officers and sergeants fussed about their ranks; the R.S.M. found faults. A flag fluttering in the distance warned us of the approach of the Olympians.

'Company commanders, get mounted,' piped Major Ardagh. The battalion grew rigid. As I stood on the left side of the company, there broke on my ears the drubbing of hoofs behind me. I leaped into the ranks as Ginger dashed by me at a stretched gallop, bearing the dumpy figure of Leader. For a second we stood dumbly open-mouthed as the mare rushed down the hill. At the bottom was a drop of some ten feet into the road: we waited for the crash. Then from the back of No. 12 platoon rose the voice of Pte. Turnbull, Leader's batman, in a passionate wail. 'Turn 'im, sir, turn 'im,' it urged. The appeal loosened us. 'Turn him,' we roared. 'Turn him, you bloody fool,' echoed Major Ardagh. If Leader did not understand, Ginger did. With a side slip and a buck, she turned and swept away towards Sir Douglas's car. At the end of a hundred yards, she turned once more and, still carrying her helpless burden, galloped past our front down the road and disappeared towards her stable.

We had only just time to stiffen and present arms before the C.-in-C. was upon us. Not until he had reached the last of No. 2 company did I realize that I was now the commander of No. 3. Darting round to the front, I was met by a kind smile and Sir Douglas's soft padded hand. 'And how long,' he asked, 'have you been in command of this company?' 'About two minutes, sir,' was all my scatter-brain would allow me to say. 'He's only temporarily in command, sir,' put in Major Ardagh anxiously, frowning me down, while I blushed, and stole away to the rear of the ballet. At last, after mutual expressions of esteem, the hierarchs withdrew and we marched back to billets to find our ravished company commander with a stiff shoulder—Ginger had gone straight to her stable and jolted him off against the doorway—and a stiff whisky and soda, being consoled by the lady of the house.

As a result of Leader's disaster, No. 3 was led by myself, on an immense and handsome black, on the day of K's arrival. It was a well-mannered beast; but it was bored. As the staff cars ran into sight, it shut up like a penknife and sat down. I was still furiously punching it in the ribs when the salute was given. In reverse of the interested geniality of Sir Douglas, the Minister for War was forbidding. Each of us accompanied him as he walked down the ranks, and to none did he vouchsafe a remark. Not a word, not a comment escaped him. At last, as he left No. 16 platoon, he turned to the C.O. and asked in a gloomy voice: 'Do the steel helmets fit the men?' We were saved. He was human after all.

At Barly, too, came my first experience of that admirable fountain of justice, the court-martial. The accused was the elderly pioneer sergeant of the 60th; the charge, 'drunk in trenches'. He was duly found guilty. As he was marched out, I hurriedly turned the pages of the *Manual of Military Law*, and found to my horror that the punishment was death, *tout court*. So when Major the Hon. George Keppel turned to me as junior member of the court and demanded my sentence, I replied, 'Oh, death, sir, I suppose.' Major Keppel blenched and turned to my opposite number, Gwinnell. Gwinnell, who was as young and unlearned in expedience as myself, answered, as I had, 'Death, I suppose.' Our good president looked at us from the top of his six feet and groaned: 'But, my boys, my boys, you can't do it.'

'But, sir,' we protested in unison, anxious to justify ourselves, 'it says so here.'

PP—C*

It was only after a moving appeal by the president that we allowed ourselves to be overborne and to punish the old ruffian by reduction to the rank of corporal in the place of executing him; but we both felt that Major Keppel had somehow failed in his duty. Perhaps as retribution for this blood-thirsty exhibition, I was thrown on my way home. The girth slipped, and in a moment I was lying on my hip in the road, watching the pony going hell for leather into Barly with the saddle balanced on its tail, looking like an absurd poke bonnet. When two days later the order came to move, and I could scarcely walk, I was given charge of the blanket lorries.

Our four weeks were over. The warm weather and the freedom from restraint had medicined us. The battalion moved with a freer air than for six months past. There were no stragglers on the march to Halloy, and though it poured with rain that night, there was no unusual grousing. We were still a long way from the fed up and far from home state of mind. On the next day we moved to St. Amand. A generous housewife provided the mess with a vast dish of *œufs sur le plat.* As we looked at those golden discs flanked by two bottles of Nuits, we vowed that life was good, especially since we were to relieve the 4th division in our old line. But my own satisfaction was abruptly dashed by the appearance of Cuthbertson, who called on me to perform his adjutant duties while he was on leave. Grimacing, I assented, and that evening dined with the headquarters' mess.

Two nights later we moved to our old trenches opposite Ransart and Adinfer Wood, relieving the Lancashire Fusiliers. Battalion headquarters lay in the shell of a brick house on a lonely road running parallel to the front line, perhaps six hundred yards to the rear. It stood quite alone, and its roof or at least the tall poplar at the edge of its untidy garden was visible to the Germans in Adinfer Wood. Usually something unpleasant fell in the neighbourhood of the house during breakfast, startling enough to drive the colonel out of it to go round the more placid front line. The telephone was in a small chamber in the cellars, where we also had our sleeping quarters. Three nights after we had come in, I got back to headquarters about 1 a.m., and flung myself on my pallet. I seemed hardly to have dropped asleep before I was awakened by a swelling tattoo. As I swam up through the waves of sleep, my first coherent sense was of the figure of our gunner liaison officer, falling headlong down the stairs, roaring 'Barrage line' at his telephonist. Then the colonel appeared at the other instrument, shouting at the companies. I pulled myself together and ran upstairs. The length of the horizon eastward was flashing and leaping light. To the right down the hill in the Monchy salient, where No. 1 joined on to the next battalion, there was crashing, grunting and roaring, not isolated noises, but continuous, and Very-lights were rising in endless succession. I ran across to the reserve platoon garrisoning the strong point to tell them to stand-to. The dark face of Sykes, one of our stout South African officers, gleamed at me in the candle-light with the expression of one who had just received a surprise parcel, and is not quite sure whether it will contain a box of cigars or an anaconda, but is hopeful. When I got back, all the companies had answered the colonel that they were quite untouched except No. 1, with whom communication had broken down; but No. 2 reported that so far as they could see, No. 1 was at peace with the world. This had not deterred the colonel from immediately sending every available man of the headquarters' staff to carry boxes of bombs to the right company's assistance. I arrived in time to see a mass of men with boxes sprinting down the road, in the darkness, although they had at least a mile and a half to go. I then found that he had despatched every runner we had, so that our only alternative means of communication had failed. He then proceeded to ring up the companies all over again. I went upstairs and joined Major Ardagh, who had lighted a cigar and was equably leaning against the wall. Gradually the noise rumbled itself out. A whizz-bang began viciously putting shells at our house, but thought better of it. In an hour dawn broke in complete silence. The line to No. 1 was mended, and it was then reported that our carrying party had disappeared. We did not find them until five o'clock, twenty men and boys, their heads on bomb boxes, sleeping placidly in a communication trench. The strafe had finished long before they had reached the front line, and the sergeant had decided that it really was not worth breaking their night's rest any longer.

Two days later the C.O. retired to England to consult his doctor about suspected rheumatism of the heart. This threw me into the companionship of our charming second-in-command, Major George Ardagh. Of his history there is little more precise data than of Siegfried's. He is said to have fought at Majuba and to have been promoted to his captaincy in the Steelbacks on his return to England. This, if it be true, would put him on the wayward side of sixty in 1916. He had retired; but during the South African War he had enlisted as a trooper and risen to command a column, with which he won the D.S.O. The news of the outbreak of the war in 1914 reached him in Upper Rhodesia beyond the Zambesi. He promptly rode into the nearest township, and arriving on a Sunday when the banks were closed, sold his guns to pay his passage home rather than wait twenty-four hours. Very small, very thin, a frail ghost of a man he seemed when he joined us; but a month of his company convinced everyone of the soundness of his heart. He was always to be found in the front line at night, sitting on a firestep smoking his pipe, or wandering round the bays guided by friendly privates, who pulled him out of the sump-holes into which he continually fell. 'Little four-by-two,' the men called him affectionately.

Now for some days I was the privileged companion of his

nocturnal wanderings. Slowly we walked the line, pausing to ask questions, dropping into a company dugout for a drink, pausing to relight his pipe which he rarely kept burning the length of three bays, pausing again to extricate the Major from the hole into which he had slipped with one of his rare oaths. At two o'clock in the morning under a misty moon, the little man stopped suddenly, as we felt our way down the uneven brick flooring of Boyau 8, and taking my elbow, said: 'I like this, you know. I like wandering round the trenches seeing men. It's far better than sitting in your dugout and getting rheumatism of the heart.' Perhaps in these nights between earth walls or walking over the down turf, the old heart recaptured something of those happy nights in South Africa and the excitement of freer days.

It was not always pleasant to stroll with the second-in-command. He had become an amateur of shells and noted new varieties with all the enthusiasm of a naturalist. At recent excavations, ominous of further gifts, he would pause and prod hopefully with a stick, oblivious of the urgent tapping of his companion's foot. So, too, he would cheerfully thrust his head over the parapet as a shattering detonation rent the air, and gaze mildly at whirring clods, barbed wire and garbage. 'By Jove, that's a funny one,' he would remark: 'I haven't seen one burst like that before'; and vainly attempt to persuade my own craven soul to share his hobby. I found I knew quite enough about shells to have no leaning towards the collection of rariora. I would admit that at a distance they might afford a certain aesthetic pleasure, especially when the enemy was solidly pounding away at a blank spot of which he had suspicions. On a still afternoon the big black shrapnel was wholly admirable. It would suddenly appear in the atmosphere, a flash, a tight black cloud, which slowly unrolled like the engravings on the title-pages of eighteenth-century French books, supporting a lyre or a basket of pomegranates and ears of corn.

Almost one expected a Zeus to spring from it towards an unsuspecting Danaë: only it was not gold which showered but smoking steel. Against this, the English shrapnel with its gay careless puff seemed a pretty toy—until one had the misfortune to get in front of it.

The heavier shells, the 150 and 210 mm., the English 6 and 8 inch, were more terrifying. A German area shoot at Ypres in 1917 seemed to touch the pitch of the aweful, even if one watched it in safety from the next acre of ground. Looking narrowly, you could see the plunge of impact before there spouted a fountain of smoke and blackened earth, and heard the agonizing split of the steel case beneath the pressure of exploding ammonal. This would fill me with terror in which my body seemed to dissolve and my spirit beat panic-stricken as a bird in the abyss of winter waves.

These terrifying portents had not yet appeared. On Cuthbertson's return I was glad to rejoin my company. No. 10 platoon I hardly knew yet. Indeed, it had no need of my attention, for since Adler had gone home wounded, Sergeant Fake had ruled it with serious affection. I was inclined to be slightly afraid of Fake, a lean sallow veteran of the Boer War, so completely self-confident was he. He had a touch of the Ironside about him, a supreme faith in the cause of England and absolute confidence in the genius of the British Army. The battle of Jutland drew no more than the comment that thank God we had an army: but the loss of Lord Kitchener reduced him to unconsolable gloom. I found him rocking to and fro in a corner of the trench saying over and over again: 'Now we've lost the war; now we've lost the war.' Remonstrance was little avail; reason, less. Kitchener was dead, and so good-bye to victory.

It was about this time that I first heard that famous melody, 'I wanter go 'ome.' The melancholy singer was Private Ting of No. 9 platoon, the company scallywag. Cockney irrepressible, newspaper vendor by profession, father of twelve (a thirteenth on the way, for luck; he sent messages to each in his letters home), admirable private and deplorable N.C.O., only the records know how often during the next years he was promoted and how often reduced: but for all his sins an unfailing, unflagging spirit. Often during the worst of the winter, I had seen him at evening stand-to on the firestep, his chin up, cheerfully shouting across No-Man's-Land to the enemy: 'Oh, Fritz, yer old sossidge. Come out ternight, Fritz, and I'll give yer . . .' a series of picturesque afflictions.

A subaltern in trenches saw little of his platoon. Though he was responsible for the upkeep of its particular sector and the wire in front of it, yet the greater part of his duties were towards the company as a whole, splitting up the night watches with the other platoon officers. There were four of us: Adler, who had returned and was now second-in-command of the company, Leader, Jerome and myself, a happy enough family under Amberton, who allowed us to quarrel and argue while he lost himself in speculative triumphs of engineering, devising a truly invincible anti-aircraft gun.

They were happy days, these last two months before the Somme. High on the airy hill-side, in the heat of the sun, one was almost persuaded that the war was but a mimic battle. Friendly gunners would invite infantry subalterns to the O.P., and show them the intricacies of their art, before blasting some new manifestation of German industry into chalky clouds. From one point further to the left, they could see the road running behind the enemy's lines, and each day would harry the Boche post-corporal as he arrived with the mail. The game, I gathered, was not so much to hit him, as they nursed him up the road (although, of course, an accident might occur), as to make him drop the letters. Not yet very good, our gunners: the driving of a salvo into the bank beside the signallers' dugout six hundred yards behind our front line required a deal of dark and technical explanation.

The days slowly pass away. A few rare shells disturb the mustard and darnel blossoming along the parapet. The men rest during the afternoon. At stand-to, this summer evening almost conjures one to believe that war is a pleasant state. The sun has gone behind the ridge; but the sky is still flushed from his passage. Across the valley, the air is turning pearl grey, with here and there brown smudges where Fritz cooks his evening meal. Adinfer Wood has lost its sinister air and wild life must be waking among the trees to business no more cruel than our own. A lark bids a reluctant farewell to the day and drops down among the tussocks on the ridge. Faintly from far away comes the hum of an aeroplane. Now that pastoral music, the rumble of wheels, begins over the countryside, both east and west, the rumble of the ration limbers, English and German, creeping steadily towards the line. The air holds the sound, magnifies and disperses it, making of it a homely background, in front of which some familiar tune whistled by the man in the next bay as he rubs an oily rag over his rifle brings a fleeting nostalgia for an English lawn, shadowed by a walnut tree, dew, and a lamp behind a window pane. In the distance, a single gun, half afraid of the quiet, speaks once, and for a few seconds tears the evening into clanging echoes. The first flare rises from the trenches opposite, curves and sinks, a brilliant lily. Suddenly far away a wild murmur breaks out, rising and falling, a tuneless, tumbling prestissimo played by a muffled orchestra. Over my shoulder to the north I can see a cataract of lights rising and falling in all the shades of the prism; now and again, a flash as of a damp match quickly extinguished, bursting shrapnel. 'Vimy Ridge again,' murmurs Leader; 'Stand down.' The darkness is blotting out the valley. 'Stand down,' repeats Sergeant Fake: 'Corporal Lennox, is your wiring party ready?' The industrialism of war engulfs us again.

There was only one brief period when a subaltern had his platoon to himself. At each relief two parties were left in support, one at the fort round the Gastineau, the other at Point 147. The fort at the latter was a ramshackle affair of tumbled-down trenches, a few rat-plagued shelters and a mass of wire, situated at a crossroad, on which the Boche would occasionally drop shells at dusk in the hopes of catching the ration carts. Like all suitable residences, it commanded extensive views, northwards up the Vimy Ridge with Arras a dim cloud in the offing; eastward it looked down the long valley which cleft our front line. Here for three days one had one's peaceful existence. A few carrying parties only disturbed the morning calm. I would lead a group laden with trench-boards, dugout frames, wire and whatnot, down Farnborough Road and across the gully. Then having had one with the Rifle Brigade company commander, I would return to a peaceful afternoon with a pipe and a book on the parados of this miniature maze.

My last visit here was enlivened by company. It had been decided to raid the trenches opposite No. 1 company; and the party of volunteers shared the fort with me while they rehearsed their stunt. They had constructed on the backward slope an outline of the enemy sector and here they rushed to and fro hurling dummy bombs. Raids had only just begun to come into fashion and the word had not yet acquired the sinister significance which it would possess within the next six months. So the party at Point 147 was gay. There were Batty-Smith, Gwinnell, and Perkins, florid ex-company-sergeant-major, with a D.C.M. won at Loos. Batty and I played fast, incautious games of picquet with a wealth of cheerful abuse, while Gwinnell and Perkins lay on their bunks indulging in those endless and irrational arguments of men isolated from the world. It must have been here that Perkins vented in response to a Kirchner drawing that superb challenge of the average sensual man: 'I don't like yer thin gals. Give me something with some meat on it . . . something *you can strafe*.'

No shadow of doubt as to their success crossed their minds.

'Come and take a stall for the night,' said Batty as I bade them good-bye, and I promised to do so.

I did not after all attend the spectacle. Ten days' leave came my way just then, to an England already a little foreign and a little queer. 'Business as usual' seemed to mean spending more money and drinking just one more than was good for you, to the health of the army or of anyone else who happened that way. London appeared a little drunk and rather vulgar. People knew all about the coming offensive on the Somme; indeed, they knew considerably more than I did. For all that, it was London in May and I was grateful for its clear sky and warm air, though not to those wise authorities who decreed that subalterns must not spend more than 3s. 6d. on a meal. The chief *plat* on the 'Officers' Lunch' at the Savoy Grill was Irish stew, without alternative.

Back in France, I was sent to La Herlière to deputize for our transport officer, Jude, who followed me on leave. He was a comic little fellow, this Jude, a kind of hobo Englishman who had come to us from the staff of General Villa's army of Mexican rebels, where he had worn cherry-coloured pants and been paid when the General robbed a bank. As soon as he saw you, he would produce a pack of cards from his hip pocket, saying: 'Come on now; play me five cold hands for five fives.'

The transport sergeant, Thompson, so obviously knew more than I did that I left it to him, except that I rode up the line with the rations each night. My quiet old grey (christened Hathi by the quartermaster: whether on account of his elephantine bulk and large hoofs or of his wise manner I prefer not to guess) scarcely eyed the lorries clanging furiously past. These streams of traffic were further signs of the preparation southward, besides the parks and dumps of stores and shells, and further back, the new aerodromes. Aeroplanes in the sky were still phenomena, we had seen so few. When one came over very high in the air, the glint of sun on its belly looking like a ripple on a lake, men still dropped their tools and gazed upwards. The planes flew so high that we rarely knew whether they were our own or enemy machines. We did not think very much about the R.F.C. in these days. In spite of the Loos fiasco, we of course believed that the big push would succeed. After ten months in France, we were still in our state of primal innocence. But even in these early days the surprised mind woke momentarily to the thought, 'but—it's a life sentence.'

A night or so later, our raiding party crept out from the right company's line and lay waiting for the 60 lb. T.M.'s to finish the breaking of the wire. A wind had risen during the afternoon and was now blowing across the front. The twenty-four men lay in the rank grass with Batty, Gwinnell and Perkins in front, waiting for the toffee-apples to lift and waver into the wire in front. The trench mortar fired; but the registration had been carried out when there was no wind. The breeze caught the bomb, carrying it down the line. It exploded a few yards from the attacking group.

'I say, guv'nor,' said Private Billett to Gwinnell: 'I'm 'it in the bleedin' arm.'

'Shut up,' growled Gwinnell. 'So am I.'

'Are yer, guv'nor!' returned Billett. 'I'm sorry to 'ear about that.'

Gwinnell staggered up, with three wounds in the leg, Perkins hit in both arms; but Batty lay still. A splinter had gone straight through his brain. Eight other men were hit, and there was no more to be done with the raid. Gwinnell, bleeding from his wounds, shepherded the men back and brought in Batty's body. And save for the burial of the quiet clay in the valley behind Point 147, that was the end.

The catastrophe wrenched many of us as no previous death had been able to do. Those we had seen before had possessed an inevitable quality, had been taken as an unavoidable manifestation of war, as in nature we take the ills of the body. But this death, at the hands of our own people, through a vagary of the wind, appeared some sinister and malignant stroke, an outrage involving not only the torn body of the dead boy but the whole battalion.

Yet though we all loved Batty-Smith, our mourning was short. Back in Bailleulval, the gramophones resumed the *Charlie Chaplin Walk*, or if you wanted more classical airs, you went to No. 4 mess, where Arthur Bliss obliged with Elgar and Schubert. We played eternal bridge, thumbed old worn books, read the papers, and scoffed at Mr. Belloc. Leader conscientiously cut Jude for five fives every morning; Cuthbertson organized a successful skit of the movies, played in the flickering jet of the cinema lantern, himself in skirt and wig. The men sat about in estaminets, or played House in the courtyards.

We worried them with continual inspections. It could not be helped. Many of them were like children, moving in a haze of their own dreams, unconnected with practical things. We made these days a refrain of socks, boots, shirts, holdalls, combs, razors, shaving brushes. 'Take that to the sergeant tailor; get it mended. Put him down for a new badge, sergeant. And see you get your hair cut—*today*, mind.' The company barber was one Joyce, an old old man, half deaf and strongly perfumed with liquor.

'How old are you, really, Joyce?' I shouted one day when he was snipping away at the back of my neck.

'Well, sir,' he answered cautiously, 'they put me down as forty-two when I 'listed.'

As a fact, his age was just about sixty. Yet when the *vin blanc* had loosened him, he would dance amid approving shouts a break-down on the cobblestones, comparable in energy to those tarantellas Sir William Hamilton used to dance with his Emma. I am glad to think that a proper blighty a month or so later sent him to England for good.

Many new subalterns had joined us during this month. Among them were two from our own ranks. The first was our bombing sergeant, P. E. Lewis, a dark, handsome man with a soft voice and a complete lack of resistance to any kind of persuasion. Before any big action he made an elaborate toilet, of which the central piece was a garment of pink silk. Towards the end of 1918, it held together chiefly by P.E.'s will power; but it bore him magically through. Besides him, there was Archbold, but he was soon to leave us for the higher atmosphere of 'Intelligence'.

Working parties had now begun again with double energy. The staff had planned to join up the heads of the long saps which protruded from our line, by a continuous trench. It was supposed that this artless demonstration would deceive the hard-bitten Boche into believing that these were assembly trenches to be manned in the coming attack. The manœuvre would not have deceived a cadet. Only on the assumption that the entire Army Command had gone lunatic could the enemy have believed that an attack would jump off from this ground; and being a deal less simple than our cheerful staff would have it, and possessed as a rule of tolerably reliable information, he did not move a single brigade to our front. But he cheerfully turned a battery on to this easy target. On the first night a company of the 60th were caught in the open under salvoes of shrapnel. In five minutes the leader of the party had been killed and thirty more knocked out. As a result of this the parties that followed employed a ca' canny policy, working inwards from the ends of the saps. Now this policy, which saved men, lowered the rate of progress. Our company commander, Amberton, having impressed on higher authorities, his capacity as an engineer, was superintendent of the work, for which duties he was withdrawn from trenches. But living in billets was comfortable and he came to rely on the reports of the officers in charge of the working parties rather than on his own vision; while somewhat naturally the man from the spot was apt to report the labours of his company in Homeric terms. At the end of a fortnight the staff concluded that the job should be finished and appointed the next afternoon for inspection. For most of us an imminence of the Brigadier was usually sufficient to set us working in the most loathly and unapproachable part of our trench at the moment when the great man arrived. There was something Olympian about General Barnes's gaze, an aloofness from our cares, which few subalterns care to court, though we knew we could rely on the Brigade-Major, Linton, to prompt us through awkward cross-examinations. But on this afternoon, the air was full of expectancy. We lurked about the saps and watched the party, consisting of a general, a lieutenant-colonel, a brigade-major, two or three orderlies and Amberton, go down to their inspection with the eagerness of children waiting for a booby-trap to work. It had, by the way, rained hard during the night. Presently those who looked over the edge of the trench observed a strange procession across the landscape, seven large rumps heaving themselves with difficulty through a shallow ditch in the grass, the floor of which we knew to be several inches deep in wet clay. It was a hot afternoon, and no doubt our friends across the valley were somnolent: not a shot echoed. The leading stern suddenly disappeared, followed by the others. They were through the perilous strait. What followed is said to be the finest piece of denunciation ever voiced by General Barnes, surpassing even his condemnation of the C.O. of our Rifle Brigade battalion when he with six hundred men, without arms and largely without boots, was left on the platform at Hazebrouck. Small wonder that our colonel, already tremulous with the terrors of his passage, quivered still more sharply, that Amberton turned a delicate green. Linton alone remained unperturbed, embracing the onlookers in a grin of human comprehension. The florid general limped away, still Olympian in spite of the mud with which his gorget patches and ribbons were daubed, while the colonel at last finding his voice, in a frenzy of nerves and rage, imprecated Amberton to the deepest hell.

In this way we prepared for the beginning of the Somme. Already the bombardment had opened in the south; and our divisional artillery joined in. The enemy retaliated by bringing up an 8-inch howitzer which shelled us without point or method, so far as we could judge. One shell would fall in our wire, the next five hundred yards away, the third on the parados, the fourth somewhere among the gun positions, a mile behind. One shell bursting on Roscommon Road threw a fragment two hundred yards which banged against my shin, cutting the puttee, but doing no other damage. I'd missed a nice blighty, as you might say. This game went on usually from noon to four o'clock. It was not dangerous, but there is no more wearying and wearing sound than the distant explosion of a howitzer and the long threatening whine of the shell as it approaches.

Into our quiet lives new phenomena were daily being thrust. For one—unpleasant blow—all leave was stopped. Then on an afternoon the large observation balloon opposite burst into flames, which turned to rolling grey clouds. The midge hovering above it jerked round and sped across our line for home. Camouflage nets and paintings hung over places 'secret as a nest of nightingales'. On the twenty-seventh of June four parties were detailed to carry gas cylinders into the sector of the battalion on our right. We rendezvoused at the headquarters of the 60th, a charming affair of rustic huts, nestling against a bank. In front lay a small garden plot, over which Colonel Chestermaster, a thin melancholy figure, his long serious face oddly adorned with an enormous French forage cap of the most vivid *bleu horizon*, stooped as he tended his nasturtiums, unperturbed by the snarl of explosives a short distance away.

Carrying parties are maddening tasks. The officer moves slowly at the head of a single file of burdened men. He shortens his pace, he loiters; inevitably there comes from the road: 'Pass the word up. Steady in front.' He halts a minute to give the stragglers time to catch up. 'Message from the rear. Please, sir, Mr. B's compliments and what the 'ell are we waiting for now?' In the meanwhile the enemy may have started shelling the trench a little further on. Insensibly he quickens his pace as he gets nearer the danger spot. Another message, ' 'alt in front'. He stops and inquires feverishly who the message is from, what's he to halt for, and why here in particular. No one can answer him. A sharp whine warns him of the approach of a shell, and as it lands over the edge of the trench he once again urges his party forward, thankful to get them past the place before another falls, and praying hard that nobody has dropped either his duckboard or the box of S.A.A. on the plea of duress of shell fire. On this occasion officers were told to follow behind their batches of fifty. Each man had a sack to pad his shoulder and a grey cylinder which he was just able to support. They toiled slowly up the trench. From the front line there came the uncanny crunch of minnies bursting. Every few yards there was a halt to enable men to readjust their loads; until there came a longer halt than usual. 'Pass it up, what's the halt for?' Answer: 'Lorst 'is guide and lorst the w'y, sir.' Spurred by a ferocious energy, I climbed forward, one step on a shoulder, the next on a cylinder, the next a jump over a head, the last a trip over a pair of legs and a headlong fall. At the fortieth figure I came on a trench junction. The fortieth figure was small, dingy, and disconsolate, seated on a cylinder, wiping its forehead with a grimy handkerchief. '*I* couldn't keep up,' it kept repeating. '*I* couldn't keep up.' 'Well, you might have looked which way they went,' I growled savagely. 'Couldn't see the b——s, sir; they went too fast, quicker'n lightning, they was. I just come 'ere. . . .' I tried my alternatives. The right arm degenerated into a gulch of slimy reeds and green water. Along the left I found the head of my party. The sounds from the front line thirty yards forward were growing more insistent. I hurried my forty on to the dump and heaved a sigh of relief as the last of the long grey objects was stowed away. The party showed the utmost despatch in getting away; it was two miles before I caught them up.

When we relieved two days later, Amberton had left us to command a guard at Army Headquarters, and the company was led by Nelson, an elderly subaltern; elderly, I say, but I suppose he was not more than four-and-thirty. At the same time arrived two cases of wine we had ordered many months before and given up for lost. In view of the optimistic hope that we should be marching forward in three days' time we took them into the line with us, half a dozen Paul Ruinart, half a dozen Pichon Longueville, some admirable brandy, some velvety curaçao, and various other correctives. It had rained hard during our relief, but now the weather cleared. The sun shone brilliantly. Work on trench preservation ceased. We should, we felt, be out of these trenches and on the other side of Adinfer Wood in forty-eight hours. Leader lay on a firestep, Nelson and I balanced ourselves in opposite angles against the parapet, Sidney chattered and clog-danced on the duckboards.

That night a small party dashed over from No. 1 company trenches into the German lines. The Boche retired to his supports and sprayed the party as they came back. Two of our men were dead, no prisoners were taken, and no enemy killed. We were beginning to realize that these raids were a hundred to one chance.

The morning of July 1st dawned in its usual heat haze. We stood down about half-past three. I had been on duty since six o'clock on the previous evening, and going to my shelter fell asleep at once. Presently there crept over me the sensation of being rocked to and fro by someone with no sense of rhythm. Waking, I found my ears battered by a distant drum. I went into a firebay and looked over the parapet. In front the German trenches lay in their familiar white scrolls across the hill-side: but to the right the wood was blotted out by clouds of smoke which poured across our front line in an impenetrable wall. Our own divisional artillery was firing hard, but more impressive was the tossing feverish turmoil beyond, an unsteady dull beating of the air. I waited at the parapet for a long time, but nothing but the cloud of smoke over the wood moved.

Breakfast came, lunch. The first sprightly communiqués were telephoned up to us. The gun-fire on our flank had lessened and we thought that our artillery must be going forward. There followed a long blank afternoon. The evening messages were less jubilant. At ten o'clock we were told to get our men into the slit trenches, which since we had no deep dugouts were our shelter against shell fire. Blake was raiding in the same place as last night. Two salvoes of shrapnel would herald his rush. I watched the shells burst. There was complete silence: but later we were told that he and his party had killed five Germans and returned unscathed.

The morning of 3rd July heaved up to our impatience. The latest reports, read over greasy slabs of bacon, conveyed little. At midday we received orders that we should be relieved by the 5th North Staffords from Gommecourt. They arrived at twilight. Two officers and thirty-five men appeared to take over our company sector of eight hundred yards. The company commander was strung up to breaking point. He placed his men over the parapet and told them they would be on duty all night. The other officer was a pale dark boy, nineteen at the most. Every now and then he shuddered. He talked of the attack below the Z. The 6th battalion had led the attack. They had been mown down. The fourth and fifth waves composed of the 5th battalion were pinned to their ground before they started. 'I lay in our left sap-head for seven hours,' he said, 'while they shelled us to hell. I crawled under the other bodies. I've had three meals and five hours' sleep since the 30th. They might have given us a rest,' he added piteously. Then the shouts of his company commander jerked him to his feet. He went along the trench, a slim shaking figure, and disappeared.[1]

We slept that night in Bailleulval. We were to be in G.H.Q. reserve from next morning. G.H.Q. reserve sounded like the last troops to finish off the war, on which cheerful thought we slept soundly.

[1] The Gommecourt Z must have been one of the strongest positions opposite the British. It had already held up two French attacks in 1915. It was never taken, but evacuated by the Germans, when they retired in the spring of 1917. It was our reserve position in 1918. It lay on a sharp hill-side, with three, if not four lines of trenches, gridwise, facing N.E. and S.E., all of which could be used as fire-trenches, since the slope was steep enough to permit the second and third lines to shoot over the heads in front. It was very heavily wired, about twenty yards deep. Between it and the British line lay 200 yards of open meadow, completely devoid of cover.

VII

'You are the first swain that ever I read of that lay on the brow of a hill when there was such hot work in the valley. You must leave your pipe and take your trumpet, Ben.'

MAT PRIOR

If I have dwelled on the simplicity of this battalion, it is with deliberate intention. Up to the beginning of July, 1916, that is, during our first eleven months, the war for us had been purely stationary; and warfare a matter of learning the job. There had been no fighting save a few encounters of patrols. All we had learned had been to try to keep our trenches healthy, and to suffer shell and trench mortar fire, if not with equanimity, at least with a cynical humour. Our wastage had not been high. In consequence, our spirits were not yet damped. Actually we knew very little; and if the battalion did not expect a walk-over, it still had the illusions bred of propaganda and the picture papers.

We marched out of Bailleulval with the band playing *The Girl I Left Behind Me*. We had garrisoned it for time enough to permit the traditional tune; though for the life of me I can recall no young face at the windows. As we followed a field track, we were amused by the sight of a German 5.9 sniping lorries on the Doullens–Arras road. The companies sang; and even the Lewis gunners towing their baby carriages did not seem depressed. This gaiety could not last. Two miles from our destination the sky opened, and water fell on us in one jet. In a trice the road was flooded; a stream, calf-high, rushed down the track. We crawled into Humbercourt as helpless as moths with sodden wings.

Humbercourt was a sweet village. Our billet was in a

long room, well windowed, looking out onto a garden sprouting with peas and haricots. 'G.H.Q. reserve for the duration,' twinkled Leader as he opened a case of champagne procured by Nelson in some indirect way.

'Come in, Quarter,' as a round serene face appeared at the door. 'Have a drink.'

'Well, as the Governor of North Carolina said to the Governor of South Carolina . . . I don't mind if I do.'

'Sing us a song, Quarter . . . go on, you old humbug, you're quite fit . . . have a glass of fizz and give us *Little Pigs*.'

The singing began, the very simple stuff we all knew: *Mandalay*, *Van Tromp*, interspersed with ribaldry such as *Coming Home from the Wake*, *The Chandler's Wife*, in which the penultimate line is refined by the energetic rapping of knuckles on the table. The sun shone out again, and through the steaming gardens came more than one subaltern to join the chorus. From the barn down the road where the company was housed rang the racket of other songs. Evening lingered, only fading with the notes of the Last Post. We unstrapped our valises and lay down on the brick floor. It had been a bon time.

On the next day at tea-time Cuthbertson appeared at the window, his cheeks flushed with exertion. 'Get ready to start by bus. Companies parade in full marching order. Draw an extra bandolier for each man from the stores. Blankets and valises to be dumped at once. Leave the Lewis gun carts.'

'How soon do we start?'

'As soon as the buses come. Any moment.'

'Where are we going?'

'I don't know, but you can guess.'

We assembled on the road as the light began to fade. The chars-à-bancs were late. The colonel fussed up and down the road, rattling in map cases, compasses, and gadgets. The men sat cheerfully enough in the last of the sunlight. Ting started *If you're Mr. Reilly wot keeps the 'otel*, and then mischievously glancing at the fidgeting C.O. broke into a thunderous:

Oh landlord have you a daughter fine
Parley vous
Fit for a soldier of the line
Oh landlord have you a daughter fine.

The company took it up. The song ran like fire in straw up the road. Soon the whole battalion was singing:

The little fat b—— he grew and he grew
Parley vous . . . .

The chorus was still rocketing from company to company as the convoy arrived. It continued while we clambered to our places. Sidney and I secured a front seat. At last we set off. Our destination was still veiled and for half an hour it looked as if we were going northwards. First we ran back towards Arras, but at Mondicourt we turned and raced down the road to Doullens. The cars clattered and swayed. The occupants yelled, shouted, and sang. We poured through the edge of sleeping Doullens. On the white hill up to Bon Air the drivers, encouraged to do their damnedest, raced, trying in reckless fashion to pass the bus in front. One broke down and was left on the hill-side, its passengers the butt of derision from each car as it passed. As the night grew colder the cheering and singing died away. I tumbled asleep, but woke as we dashed through a silent faubourg in Amiens out on to the broad road to Albert. Sidney's teeth were chattering with cold. I pulled him under the pent of the dashboard and held him in my arms until he fell asleep. A red lamp and a sentry beneath tall trees glimmered for an instant in the bleached dawn, Fourth Army Headquarters. Our headlong pace never slackened. Behind me a platoon, heaped in untidy bundles, slept: between them rifles and Lewis guns stood sentinels. At last on the straight dusty road the pace checked. The chars-à-bancs drew to the side. A finger-post, in an off-hand way, announced ALBERT 8K. We lumbered stiffly to a hamlet half a mile off the road, Bresle its name, a tiny place with few houses and fewer inhabitants. Its barns had been converted into bunked baraques, but even so it could not hold a whole brigade, and our other three battalions were coming in. Smith led No. 1 company into the church. An hour later he was assailed by the priest; but he refused to move his men, though Blake grew angry at this sacrilege. Two canvas huts sheltered the officers. The cooks set to building fires and boiling water.

'What about breakfast? What's that you say? Left the rations behind? Well, of all . . . D'ye hear that, Guy? We haven't got any food.'

Leader and I slid away to investigate the local Harrods. Two tins of sardines, one of condensed café-au-lait, two bottles of inferior Beaujolais, four bars of chocolate, and two packets of *petit beurre* biscuits rewarded our enterprise. Later comers found the shop bare.

We waited dully all day. The men played House. At least three shirt-sleeved *parties* lined the ditches on the way to orderly room. The air rang with raucous cries, of Legs eleven, Clickety-clix, Top-o'-the-'ouse. Towards evening the 60th and ourselves were ordered to detonate a couple of thousand Mills bombs. This treacherous work was usually carried out by small parties in some embattled recess: but now there was need of haste. Three hundred men squatted in rings of six or seven beneath the thin weary trees of the *place*, working as if possessed. We moved from group to group, looking over shoulders to see that the safety pins were properly split and bent back. Suddenly there was an explosion and a shout. Pieces of iron hammered and slapped against walls. Three of the 60th were lying in a bloody group: one holding his stomach was screaming. Stretcher bearers ran up and carried the wounded away. The detonating went on without pause.

As evening fell we were ordered to dump our packs at the Q.M. Stores and fall in with two days' rations. As we fell in, Cuthbertson came up to me, and said: 'You stay here with the orderly room—in case I'm hit. Report to the quartermaster.'

He hurried away and I retired into the doorway of Fairburn's billet. I felt sulky, and at the same time relieved, and again—oh, fed up. As I watched the companies marching fast through the dusky afterglow, hurrying as it seemed with a tight-lipped urgency, my heart was very sore. Fairburn was as gloomy as myself. During dinner we speculated morbidly on whom we should lose. 'If only that —— of ours. But he won't: you'll see, we'll have him for always, Guy.'

The transport came in next day and we received a brigade order to move to Albert. There was no news of the battalion except a rumour that they were in the line. Fairburn and I rode to Albert that afternoon, clattering in under the leaning Virgin, and found a house in the street that leads out to Bapaume. There were beds on the first floor. Said Fairburn, looking out on to the stinking, garbage-strewn cobbles, 'Well, this is a bit of all right.'

Whoop, crash. A shell banged into the yard of the factory across the road. Planks and pieces of timber whirled in the air, clapping down on the stones. The clerks were arranging the front room for my office. My batman put his head in and said: 'There's Turnbull from Number Three wants to see you, sir—and Mr. Leader's dead.'

My mind shot out to the cheerful, comradely Leader. We had scarcely considered him last night: his grin, we felt sure, would bear him through all tribulations. Red-headed Turnbull, his creamy skin pale beneath his freckles, his eyes shadowed with grief and fear, slipped into the room. His uniform was plastered with clay, and he had no rifle.

'It was after the attack, sir. They were bumping our line cruel hard with 5.9's. Captain Nelson and Mr. Leader was standing side by side. The Captain bent down to do up his puttee. A shell burst on the parapet above them. It missed the Captain, but it knocked Mr. Leader's brains out. Yes, sir, we buried him last night, back of the parados. The Captain was wounded too. The Adjutant sent me down to see about Mr. Leader's kit, getting it home—and there's a note for you.'

Cuth's note said they had attacked and had taken all their objectives with comparatively few casualties, Leader killed, Nelson, Bliss, P. E. Lewis, and Morgan wounded. The battalion would reach Tara Hill during the early hours of the next morning.

When I found them, the whole battalion, except the cooks and the half-dozen officers who had been left out, was asleep. They lay stretched on the hill-side, their uniforms daubed with chalk, their faces and hands brown with mud, their hair tangled and their unshaven cheeks bloodless, the colour of dirty parchment, just as they had fallen in attitudes of complete exhaustion. Every now and then a figure moaned or beat the air with his hand. I found Cuthbertson engaged in an elaborate toilet. Even he who was ever the mirror of fashion was unkempt.

'We went up that night,' he said, 'and got orders to attack at half-past eight in the morning, to the right of and above La Boisselle. We went over. There was a lot of bombing up one of the communication trenches. That was where P. E. got his: but we got our line all right. We caught a lot of Boche there. Then we got astride the Bapaume road, where we had a marvellous view of the attack on our left. We could see the Boche in Ovillers packing up to go, but he was too far off for us to hit. We settled down in the line and then they started shelling us. That was where poor old Leader was killed and the others wounded. The men stuck it very well; but—oh, my God, that ——! I got him to go round the line once; he ran at full speed, keeping his head down, and then retired to his dugout. About three o'clock that night, I'd just turned in when I saw him get up. He carefully put on his gas-mask, his belt, his revolver, map case, compass, and field-glasses. I was so surprised that I asked him if he was going round the line. "Oh, no, no," he said, "I'm only just going to the water-closet." We *must* get rid of him. Little old Ardagh is furious with him. *He* was up in the line all day, running about looking at shells.'

While he talked there was a sudden stir. A few men rose, others woke and joined them, collecting in a mob round a khaki figure with a camera. Pickelhaubes, German helmets, Teutonic forage caps, leaf-shaped bayonets, automatics, were produced from haversacks. The faces which ten minutes earlier had seemed those of dying men were now alight with excited amusement. 'Come on, come an' have your picture took,' echoed from man to man: and amid much cheering, the official press was obliged with a sitting.

I sat down with Blake and Sidney Adler, near the crest of the slope. From here we looked down over the clustered red huddle of Albert. The front line was perhaps three thousand yards forward, yet the slope was thick with the infantry of four or five divisions. The enemy could not see over the crest without balloon or aeroplane observation, and no balloon could stay in the sky. Our aeroplanes were now strong enough to see to that. In between the lumps of infantry British 18-pounders and French 75's, tucked into shallow emplacements, were cracking and banging. A 60-pounder at the side of the road stirred the dust into whorls at each discharge; horses passing by shied and fled up the hill. There was a dressing-station by our side to which Ford ambulances came and went unceasingly and unhurriedly. Once or twice German shells fired blindly exploded on the road.

In the morning sun, every figure, every stunted tree, was

illuminated with a clarity of outline as in a Manet picture. The round white rumps of men seated on latrines facing the town added points of light to the drab tint of the worn grass, the baked leaves and the dusty creamy track. The crowd shifted and heaved. But for the guns spitting and flashing and the half-naked men, it might have been Parliament Hill on an August Bank Holiday. Notre-Dame-des-Brebières clung tenaciously by her toes to the ruddy campanile. She was not yet to fall.

Blake's face was slack and haggard, but not from weariness. He greeted me moodily, and then sat silent, abstracted in some distant perplexity.

'What's the matter, Terence?' I asked.

'Oh, I don't know. Nothing. . . . At least. . . . Look here, we took a lot of prisoners in those trenches yesterday morning. Just as we got into their line, an officer came out of a dugout. He'd got one hand above his head, and a pair of field-glasses in the other. He held the glasses out to S—— you know, that ex-sailor with the Messina earthquake medal—and said, "Here you are, sergeant, I surrender." S—— said, "Thank you, sir," and took the glasses with his left hand. At the same moment, he tucked the butt of his rifle under his arm and shot the officer straight through the head. What the hell ought I to do?'

He tore a withered blade of grass out of the ground and chewed it angrily, his eyes roving over the barren landscape. I thought hard for a minute.

'I don't see that you can do anything,' I answered slowly. 'What can you do? Besides, I don't see that S——'s really to blame. He must have been half mad with excitement by the time he got into that trench. I don't suppose he ever thought what he was doing. If you start a man killing, you can't turn him off again like an engine. After all, he is a good man. He was probably half off his head.'

'It wasn't only him. Another did exactly the same thing.'

'Anyhow, it's too late to do anything now. I suppose you ought to have shot both on the spot. The best thing now is to forget it.'

'I dare say you're right.'

He got up and moved stiffly away. I turned to Adler, who was carefully powdering his feet. He was bubbling over with cheerfulness. Late on the previous night. Nos. 3 and 4 had been pushed forward suddenly to take a line of trenches vaguely spoken of as lying a few hundred yards ahead. Either because the actual objective had been blotted out and the trench they eventually reached was past the one against which the attack was directed, or because our artillery was firing short, the gutter in which they eventually settled was being whipped by English shrapnel. They stood it for two hours, and then after messages had failed to stop the gun-fire they were ordered to come back to the starting point. They brought back the dead and wounded through a storm of low-burst shrapnel, quick flame and hailing bullets.

There was already a change in the battalion. In the first place there had come to the men, now that they were awakened and had shaken out of them their first drugged nervous slumber, a new confidence, almost a jauntiness. They had come through their first battle successfully; they were all right. Secondly, between those who had been in the show and those who had not there was a gulf fixed. It may have been due to a certain delicacy on the part of the latter; but the gulf existed.

There was enough to occupy one in Albert with the constant stream of messengers coming to and fro, the melancholy business of the casualty lists, next-of-kin, sorting out these humble parcels of the personal effects of the dead, the creased, greasy letters, addressed to No. 6494 Private Smith, On Active Service, B.E.F., the knick-knacks and trifles. There were letters to be returned. One addressed to Leader in a sloping French hand I put on one side. I had to tear the envelope to discover the address and saw the first passionate lines. Strange that my ugly stolid little friend should inspire such. I thought of him looking at me over a mug of hot milk and rum at stand-to in the dead of winter and with a grin of his terrier mouth croaking 'Chin-chin. Happy days.' I stumbled an hour over the appropriate letter.

Three nights later the battalion went up again, this time in support. By now we knew that our division had been split up, and the infantry loaned right and left. Our whole brigade replaced four broken battalions of Fifth Fusiliers in the 34th Division, whose general was described as a fire-eater. The area was hotting up. The enemy had succeeded in getting observation over the ridge and had seen enough to justify him in shelling both sides of the road freely. One of our officers had been very slightly wounded in the hand. From the dressing station he was carried away on an ebb tide of wounded, and before we knew of his wound was in England. Adler fell into a trench while leading a carrying party and broke his collar bone. Our street in Albert was becoming uncommonly nasty. 5.9's would scream down out of the hot sky, smashing among the flimsy brick houses. The water-main, cut by a shell, burst into a dusky fountain a hundred yards from our door. Fairburn shook his head and decided that the stores would be more conveniently situated with the transport. I missed his company and felt unhappy at night alone in my cock-loft when the shells came over.

The sordid street never slept. The noise of wheels was ceaseless. Up and down, all day and all night, passed lorries, limbers, G.S. wagons, ammunition columns, ambulances. At the sides marched weary infantrymen stupefied with battle, dragging their feet as they came out to rest. Over it hovered and sank stagnant dust from road, broken brick, dried paint, stirred into lifeless movement by the wheels, only to fall back. Through it all, the yellow smell of garbage, and beyond the guns thud-thudding, bruising the tired air. The 2nd S.W.B., short sturdy Welsh miners, occupied houses all round us. One platoon was billeted on the first floor next door. They sang choruses in fine deep voices; the tone was beautiful, but they sang all day and half the night, and at that one song. It had a refrain which sounded like, 'Hop along, sister Mary, hop along.'

I also suffered another disillusionment. The bed on which I camped was, I discovered too late, infested. I was lousy. Hordes of minor parasites ran about my body, in and out the seams of my breeches. In vain I attempted to hunt out the tribe by hand. It required a Briareus to deal with the plague in this fashion. I surrendered and hoped I might one day see my kit again.

In the meantime the battalion near Contalmaison Wood was enduring pertinacious shelling and constant casualties. Each morning a list came down with a fervent appeal from Cuth to send up every man who returned from leave or a course. The big guard of half a company under Amberton had already come back. So, too, had Ned Kelly, a Punch-faced elderly subaltern with a row of ribbons from previous wars. His words were a sharp chirrup, precise as a thrush's. Borrowing a steel hat and a gas-mask he went up the line with a mackintosh over his arm and a little swagger cane, as cheerful as if he were going to a city dinner. He reached the battalion in time to join in one of the ghastly mistakes which break soldiers' hearts. A big attack on Pozières had been ordered. One of our battalions had already made an effort against this stronghold. The few who got as far as the orchards had been killed by machine-guns. Today the Rifle Brigade were to take part in a big encircling assault at 11 a.m. and the 13th were to support them. At the last moment the plan was cancelled; but the message reached neither battalion. So at zero they started with their flanks in the air and no protecting artillery. At once every German gun covering that section was concentrated on them. The Rifle Brigade struggled forward in the teeth of the storm, half-way to their objective. By that time their colonel and their second-in-command had been wounded, and all four company commanders killed. The attack withered away and stopped in a sunken road. Behind them the 13th moved forward a hundred yards, and seeing the catastrophe in front, lay down. For an hour they endured a barrage in the open: then the news of the cancelling of the attack reached them and Major Ardagh, who led, ordered them to fall back to their jumping-off line. The casualties were heavy. Williamson was severely wounded, and Blake, while both the sergeants whose conduct in the earlier attack had made him bite his nails, were dead. That afternoon I received a further urgent call for men from the adjutant. While I was reading it, Leader's Turnbull reported. His expression was worn and anxious.

'What am I to do, sir?'

'I'm afraid you must report to the company, Turnbull. . . . I'm sorry. Every available man has got to go. I'd like to keep you; but you see. . . .'

A docile resignation crept into his face. 'I suppose so, sir.'

At that instant there was a terrific explosion immediately overhead. Turnbull yelped and crouched. The hanging lamp over the table hovered for an instant and then crashed down. Bits of hard substance went banging into the floor and about the walls. There was a yell from the street, followed by shouts of 'Stretcher bearers, stret-cher bear-ers.' The passage was filled with dust and the stairs choked with débris. I ran out into the street. The shell had hit the roof exactly at the junction of the two houses. Screams and groans were echoing from next door. S.W.B. stretcher bearers ran up the street. From the wreckage of the upper storey they pulled out two-and-twenty Welshmen, unconscious, pale, and shocked. The orderly room emerged from the basement with self-conscious grins. My batman led me upstairs to look at the damage. Both rooms were wrecked and the contents of my pack tossed hither and thither among the fallen plaster. A pair of scissors had been neatly cut in two. I reflected on the prescience which had induced Fairburn to seek more pastoral surroundings. It was his hour for a nap, and the shell would have burst over his head. In the turmoil, Turnbull had disappeared.

I slept on the floor of the office that night. Next morning's runner from the line grinned when he saw me. 'We was laughing up there,' he said, 'to hear orderly room 'ad been done in.' I glanced down the casualty reports. One name stood out above all the others. 'No. . . . Pte. Turnbull, 3 Coy. S.I.W.'

On the night of 20th July, the battalion was relieved. That afternoon I removed the orderly room to the transport lines. My first action was to strip, walk naked into the middle of a small patch of standing corn, and drop my garments among the wheat. No doubt, by the time the harvester found them they would be clean. Next morning we trudged solemnly back to Bresle. On the way, an ambulance passed us. On it was one man with a bandaged foot. I caught his eye and waved a hand. Turnbull answered me with a melancholy grin as he was swept past the dusty, depleted companies. I have no doubt that those entirely efficient generals and staff officers on whose manner I should have modelled myself, would have reprehended so gross a failure in discipline. Yet I could not do otherwise. I had known Turnbull for a year. He had served—I might almost say, had shielded—an intimate friend through troubles and stresses. Perhaps with Leader's death something cracked in him. The loyalty to one man had been too concentrated, and with his end, it died, leaving him with no other creed. Into the vacuum rushed the need for escape. A bullet fired deliberately at the foot was the only way out. Perhaps those who call this man a coward will consider the desperation to which he was driven, to place his rifle against the foot, and drive through the bones and flesh the flames of the cordite and the smashing metal. Let me hope that the court-martial's sentence was light. Not that it matters, for, in truth, the real sentence had been inflicted long ere it sat.

Bresle was no shady sanctuary, such as Barly or Bailleulval had been. It had never been more than a slattern village. Its tumbling by the British Army made it more sluttish than ever before. The sun poured down on it. Its trees were parched. There was dust perpetually sweeping its one street on hot winds; and it was empty of feature. Every hut was lousy and there was a constant waft of disease. Once more the cries of the House players rattled up and down the street. Leave to Amiens was sparingly granted. Few went and those chiefly the newly joined. Occasionally we rode to Corbie to sit in a crowded café. In the evenings we gathered in the orchard round a table simply constructed by digging trenches round a plot of earth, drank whisky, and talked. The earth was warm, the leaves brown: the sky was airless beneath a sulky orange moon and deepened our sombre mood. Death glanced sourly at that orchard and pricked a name upon his tablets. We talked a little of vanished friends, of dead men. 'Poor little beggar . . . rotten luck . . . he was a good man . . .' were the poor phrases in our mouths. But we had not yet reached the state of baffled exasperation we were to acquire during the next year. Under the stimulus of Cuth's good whisky and the quartermaster's talk, we might soon be singing some catch, breaking off to call: 'Now, Fairburn, tell us the elephant tale.' And wrapping his cloak still tighter round him until he appeared more Falstaffian than eve, the quartermaster would begin: 'When I was stationed at Umballa in 'ninety-eight, there was an elephant which had the colic. . . .'

So a week passed. On the 30th July we moved up to Albert once more. A few drafts had come to us, but except for officers we were still woefully under strength. We were also fed up with being away from our own division. The 34th, to which we had been loaned, now only possessed one of its own brigades, its eight washed-out battalions of Tynesiders having been sent up north to our own division. Some hooted with derision when the divisional commander was killed near Mametz Wood; it was reported that he was souvenir hunting. And why not hoot? What was this Hecuba to them?

On the 31st the battalion moved up the line. I went with them as far as their position near Mametz Wood. Then once more I returned to the transport lines to wait on Cuth's becoming a casualty. The transport lay in the Happy Valley; I wonder what Johnsonian so named it, and for that matter why. Its brown banks seemed to hold a million men and a million animals. All day long the dust, brown and golden in the sunlight, rose and choked the blackening trees. All day long carts, wagons, men and horses went by, an endless bistre frieze. All day long a Royal Scots band practised *The Broken Doll.* It was the meeting-place, the market square of the army. Broken divisions, coming back, paused here one night before release to quiet sectors. Fresh divisions bivouacked on its stale earth before being sent up to their ordeal. Friends from other days strolled over as they waited, to ask the news, have a drink, and pass out into the rosy twilight dusk. Fairburn returned brimming with happiness, having stumbled on X battery, R.H.A., the only Indian troop, with which he had served on its formation some centuries earlier. One day cavalry went up the road to go into action. An excited crowd gathered to watch them. They passed back the same way that evening, going westwards. This time the crowd was derisive.

There was sickness in this hot stifling valley. Four

out of a draft of five officers disappeared with dysentery within a few days of joining. Bloated flies poised determinedly over our food and swooped upon it. One sickened of these carrion eaters and inevitably of the food they would contaminate. That recurrent piece of stewed beef with its enormous satellite boiled onion, which appeared morning and evening in undisguised hideousness, became nauseating, even when dowsed with Worcester Sauce and gulped with the aid of neat whisky. I found, too, that I had dysentery. A local medico across the valley presented me with five black pills which he averred would cure an elephant. He was right. I stayed with the transport and went on waiting.

Waiting thus, I was damnably unhappy. It was all very well to remind myself that I was obeying orders by remaining at the transport lines and acting as kitchen maid to the battalion. I did not disguise from myself that I was at the same time relieved to be in this safe place. The past twelve months had not revealed in me any love of modern warfare. I loathed shells. I had none of that active energy which makes your true fighting man cry, 'I adore war!' The sight of the rigid bodies of men I had known quivering with vitality, bodies now 'blue and wan, woefully arrayed', made me shudder and stirred in me a hatred of existence. Heavy shells froze me until it was only by an act of will that I could move from a state of lethargic suspense, even as I cursed myself for the weakness.

Now to be once more left out of the line, while more recently joined officers went into action, seemed to me a stain on my pride—or was it my vanity? I was too young to accept it with philosophy or cynicism. It gnawed at me while I sat in outward tranquillity beneath a bank in the valley. I began to hope for some accident to befall our adjutant which would send me up to his place. I eagerly scanned each casualty return to find his name. Other names appeared, Amberton's, and that of a boy in our own company, only with us a few weeks. But our adjutant continued, it seemed to me miraculously, to survive.

Instead, we received news of —— ——'s final withdrawal from the battalion with diarrhoea. He was last seen running down the road past Mametz Wood, his belt in one hand, his stick agitated in the other, calling on his batman to follow him, while the battalion ensconced in the angle of a quarry jeered. It was divulged later that our brigadier had declared in writing his wish never to see the fugitive's face again. I felt a certain sympathy for the wretched man. He had been a wash-out from the first; had succumbed without any effort to the first strain, and yet by arrogant stupidity had alienated the sympathy of every person who might have brought him to a counselled leadership. Nevertheless, such is the incalculable alchemy of the human soul, his failure had resulted in a curiously democratic control, which had effected a more complete harmony, confidence, and loyalty than was often to be found in units more capably led.

The battalion was now holding the line opposite the switch trench between High Wood and Pozières. They were asked to do nothing except patrol, dig, and endure continuous shelling. It was here that a subaltern was annihilated by a direct hit from a whizz-bang. A booted foot and some bloody earth were all that were recovered to be placed in a sandbag and decently interred. The adjutant inherited the ambiguous task of explaining to his relatives exactly why it was not possible to send home his personal effects.

But even these things end. On the night of the 13th August the battalion was relieved, and on the next day we tramped for the last time along the Amiens road to Bresle.

VIII

'And then I was sent off to South Wei,
Smothered in laurel groves,
And you to the north of Raku-hoku
Till we had nothing but thoughts and memories in common.'
RIKAHAKU-POUND

We stayed at Bresle four days: four days of constant inspections of all the gear and harness of the modern soldier, discarding, repairing, renewing. Those who had come through were happy, glad to have escaped and optimistic of a rest in a quiet sector. Drafts came up. Some of our lightly wounded rejoined. 'Glad to be back here, sir. If it hadn't been for Sergeant-Major Bailey we'd ha' been Cameron Highlanders by now. Taking everything they was, at the base, Sussex, Fusiliers, Dorsets, shoving 'em into kilts and sending 'em off to the Jocks. But Sergeant-Major Bailey remembered us Thirteenth chaps, and marked us for the old batt.'

We moved north by devious routes. The battalion and the billeting party played a complicated game of cross-purposes under the direction of the circumnavigation department. I almost thought the battalion had won, when it passed me all forlorn on the railway tracks at Fontenettes by Calais at 2 a.m. on the third day. However, I reached Estaires with an hour in hand.

The battalion was reorganized and No. 1 company fell to me, Walter Spencer taking over No. 4. Within twenty-four hours we were inspecting our 11th battalion's trenches at Armentières at the top of the Lille Road. These trim sandbag bulwarks seemed reasonably clean and safe. No guns fired. Pleasant orchards through which birds fled and twittered lay behind the trenches, and a mile back an estaminet offered decent refreshment. We rejoiced as our No. 19 bus carried us back to Estairs. But within two hours, our happiness was dashed. Orders were issued that we should return to our division, and that the two Fifth Fusilier brigades would take our place. A day later, as our train meandered in the maddeningly purposeless manner of troop trains through the back areas, southwards once more, we passed another bearing one of the battalions to take over our cushy line. 'Where have you come from?' someone shouted. 'Vimy Ridge,' came the reply. 'What's it like?' 'Hell,' answered the voice amid a roar of laughter. But the day was too fine and warm, with a brisk wind, and we were not disturbed by this *schadenfreude*: our determination to enjoy the moment was justified when at last we found ourselves in the mining town of Divion. A bon place, you would say, with passable billets and a decent estaminet or two. Even in the few days since they had passed Mametz Wood for the last time, the physical condition of the men had reasserted itself. But they were not anxious for a repetition of their experience. Still, No. 1, in spite of casualties, was much what it had been. The company-sergeant-major and three of its four platoon sergeants had survived the battle; and all were willing soldiers.

In a week we were on the move again through small sordid towns, Bruay, Barlin. This was to us a new country, a ghastly blasted region with its slag heaps, latticed towers, and pit machinery. The rain fell in torrents. We limped soddenly into Hersin, a squalid dump of miners' cottages. The company was billeted in houses presided over by grim slatterns of repellent aspect but of amorous nature. The operation of drying one's body was fraught with embarrassment. Most of us were glad to depart from this sordid village, which Zola would have loved to describe. By platoons at intervals of 200 yards we marched slowly down the slope into Bully-Grenay beneath the eyes of a line of observation balloons.

At first, Bully-Grenay appeared the neatest of villages. Some pioneers of culture had attempted to lay it out as a garden city. Small red villas stood in festive gardens. People, as distinct from soldiers, went to and fro. It was only on closer inspection that the flaws in this Eden began to appear. At lunch, a 60-pounder, coyly sheltering behind a hedge of pea-sticks in the next garden, suddenly leaped into noisy activity. Our house shook, the windows rattled, the plates trembled in anticipation of back answers. We heard them come, passing viciously overhead. Later, I noticed one lad, a new draft, looking shaken and wan. 'Not surprising, neither,' said C.S.M. Dell, 'those four shells landed all round him in the middle of the square; and all he's got is a hole in his water bottle. . . . Here, pull yourself together, lad. That's the cushiest wound you'll ever have.' A great man, Dell; first remembered as a small innocuous company clerk, bending a curly tow-head over the pay and crime sheets in the company orderly room at Worthing two years before. By swift metamorphosis, he appeared in France as C.Q.M.S., prompt, efficient, and the owner of a brisk humour. When, during the first winter, our elderly C.S.M. retired to the base full of age, sciatica, and rheumatism, Smith had discerned in Dell the man to run and hold No. 1 company. Yet though his tunic flamed with a fresh D.C.M. ribbon, nothing could ever make him into the semblance of the swaggering regular sergeant-major. But he could handle men, and somehow conveyed a sense of fierce authority. I had the impression of a harassed but efficient mother of a reckless family.

In the next day or so, we reconnoitered what was to be our trench line, not sorry to be out of Bully. There was a treacherous air about these smug cottages. Rumours of spies assailed us, but we treated them with familiar scorn. What need of spies had our would-be murderers? Their balloons hung, vulturine, in the sky all day, looking down on to every open space. Troops were forbidden to congregate or to move about in parties except out of observation. We carried out inspections in the lee of empty houses, and our parades were confined to extended—very extended—order. In this game of I-spy, the odds were all in favour of the spy, and the only warning that he had seen something was the hurrying shriek of a 5.9. Not that shells fell frequently, but the German gunners usually chose the moment for these manifestations with a fiendish regard for our discomfort. A whizz-bang slapped into No. 2 company's mess as glasses were being raised to lips, causing serious consternation.

Calonne North, a mile-long, featureless conduit, led us to the front line. At the eastern end a Xanadu rose. Calonne and its environs would have rejoiced a Churriguerra by its wild and unpremeditated architecture. Not the most baroque of builders could ever have designed this fantastic minehead with its cluster of stark mad houses, its corridors, tunnels, and aisles. You passed through such a Covent Garden as might have been before the dukes of Bedford began to build, a small square with young trees beneath which the cookers sheltered, and lent it the air of a sleepy market place. From here various ways led to the front line. Birdcage Walk brought you, surprisingly, to the Marble Arch, while the First Commissioner of Works would have been shocked by Boyau Thomas cutting clean across Hyde Park. For ourselves, we took the less urban route through Essex Trench, past West Ham Lane, into Durham Quad, at the corner of which lay an angle of the fire-trench. In this mixed geography, it was not odd to find one's support line the Hoxton Road, and behind it the Horseguards' Avenue.

The company sector was of the most fantasticated corruption, a series of salients and re-entrants. On its left lay the Béthune–Lens railway: a barricade formed an immovable buffer-stop, but no engine tested it. Two sap-heads at this point were within the range of the Boche rifle-grenade, highly unpleasant posts, until Glanville put a Stokes gun in Hoxton Road. Half a dozen canisters spinning in the air at once, cooled Fritz's advances. From here ran a chalky ditch with a treacherous parapet of ragged sandbags, and in front of it a torn lace petticoat of wire. At the corner of Durham Quad the trench suddenly turned towards the enemy, and you came round by the school. With its eastern wall eaten away as by giant rats, it was closed for repairs. Its other wall still stood, balancing by a feat of equilibration the roof from which slates would slide and clatter. Here the trench walls rose to ten or twelve feet, a solid bastion of rubble with the firestep at head level. Then after seven bays or so, you passed into the shadow of the crassier, a gigantic double-bar joining the many clef lines of the trenches. Its sulky black hulk dominated the landscape as far as its larger brother, the Double Crassier, two miles to the north. Its summit at our end was festooned with a crown of ironwork, which flapped and creaked in the wind. In the rough weather slag would tumble down its sides, startling nervous sentries, as Gideon's cake the Amalekites.

The German line conformed to our shape, a lifeless place, held by Saxons: its back-cloth, rows of dingy workmen's dwellings, stared at us with pierced eyes; yet, like blind men, sensitive to movement, which was rewarded with pineapples or a few shells. Cité de la Plaine the map called it; but no fire from Heaven consumed this Gomorrah in our time, although our guns made practice on it. For a time a tower of latticed steel stood at the corner. One morning a 60-pounder blew away its legs, and mid cheers from the spectators, the mass of ironwork slid and crumpled, like one of Mr. Wells's Martians. Our gunners were furious at this intrusion of the heavies; the tower had been their datum line.

To our rear down communication trenches walled with pit-props lay Calonne, fortified as a mediaeval stronghold, where machine guns, which never rattled, were mounted at loopholes, where observers, who never fired, watched all day. Behind its façade lay Durham Quad. No college at Oxford boasted better cloisters than this small square. A trench to cellar level ran round three sides. Black deposits of coal showed the soil we were on, but great thickets of nasturtiums, now that man no longer tended them, luxuriated over the banks, and brave asters nodded their rose and mauve petals. Our dugout, a cellar at the trench corner, was not gas-proof nor had it much head cover, but we were calm enough to think that the ruins of the house above it would prove a good bursting course. Outside the door an acacia swayed forty feet above our heads. On the fourth side of this quadrangle lay the cloister. It had been constructed by the simple means of driving holes from house to house through the ground floor walls. Dust of lime and brick lay thick upon its pavement, printed with the tread of a thousand hurrying feet. With the autumn sun pouring through the rents in the walls it was as pleasant an alley to pace as you might find from Lens to Canterbury.

The worst offence in the neighbourhood was the rats, great beasts as big as kittens, which ran to and fro over the parapets and squeaked behind the boards in the dug-out shafts. Dell was their deadly enemy. As we strolled round the line at night, with an 'Excuse me, sir,' he would brush by me and lunge with his bayonet at a scurrying shadow. Not infrequently, he would turn back to me waving a struggling trophy, which torchlight revealed as the scrofulous and mangy progenitor of vast litters, now gorged on French corpses and offal, too obese to move with the slippery agility of the young fry.

John Marquard, one of our quiet soft-voiced South Africans, a Transvaaler, and I spent hours exploring these ruins, chewing the biltong with which his folk kept him amply supplied, as we loafed into empty houses whose caretakers had long died. A grave, passionless man was John, brooding as a line of kopjes. He looked very boyish with his long awkward frame and fair hair, and very steady. He possessed in high degree that primitive simplicity and integrity of life which Hyde found in Falkland. I think of him standing upright in a tangled mass of wire, silhouetted in the white glare of a Very-light; and as a machine-gun titters, hear his sober voice: 'Steady, man, don't move.'

In this sector normal conditions asserted themselves. The new drafts (not so new either, for many of them were returned wounded) became assimilated. We went back for a week to Coupigny; and such being the toughness of habit, to shoot our annual course. It was during this week that the battalion showed itself capable of dealing with any situation. During a sudden inspection by the divisional commander, Colonel Ardagh was requested to form a line into a square. Not having studied the drill-book since he was on the Steelback's square in his youth, the Colonel in a broken voice murmured: 'Form square,' and waved his arms. Whereupon with no more ado than if it had been asked to slope arms, the battalion performed the complicated manœuvre without a hitch, though with many *sotto-voce* comments from subalterns and C.S.M.'s. We were not going to let little Four-by-two down.

From Coupigny, civilization, or at least a simulacrum, was rediscovered. There were places in the neighbourhood where one could dine, not merely feed. In the distance was Béthune, to which our youngest made painful journeys, lorry-hopping, to return in the small hours pink-eyed, woebegone, and exhausted. One pasty-faced newcomer, R., made himself notorious by the frequency of his visits until he became a casualty to this mode of life. The rest of us rode the hills at the base of the Vimy Ridge. Once I visited the Lorette spur, a grisly graveyard of fallen trenches and mingled bones, nameless, unrecorded. 'We cannot hope to live so long in our names, as some have done in their persons.' Sir Thomas Browne would doubtless have forged a trenchant aphorism; but in the face of these heaped relics I was tongue-tied. As I stood beside a crumbling ditch, filled with helmets, *cantines*, long rifles, and these somehow less than human bones, a heavy piece of earth, grass-grown, fell, loosened by the rain, from the top. In the cavity lay something which had once been blue, faded to fleece colour, stained with earth. Nature was working fast upon it. It was enough. 'We reckon more than five months yet to harvest; had we but eyes to lift up, the fields are white already.' I turned and went heavily back to Coupigny.

Our week over we returned to the line, and it rained, but we were cheerful enough. The Debatable Land between the lines was practically our property. Our junior subaltern, a red-haired happy lad named Jolly, investigated a German sap-head on two successive nights. Dell and I explored a number of ditches, which led nowhere. Once a flare fell within a yard of my hand. 'Be careful,' muttered my companion, as we lay breathless beside this hissing incandescence; 'they burn.' I had no intention of experimenting and was thankful enough that the light had not betrayed us to the watcher who fired it. The brigadier visited us augustly but refused Colonel Ardagh's invitation to join him in an inspection of the enemy trenches from the most elevated and conspicuous point in our line. Linton winked at me. Colonel Ardagh was apt to be difficult. Always a little vague, he would insist that a crunched, flattened, and abandoned sap-head was the way to the next company, and was only convinced of his error when he found himself faced by our crumpled wire and the Boche trenches.

Behind the front line the war was getting more and more a matter for experts. Novelties arrived almost daily. A vast trench mortar, known as the Quarter-to-ten, planted itself in the rear of the next company. Its first missile landed neatly between our front and support lines, pocking the ground with a pit capacious enough to bury five mules. We were now forbidden the use of the telephone. I Toc listening sets had been installed in the neighbourhood. What they heard of Fritz we never knew; but Comic Cuts provided the following dialogue which had been picked up between brigade headquarters and one of our battalions.

B. M. 'I say, what time do you stand-to in the morning?'

Adjutant. 'I'm not quite sure, I'll ask a company. (*Pause*) I've asked A, who says five-thirty. B says five, but he's only a bloody fool.'

B. M. 'Thanks, I'll call it five-fifteen.'

During the day there was a frequency of visitors. Smith, now second-in-command, serenely enjoying the diluted pleasures of his position. A sapper might follow, anxious for topographical advice on a drainage scheme. Then Glanville or Sykes, with a suggestion of a little shoot on some sore point where a minnie had been located. Padre Leeson, our devoted Catholic priest, might drop in on his way to visit his sparse flock. These Catholic priests impressed one. Leeson never dropped a word of religion in my hearing; but one felt a serenity and certitude streaming from him such as was not possessed by our bluff Anglicans. Already there was growing a dislike of these latter. They had nothing to offer but the consolation the next man could give you, and a less fortifying one. The Church of Rome sent a man into action mentally and spiritually cleaned. The Church of England could only offer you a cigarette. The Church of Rome, experienced in propaganda, sent its priests into the line. The Church of England forbade theirs forward of Brigade Headquarters, and though many, realizing the fatal blunder of such an order, came just the same, the publication of that injunction had its effect.

The padre would saunter on his way, his old maid's curls brisking in the wind, and perhaps about lunch time, a gunner would climb down from his O.P. in the corner house and regale us with tales of a certain Col. Cubitt, a descendant, so the stories seemed to indicate, of the famous John Buncle of Warwickshire.

As night fell, I might be joined by Uncle Lander, the new commander of No. 2 company. Together we paced the long line of the sector, talking of many things apart from our present tasks, pausing every now and then to question a sentry, stopping to lean against a traverse, while my companion reinforced his arguments by flamboyant gesticulations of a walking-stick, grotesquely simulated by his squat shadow, lingering with elbows on the parapet to quote some half-remembered verse, or to admire the Alpine whiteness of our chalk defences in the moonlight. Uncle was an artist, an ancient of Chelsea and an ardent advocate of the *vie de Bohème*; in earnest of this he painted in sepia, ochre and scarlet on the whitewashed walls of his cellar a fresco in which a life-size subaltern and a girl in her shift toasted each other, while an elderly triple-necked and red-tabbed general knelt in attitudes of supplication behind. It was voted a speaking likeness of our highly respectable divisional commander.

Uncle was one of two senior captains who had recently come to us from England. Their arrival had caused much heartburning among us juniors. Those of us who had companies were anxious lest we should be superseded. Both of them behaved with admirable tact in an awkward position and we liked them well, but all the same I was not going to surrender the company without a battle.

The tangle was resolved by our adjutant. He drew me aside and pointed out that I must inevitably lose the company. The officers who had been wounded were not being struck off the strength quickly enough to promote us, and the reserve battalions were sending out more and more senior officers. He suggested I should be attached to the staff as a G learner, which would solve both mine and the C.O.'s problem. The lure was too tempting. The fact that

I should lose the company if not now, certainly very soon, tipped the balance. I agreed and my name was sent in. I was not very clear as to what it meant. I think I saw myself as a rather kindly brigade-major, encouraging my seniors. For I still cherished illusions. In the meantime No. 1 was my charge and delight; and in that I forgot the staff.

For the company was no longer a band of amateurs, working out its salvation from its mistakes. The Somme had given it the touchstone of experience, the necessary touch of pride. We were no longer humble seekers after the right way. We knew. Our way was the right way, and damn what the 1st battalion does. We had never met it or any other of our regular battalions. Our tradition we had made for ourselves, and by that we would hold. We could meet others on equal terms and yield nothing. Each company now had its hard core of veterans, and the battalion was welded into a homogeneous unit.

Observe these four figures striding down the street, the C.S.M., the C.Q.M.S., Sgt. Brown, and Sgt. Baker. Their boots, their buttons, and badges glare; their webbing belts (these old hands have discarded the New Army leather, having 'won' the correct and smarter webbing down south) khaki-blancoed to a smoothness of texture a painter might envy. They salute with a swaggering click and a stony eye which the Brigade of Guards would not disdain—that is, except Dell, whose glance twinkles as one playing a part to amuse the children.

From my window I can see the street and a group of men lounging and talking by the gateway into the courtyard. They are never actually still. The group sways, breaks and shifts. They laugh and move with the restless grace of young cats, with the jaunty ease of perfect health and self-confidence.

For the moment they are at peace, and—dare one say it?—contented. They have three more days in billets and at the end a cushy line. Wisely, they do not think far enough forward to the inevitable next week or next month, when they will cower in mud, feel that hard flesh wilt and melt under the blast of high explosives, know again hunger, thirst and fear, inactive suspense, numbing terror against which there is no charm, no amulet.

There was a concert held at Bully-Grenay, one of the unforgettable nights. The small hall was crowded. Beer and rum punch—one wondered whether the quartermaster distilled the spirit or merely pinched it—were sufficient. We applauded the sentimental tenor and sang the chorus with a wealth of feeling which we should deny in the morning. We cheered Sergeant Hyams of the Lewis Guns in *O-O-O, I'm an Eskimo*, a song of suitable simplicity. Fairburn sang *Mandalay*, and later, under pressure, *Little Pigs make the best of pork*, with vehement gesticulation. But these only led up to our adjutant. He will never again have such an audience. *Winters' Nights* is a ragtime melody, the words negligible; but it will make an exile dream. Cuthbertson sang it so quietly that the dreams were undisturbed. In the end we were crooning the tune, would have sung it until we rocked asleep. In a moment's pause Boche shells could be heard tearing the night outside and dropping with subdued crashes in the square. But no small strafe could have disturbed us: we lay back and sang.

Autumn was coming in, and we stood-to at dawn in white mists which peeled slowly away and kept us waiting. From the south came the earliest stories of the hush-hush cars, in the attacks of the 15th September. They were well-garnished newspaper tales and we began to expect the advertised break-through. Yet there was a churlish expectation that the reports would prove to be highly coloured. The war was not going to end quite so easily, we felt. Within a few weeks our refusal of the G.H.Q. illusionist's tricks was confirmed by the arrival of a Canadian reconnoitring party. The 15th September had not been the jam with which these parental authorities tried to disguise the powder. The Canuck captain who took over from me lumped the tanks and the French Canadian battalions in one almighty explosive sentence. It was a long sentence, about a minute in duration and of a blasting searing quality. Otherwise he was efficient, cheerful, monosyllabic and thirsty.

This relief was unexpected. We had looked to stay in these quiet pastures for another month. But we had grazed long enough, and as Smith put it, we were fat enough for the slaughter. Rain clouds, heavy with expectant Walküre, blackened the evening sky as we marched from Bully-Grenay to Hersin. We passed a sinister platoon of the recently cursed French Canadians. A pullet swinging from a rifle muzzle and the wolvish faces of the men recalled Callot's *reiter*. They stared blankly and refused our greeting; but several broke from their ranks to accost in their clipped dialect some women who were standing beside the road.

Next day we were marching. It was the 18th October and the smell of autumn lay heavy on the air; a chill colourless morning, but the sun broke through as we passed a lonely sentry before a lonely handsome château near Ranchicourt, an army or corps headquarters; at least, something too august for our acquaintance. Our trench-cramped limbs were already growing aware of their novel freedom. We stepped lighter and with a rhythmical swing. That night we came to Magnicourt-en-Comté, and there we lay two days.

When we moved out, there was a nip in the air. The first frosts had come. Beeches showered us with copper and yellow coin. Briars shaken by our tread flung us the crystals from their sprays. The way was lined with brave colours; streamers of travellers' joy waved in the faint breeze and hawberries shook their crimson heads at the tramp of our boots. As we passed under a tunnel of dark trees, the band broke into its thunderous jollity. Blow, fife; rattle, drum. On this morning the clatter of *Brian Boru* is better than all Beethoven's nine symphonies. Even the immortal Ninth pales before the chorus: *And we'll buy a pair of laces orfer pore—old—Mike*. The battalion is moving as one man; very strong, very steady, with a sway in the shoulders and a lilt in the feet. We have regained our youth; we have recovered the innocence with which we came to France, an innocence not now of ignorance but of knowledge. We have forgotten whither we are marching: we do not greatly care what billets we find tonight. We are content to live in the moment, to feel the warm sun, to enjoy the strength of our bodies, and to be lulled by the rhythmical momentum with which we march. We are no longer individuals but a united body. The morning, the sun, the keen air, and the rhythm of our feet compound a draught more heady than doctored *vin blanc*, than the forgotten kisses of the girl in the billet. Few had forebodings of their destiny. At the halts they lay in the long wet grass and gossiped, enormously at ease. The whistle blew. They jumped for their equipment. The little grey figure of the colonel far ahead waved its stick. Hump your pack and get a move on. The next hour, man, will bring you three miles nearer to your death. Your life and your death are nothing to these fields—nothing, no more than it is to the man planning the next attack at G.H.Q. You are not even a pawn. Your death will not prevent future wars, will not make the world safe for your children. Your death means no more than if you had died in your bed, full of years and respectability, having begotten a tribe of young. Yet by your courage in tribulation, by your cheerfulness before the dirty devices of this world, you have won the love of those who have watched you. All we remember is your living face, and that we loved you for being of our clay and our spirit.

So, marching, we came to Magnicourt-sur-Canche, on a hill-side with the grey water of the Canche rippling against wooded banks. There were trout below the bridge. I wondered if they would rise to a Ministerial Deevil, the fly the last trout I hooked had fallen to. But these thoughts should be banished in October. Let me, instead, recall the proud four-poster bed under whose lace curtains I smothered, and the tessellated pavement on which it stood. 'Fit for Sir Douglas himself,' commented my herculean batman, Johns, as he produced a mug of tea in the morning.

The battalion threw the eighteen miles to Gézaincourt over their shoulder as easily as apple rind. Some of us explored the Bon Air that evening. Uncle cut jests in evil French with the villainous old dame.

The next day was painful marching. The weather had changed. Out of a dull sky a chill wind blew with a hint of showers in it. Four miles from Puchevillers, it turned to rain in good earnest. We reached the camp wet through.

What a camp it was! It had been the temporary accommodation for troops for 1st July. No doubt a pleasant enough place in midsummer, this six-acre orchard with tents under germinating apple-trees. Since then it had been used by every arm of the service. There was no grass. The ground, churned and stamped by hoofs and boots, was six inches deep in mud and horse droppings, and smelled stale. The trees were plastered with mud, lacerated with ropes, and the bark torn with the teeth of mules. The men sheltered in threadbare tents; the officers in two leaking canvas huts. And it rained. It rained remorselessly: it was neither heavy nor light; just rain; it never altered its tempo; it never changed its tone. In the rare hours it ceased, its irritation was supplied by heavy drops slapping on the canvas. It was cold, too. We crouched miserably over braziers filled with wet green wood. The smoke filled the barracks, and flavoured our food and our tobacco. Our clothes were sodden, our kits damp. There were no means of amusing the men, no place to see them. Our spirits fell to the bottom of the scale.

We were waiting for Z day. Z day was postponed, and then postponed again. On a raw grey afternoon, the colonel rode out, accompanied by Smith, four company commanders, the adjutant, and Archbold, the intelligence officer. The horses after long days of idleness were fresh. They bolted down the road to Toutencourt, Archbold and Cuthbertson leading, our frail little colonel with difficulty holding in his pony, and Uncle, no centaur, bumping ferociously and growling between his teeth: 'Whoa—Whoa—you beggar—oh—oh—oh—stop, you brute, and let me get my giglamps straight.' We passed through unenchanting villages where the walls were splashed to the eaves with oily mud by the lorries grumbling to and fro. Pools of dark fluid covered with iridescent scum lay across the road. Labour battalions and Boche prisoners were struggling vainly against the advancing tide. These villages, Varennes and Hedauville, were packed with troops resting, pale drab men who walked listlessly. Beyond there was the unsteady tossing of the gun-fire round the Thiepval ridge. At last we moved into open country and surveyed a long grey hill whose top was vanishing in the drizzle. 'This is our rendezvous,' said the colonel. 'Can you find your way here again?' We surveyed the dismal ground. The tall elms of Englebelmer seemed at peace; but every now and then the mist reddened as a heavy coughed its shell into the air. The rumbling and tossing of gun-fire was growing stronger, pulsing into an uneasy rhythm. Yes, we nodded. 'All right, go home.'

The ponies needed no urging. In a minute we had scattered over the turf. The mist had turned to rain again, and night was falling. Harding, a grim colonist, and I galloped ahead and by hard riding reached our melancholy camp by five o'clock. The others gradually came in, until only Uncle was missing. We clustered round the smoky brazier and speculated on his fate. Seven, eight o'clock passed: and then about nine, through the hum of rain and the splash of drippings from the trees, we heard the sock-sock-sock of weary hoofs picking their way through mud, and the voice of Uncle raised in melancholy song, 'Be it never so 'umble, there's no-o place like 'ome.' He had been left at the start. He had reached the Hedauville crossroads, and ignorant of his direction, turned down the road to Albert. Discovering his error after four or five miles, he turned back. Reaching Hedauville a second time he once more failed to discern his right road and rode due northwards to Acheux. It was now dark and the rain on his spectacles made his difficulties even greater. He passed through Acheux about 6.30 on our reckoning. Somewhere north of here he dismounted from his horse to examine a signpost; and then cramped and soaking was unable to mount again. He plodded along a dark muddy road. The few wayfarers he met were quite ignorant of the existence of Puchevillers. At last he found a military policeman who had not only heard of the place but was able to hoist our poor friend into the saddle and put him on the right road. At a conservative estimate we reckoned that Uncle had covered about thirty miles in his Odyssey. Happily we were not short of whisky.

The next morning we heard that Z day was once more postponed and that afternoon an order was handed to me: 'You will report at 63rd Bde. H.Q. at Terramesnil this evening for a course of instruction in G staff duties.' It was the intervention of a kindly fate: and I resented it. I knew we were on the eve of a serious engagement. But for the weather we should have been in it a week ago. I had no illusions—those cheerful staff illusions—of what was encouragingly termed a walk-over; and I disliked being shelled as much as anyone has ever disliked it. But I did not want to leave the battalion or the company. It was flagrant desertion to leave at this point. Afterwards would be another matter, but at the moment I had no relish for the wary and pious discretion commended by Sir Thomas

Browne. I sought out the colonel and had a short passionate interview under the streaming trees.

'May I stay till we come out, sir?'

'No. You've got to go. It's an order. My dear boy, don't be an ass. You've got to obey.'

'Couldn't you ask Brigade, sir?'

'No. I don't see how I can. It's an order. No. No. No.'

He wandered off into the rain and I flung away angrily. I said good-bye to a few friends in the hut who looked at me enviously, to the C.S.M., whose eyes I could scarcely meet, to the company pony. Johns rolled up my kit and we bundled it on to the mess cart. The six miles to Terramesnil were some of the most wretched I have ever driven. I was worn with misery as we drew up at the red lamp of the Brigade H.Q. A light shone from an open door and beyond there was a dry clean room with a blazing fire.

INTERLUDE

THE PROFESSIONALS

'Yet what here ye tell
Of our grande counsell?
I could say somewhat
But speke ye no more of that
For drede of the red hat.'

SKELTON

IX

'Apollo . . . made the Soldier's trade a Mystery as the Butcher's is.'

SELDEN

ONCE more Z day was postponed. It being the third or fourth postponement, it was at last concluded that the troops could not remain in their present inglorious squalor without either mutiny or plague. The division was withdrawn a few miles back into billets. Brigade headquarters came to Beauval. It seemed paradisiacal to eat well-cooked food off good tables, with decent napery and glass. This was a happy staff. Both the general and the brigade-major came from the same battalion of the H.L.I., and had served through the Retreat and First Ypres together. They were of that superb type, the best kind of regimental officers, devoid of personal ambition. They knew all the miseries which can afflict men in the field. General Hill was of the line of those Stuart portraits you may see in the galleries at Holyrood, with the hooked nose and the long jaw. A worn, pensive man, speaking infrequently in a gentle voice, uncomplaining, but, one felt, tired in body. Brodie, much younger, was somewhat of the same feature, but sandy-haired, with a long jaw and a pugnacious nose (confirmed by the ribbon of the V.C.), and in colour freckled like a wild strawberry. Sometimes, but very rarely, they talked of the past. 'I say, General, do you remember the donkey on the common at Mullingar?' What the story of this was I entirely forget, but it lingers in my mind with Arion's dolphin and other fabulous beasts. The only time the Retreat was mentioned was when Brodie said: 'There was a château there with a fountain and goldfish in it.

Remember, we bathed, and, by Jove, it was cold'; and the general chuckled.

The staff captain was Codrington, who a few years before had attempted to drill into me the rudiments of coxing an eight on the Isis. He had commanded a squadron of Yeomanry and been shot through the body at Ypres. He was a complete compendium of all military matters and lore, very deliberate and very thorough. Besides these, there was the brigade bombing - cum - intelligence - cum - bottle-washing officer, Simpson, a cheerful leery old-young man, glad to be out of the line—and the Baron. Proust would have loved the Baron, would have seen nothing amusing in him. In far-off days, the Baron, clad in lemon gloves, with a silk hat beside his chair, handed camomile tea to the ladies of the *ancienne noblesse*. Perhaps I am wrong. He was, now I come to think of it, a Bonapartist, which permitted him to serve as a decoration of the Quai d'Orsay —I can never imagine him to have been useful. Nor do I think he had ever before the war lived in an unheated room or existed except in a capital city. With his tiny feet, encased in peculiarly national boots, his gloves, his small very silken moustache, his ungainly seat on a horse—he spent his days trying to find an animal which would suit him—his scent, his love of Biedermeier music, he was a touchingly maidenly figure. The staff made a pet of him. The infantry spoke of him in derogatory terms.

I was only just beginning to be aware of my total incompetence and ignorance when the order came to move. We went in a thick mist to a small camp on the outskirts of Lealvillers. It was a desolate place. Two mornings later the attack up the Ancre began. We spent the day moving restlessly in and out of our huts listening to the gun-fire. The scanty news was, as usual, optimistic. No one offered any commentary. On 14th November, Brodie and the General rode away into the fog. At noon Simpson and I were told to bring the headquarters staff to the hill by

Englebelmer which I had marked nearly a month earlier. We reached it in a persistent drizzle which turned the afternoon to evening. The hill-side, which had been bare three weeks before, was now covered with every type of soldier and every kind of vehicle. There were two tents on the hill surrounded by a glittering staff. I stumbled on Brodie and our brigadier. The latter was wrapped in his mackintosh, trying to get some sleep. He looked like an elderly Scottish shepherd. Brodie was conning some pencil notes. He told me to sit down and take down the orders for the brigade from his dictation. At the same time he wrote swiftly in his own field message book. The orders were for us to relieve a brigade of the Naval Division in Beaucourt with my own old brigade on our flank.

'So they've been in it already?' I asked.

'Yes—attacked this morning. Have you finished? Then come along. I haven't got our orders yet.'

'What are these then?'

'Verbal only. I've taken them down from their G.S.O.1's mouth. They're damned silly and he won't want to sign them: but he's going to.'

'But——?'

'When you've been a bit longer in this game, you'll have learnt to trust nobody without a written order. If things go wrong, they'll go back on you. Besides, this isn't our Division.'

It was a long time before Brodie got his signature; but he came back triumphant. The General and he set off at once, telling us to follow with the headquarters staff to a dugout at a map reference Q. 18A. This was in what had been the German line two mornings before, on the Albert–Achiet railway. It may have been half-past four when we set off and the darkness was coming down fast. Our faces were covered with wet masks of mist. We moved very slowly. There were infantry on the road, and every hundred yards there was a halt. One could just see helmeted figures and the grey glisten of the ground-sheets twisted over their shoulders. In between there were limbers and pack animals. We slipped past the crowd in Martinsart, but we were soon stopped again. The road was densely packed with traffic moving both ways. Another hour perhaps, and we came to Mesnil. Here a battalion was halted. As we pushed past it and drew near the head of the column, there was a cry of 'Gas! Gas!' German shells were falling somewhere close by with a little chirruping explosion. The leading ranks of the battalion were a disorder of men struggling to adjust their gas-masks through the tangle of their equipment, ground-sheets, rifles, tools and helmets. One boy was seated on the ground sobbing. A man beside him said: 'Aw, chuck it!' We extricated ourselves and got on to the long steep road down to Hamel. Here, if it were possible, the press of men was thicker. Our march dropped to a walk, to an advance of a few paces, to a definite halt. Is it my fancy, or did the moon rise that night? In any case it seemed lighter and fresher on that hill road. In the arch of the horizon flares were gliding slowly up and down. Shelling seemed to dance in perpetual flames over one or two points. We descended slowly into the valley. At the bottom skeletons of long-dead houses glimmered against the light. We moved over what had been the front line and our pace slackened again. The road had been driven and beaten into enormous craters, ten feet deep or more. The bottoms of these pits were of sodden loose earth; carcases of men and animals lay in them. Paths led gingerly round the edges, past which thousands of men crept in single file. From the right the churr of a fast-running stream persisted over other sounds, and through thin perished trees the pools of a marshland glimmered in a wild pattern. It was cold now. A sharp frost had set in. I came up with a party of 13th officers, going up to replace casualties. I asked eagerly after the battalion, but they knew very little, except that the colonel and Uncle had been hit. As we talked, a stretcher halted for a moment by our side. I caught a glimpse of the unconscious face of a boy in my company, handsome brave young face, peaceful as in sleep. 'Where's he been hit?' I asked the stretcher bearers. 'Bayonet in the guts, sir. The Fritzes fought all right this morning before the company settled 'em.' 'Who else?' 'Ser'ant Brown's dead and Ser'ant Baker's wounded, and Sarn-Major Dell, badly 'it in the leg, weren't 'e, chum?' 'Yes and a lot more too. Ain't much of Number One now.' The block shifted, and they passed on with their burden while we went forward. It was one in the morning when we found the red lamp in a trench gully. I stumbled over something and fell upon the body of a dead German. It was rigid, with elbows raised and one leg up, the posture of a runner; a statue knocked from its pedestal.

A few hours later I was walking further up the road with Brodie. Dead men and animals were strewed on all sides. Ahead lay a steep bank and between it and the river the relic of a station—one wall and rails twisted and torn into wild arms thrust in appeal towards the sky. Under the lee of that bank a battalion was lying, its men clustered up its side like gulls above the sea. Every now and then a shell splashed in front of them. This was our first point of call; but between it and ourselves a quite considerable barrage of light shells mixed with 5.9's was falling. We marched along gaily, getting closer and closer to it. Nosecaps and pieces of shell came hurtling past. 'Surely he's not going to walk through this?' I thought. I glanced at my companion. The V.C. ribbon seemed to make that hope less sure. Setting my teeth for a wild scurry, I tried to maintain an appropriate impassiveness. Then Brodie suddenly remarked: 'I think this is a bit *too* hot,' pulled out his cigarette case and sank into a shell hole. I gratefully agreed and imitated him. In the end, since the storm showed no signs of abating, we worked our way round its northern end and turned back to the cliff. The 13th M.O., Proctor, had his aid post here: or rather, here he attended to the sick and wounded. There was no shelter. The stretcher cases, which the field ambulances' orderlies had not yet brought away, lay pallidly, well doped with morphia, in shell holes when possible; on stretchers in the open, when their wounds were such that they could not crouch but must lie stretched out. The high bank protected them from direct hits from shells, though there was always the possibility of the back blast. Proctor, white, with red-rimmed eyes, unshaven and dirty, grinned at me through his spectacles. 'My God, we've had a night. The C.O. copped it as they started from the top of this bank—smashed femur. Poor old Nunky got his working elbow drilled. He was pretty bad; but he managed to say, "I suppose I'll have to write serials now." Casualties coming down all yesterday. Number One got bumped to hell after they got on their objective. Me? I'm all right, bar diarrhoea. Caught a chill and kept dashing out all night into a barrage to find a shell hole.' Brodie beckoned me and we went on. Shells were tearing over our heads and crashing into the station thirty yards away. We clung to the side of the bank, picking our feet delicately between the débris of a Boche wagon team, bones, blood, and guts of horses, the heads with ghastly staring oyster eyes. Above this shambles hung the stench of blood and a strong sweet odour of an apple loft, the smell of gas. Pieces of shell and chalk rattled continually about us until we pushed our way into a narrow chamber, a passage dug into a bank, which was the 13th headquarters, and squatted rather breathlessly in front of Smith.

Brodie's business was to sift out the battle, to find where our troops were and where the Boche was. The fight was two days old and already, as usual, it was held up. Reports conflicted. The enemy's position was only guessed at, and, worse, even the line of our own front was vague. A battalion holding one sector would plot out a line of points indicating its posts. The battalion on its right or left, trying to get into touch, would deny the existence of these posts. It was nobody's fault. In this muddy wilderness where every natural and human feature had been either blotted out or twisted to unrecognizable form, and when the attempt to recognize those features could only be made through the blackness of a November night, through an atmosphere whipped with bullets and torn by explosion, where to leave the known plunged the seeker in ten paces into the unknown, and sent him perhaps blundering into a nest of Germans, no man could be blamed for inexactness in plotting points on a map. Throughout the days we remained here, the exact disposition of the division front was never accurately cleared up.

My own province in this tangle was indefinable, a mixture of scullion and aide-de-camp. To run with messages, to accompany the general on his visits to battalions in whose headquarters he would talk in his quiet impersonal way, as if the attacks were a matter of going down to the club for a drink and game of bridge, to sit up at night beside Brodie and protect him from unimportant messages, to bully the servants into filling in the crater of an 8-inch shell in the roof of the dugout. It was during one of these nights, the night before an attack, that the legendary Colonel Cubitt made his appearance. He arrived about ten in the evening and immediately started talking. When he stopped I have no idea. Between cat-naps I was aware of fragments of a discourse uttered over a pint mug of Harvey's port. 'You've got Carton over the river, General—first-class man—with me in Somaliland—got six wounds—probably get another tomorrow—you can't kill him. . . . Three things I never forget: a man's initials, every Derby winner since it started, and every horse I've ever seen. . . . He said I wanted eighty horses cast. I told him to go to hell. I'd get rid of three. What the hell does he know about a horse, the artful little beggar? Look at the way he rides. God's truth, I had him out of my lines in two shakes of a. . . .

Divisional commander wanted me to apologize. I told him I'd resign my brigade first. . . . ' It went on and on, a stream not to be turned. Our general's quiet comments were but stones in the brook which flowed over and round them. It was three in the morning before our guest swung up the stairs.

There are incidents which stand out in the six days' muddle which is a battle. Our brigade attacked and got part of Puisieux Trench; withdrew because some other troops had failed; attacked again and failed. Some other brigade withdrew because we had failed. Another attack secured an intermediate line out of which our own heavies blew our infantry. A few memories stand out sharply during those long hours, of mud-plastered men, with livid twitching skins, who drew dirty scrawled notes from their pockets and waited, panting, while the answer was written; of a large gunner F.O.O., blackened by an explosion, cursing, in a hoarse, shaking voice, our heavy artillery, which had killed five men at his side; of tired officers in battalion headquarters, poking with mud-caked forefingers at soiled maps, trying to elucidate exactly where it was that they had met the enemy, and, above, the sharp rap of a whizz-bang, bursting over the doorway every third minute.

One sat or stood waiting, humbly, through hours which scarcely melted, for something to happen, something which would bring this eternity to a conclusion: but, one felt, there would be no end. Beset by the aromas of humanity, German and British, cooking, and foreign cigars, which struggled, like the human powers, in an endless battle, I tried to read *Jude the Obscure*, and found the tragedy of the young craftsman extravagantly mawkish beside the long crucifixion of the men in the front line. Above our heads five tanks petered out and stuck immovable in the mud. Their presence induced an extra ration of shells from the distance. When the battle sank to stagnation, we explored trenches and derelict shafts. Dead lay everywhere, three British to one German. One magnificent Boche giant lay on the lip of a trench, a blond moustache and imperial still jutting in defiance. In front of him lay three English soldiers, killed by his bayonet. Burial parties of cavalry were still working over the old front line, unable to cope with the rush of business. On all sides lay a blasted waste, a barren frozen sea, pink, golden, and cream in the afternoon sun, with the austere beauty of a dying planet. Nothing moved on it, except that now and then the black cloud of a 5.9 blossomed and faded. From the river rose the sobbing of water hurrying through the black iron-bound marshes.

At last there was a relief and we moved back to Kentish Caves, dark warm recesses in the bank at Hamel: and presently they sent us back to refit. My education was taken in hand: but the best of that fortnight at Beauquesne was the long rides which Brodie took me on his spare horse over the grey downs. Brodie never talked about the war, but he would tell me a lot about the army before 1914, describing it as a paradise for men, in which a subaltern thought very little, but kept very fit, hunted two days a week during the season and never looked at his passbook until Cox's informed him he was vastly overdrawn. 'By Jove, I should have been in the soup if the war hadn't started and let me get straight.' There was a very simple direct charm about Brodie. 'You read a great deal,' he said, looking at my small battered library; 'I only carry two books, the Bible and Jorrocks.' After all, those two classics do fill most of a man's needs.

As soon as we had refitted, we started northwards. Winter had come in, but there was still the breath of life upon the fields. We passed Doullens, and after crossing the Canche came by slow marches to the locality of sandbag breastworks. We reached our destination three days before Christmas. The Baron and I raided Béthune to bring back cases of what Brodie called the Widow Click-clock, turkeys, and a parcel of Schumann, which, with sentimental eyes upraised, the Baron played delicately upon a tinny cottage piano. Leave opened and I was sent off in black bitter weather.

With each leave that fell to my lot now, there seemed to be a notable difference in England. Or was the difference only in myself? Though the weight of the war had pressed on me much more lightly than on others, it was heavy enough. I was being forced like a plant in a hot-house. The ingenuousness with which I had set out was being sweated off me. I was growing up faster than I knew. And as this process went on, I drew further away from England. It was—I think it still is—impossible to make those who had no experience of this war, understand it, as it must be understood, through all the senses. Sitting in a shelter of sandbags and corrugated iron, shivering with cold, looking out at the wrinkled frosted clay of a trench wall, hearing the sky rent by explosions and hammered by gun-fire, smelling the hundred stenches, animal and mineral, fixed in the mud, tasting a tongue sour with perpetual tobacco smoke, I let my mind retreat further and further from thoughts of home. I could find nothing to say in letters. All communication was as 'dissed' as though the lines had been broken by a shell. So on my arrival in London, I was as foreign as a Chinese, could observe the natives with unfamiliar eyes and bitterly enjoy all the prejudices of another civilization. As the war trailed its body across France, sliming the landscape, so too it tainted civilian life. London seemed poorer and yet more raffish. Its dignity was melting under the strain. It had become corrupted. There was a feeling of hostility growing up between the soldiers abroad and the civilians and soldiers at home; the good-timers, the army abroad thought them, profiteering, drinking, debauching the women. There were ugly tales of money-making in coal, wheat, wool, tea, and other necessities far above legitimate profit, stories of farmers' profits, of breweries' winnings. The 1914 values had gone bad, and instead, the English were learning to respect one thing only, money, and easy money by preference. It was better in France. There a man was valued rather for what he was than what he achieved. One found germinating in one's mind the seed of a hatred for these home-keeping English. One might have recalled that it is the habit of the English from the days of Marlborough to trade with the enemy. Was not Napoleon's army shod by England? But the habitual rapacity of man seemed no excuse when it was not a dynasty but the whole nation in arms. Such gloomy thoughts entertained me as we slowly rolled through the icy dark towards the line in a train from which the windows had long since vanished.

X

'The head of it is a rainbow, and the face of it is flattery; its words are charms, and all its stories are false; its body is a shadow, and its hands do knit spiders' webs; it is an image and a noise.'

JEREMY TAYLOR

On my return, I was told that my education so far as concerned the brigade was considered finished. The first person who disbelieved the dictum was myself; but I meekly acceded to a transfer to Corps headquarters. My emergence from the desponding slough of war was nearly complete; only, I had left half my heart behind with a group of men now shivering behind frozen bags of earth on duckboards that were a mask of ice. So in bitter January weather I was driven by car, first touch of a new civilization, to a gentle village perched upon a wooded hill-side and dominated by a princely château. A pathetic sun between the showers tried to reassure me.

It was rather like being taken from lodgings in a small suburb to a mansion in Mayfair. Well, hardly Mayfair; Kensington, rather. Everything here ran on oiled wheels. There was the staff-sergeant-major, impeccable and expert as a foreign office clerk in helping Labour Ministers over the difficulties of protocol, réclame, and other traps for the inexperienced. There were the clerks, each of whom knew the exact worth, gravity, and distinction of his position to the lightest hair. There were the generals' servants, the chauffeurs, and other permanent retainers, all true Susan Nippers, and all superior to the mere batmen of hangers-on such as I. (Mine, incidentally, during three months at brigade had built up a kit of grosser proportions than my own.) With my soiled and leather-patched garments of trench life I felt very provincial.

It is unfair to make fun of brigade and divisional staffs, of all those sorely-tried and overworked officers, who, from having been happy thoughtless subalterns and company commanders, were suddenly thrust by the fortune of war into positions where they were called upon to perform superhuman feats of imagination and tact, of rapid thinking and quick acting, difficult, even for a Cardonnel. And Cardonnels are rare.

But the higher formations are fair game, these monstrous tumours swelling with supernumerary officers and self-importance. A Corps staff which had been well dug-in for a year on a quiet front, resembled nothing so much as the menial hierarchy of a ducal palace—with the duke away. Never having had a division on their hands for more than a month or so they had come to regard them as persons to be employed but not encouraged. Their interest lay in the smooth airs which caressed Army and G.H.Q. They were in constant touch with the higher aspect of war, shown to them by visitors, delicious information as to what Foch thought, how the French wanted a single command under Nivelle, how old So-and-So was at last about to be sent home, what Lloyd George had promised the Italians, and how his lavish promises did not suit the French. In short, it was a rare atmosphere, which the fears and anxieties of troops in the line never poisoned.

This is as it should be. After all, the men who are planning attacks or the details of defence cannot afford to be distracted by sentimentalism or sympathy for the tools they use. But the failure of the Somme had bred in the infantry a wry distrust of the staff; and there was fierce resentment when brass hats descended from their impersonal isolation to strafe platoon and company commanders for alleged shortcomings in the line. The Old Army could not grasp that the New Army cared nothing for soldiering as a trade; thought of it only as a job to be done, and the more expeditiously the better. The man in the line wanted practical help; but in its place he too often received theory based on a type of warfare which had passed away with the Old Army before the end of 1914. He resented the staff's well-meant but frequently out-of-date admonitions. It made him mad

> '*to see him shine so brisk and smell so sweet*
> *And talk so like a waiting gentlewoman*
> *Of guns and drums and wounds. . . .*'

Such bald unjointed chat produced some true Hotspur animadversions. 'If that perky swashbuckler shows his nose in my trench again . . . ,' an infuriated company commander would rage. Meanwhile the rouser of this bile would be equably pursuing his way back to his château and his lunch, conscious of a good morning's work.

I was very aware of both sides when I was commandeered by one of my superiors to assist in a jaunt round the line. The red and white brassard of Corps staff, the undeniable elegance of the wearer, his specially padded and exceptionally clean tin hat, his glowing boots, his thick manly stick, made one think of dowagers slumming. Further, out of long absence from the focal point of war, he was often extremely sensitive to the ordinary noises of the line, the crack of a bullet and the purr of a minnie. I felt painfully embarrassed as my senior crept gingerly along the duckboards, cringing slightly behind the sandbags, under the solemn gaze of half a dozen old sweats, unconcernedly cleaning rifles, cooking, shaving, or writing letters, smoking their pipes, and altogether at ease in this cushy sector. I was therefore delighted when, one grey afternoon, the G.S.O. 3 and I were penned up in a famous sap-head while Fritz conscientiously lobbed some twenty little pineapples at the trench end. This unseasonable pleasure was further heightened when, as we hurried back, a 5.9 whooped over and crashed into some ruins a hundred yards away, and my companion, throwing dignity to the winds, took to his heels and galloped with the grotesque gait of a terrified foal through the water dismally covering the duckboards. It required considerable persistence to clean himself to a seemly state before he reached the car.

Modesty was not this young person's strong suit. Two years and more as a personal A.D.C. had taught him all the clichés of criticism and allowed him to dilate frequently on the policy of the War Office as opposed to the policy of G.H.Q., and of the Government as opposed to both, and of the French as opposed to all three, with the same freedom from self-consciousness with which he would criticize the very able and experienced colonel of a regular battalion in the line. I was glad when the presence of the G.S.O. 2 imposed silence on our suckling Mars.

This existence was indeed a *vie des coulisses*, and the ballet effect was heightened by the curious visitors we received. In addition to the minor members of the Army staff, 'pregnant with circumstance', we were, being in a passive sector, the frequent host of our allies' representatives. These resplendent figures would clank into our white-panelled chamber, and we would match our mutually indifferent French. I recall an overwhelming bevy of four exuberant Russian colonels, all magnificent animals, jingling with orders. One was very fair with a wide fan of blond beard: he bowed and smiled, and I think kissed the G.S.O. 2, while another, a swarthy Tartar, wore a scarf across his forehead where a bottle had cut it open. There followed two harassed-looking Portuguese generals, bear-led by a long-nosed and voluble gunner brigade-major who whispered: 'They've given me the Order of the Aviz, which, I'm told, means "the bird"!' The Portuguese were succeeded by a plump little partridge of a Roumanian army-commander, who had been translated to Allied propaganda after his command had bolted over the Vulkans. His gold-laced jacket could scarcely restrain his pouting chest, while his A.D.C., a dark and girlish flasher, wore a glorious sky-blue cloak down to his ankles. This lad carried, loosely tacked to his chest, the M.C. ribbon. When questioned about it, he said it was given to him on his arrival in England, and deftly turning it up, showed the words FOR VALOUR scrawled in indelible pencil on the reverse.

I could continue the catalogue of these visitants, all of whom were taken down to see a specially prepared 6-inch How fired from a very safe place; but my time is short.

One other of a different kind I recall is the Chef de Mission Française from one of our divisions. On the last occasion I had seen him, he was in charge of the French class at my private school where, by bribery, he had tried vainly to control a group of fifteen irreverent and fearless children who had bullied him so brutally that an English master had to be imported to preserve order. Now he strutted, all gorget patches, cherry cap, and gold lace, into G office, and was insolent to brigadiers because he had not yet received the Military Cross.

One heard in a subterranean way a good deal about decorations. The A.D.C. who ran the domestic details and the cars (bless him! even a shabby subaltern could get a car at this place) had been shot in the stomach at Loos. He managed the estate with all the tact and efficiency of a professional factor, and constantly bewailed the fact that the staff had a stable full of ponies but were too fat and lazy to exercise them. He spent hours and fivers erecting jumps in the policies, which no one but himself tested. One day he said, à propos of nothing at all: 'The old man has just offered me the M.C. for the fourth time. I've refused again. Damn it, if I couldn't get one with the Brigade of Guards I'm not going to pick it up this way. He's given one to that little squirt he's just taken on. It isn't decent.'

Like Captain Boldwig's estate it was all very high and mighty and great; and at the same time rather pathetic. Divisions were always insisting, like intelligent children, that their own methods were right, and being reproved in the mother-knows-best style. I have a distinct recollection of the G.S.O. 2 murmuring into the telephone: 'But you ought not to have done it, old fellow, except on an order from *us*. 'Tell you what, I'll send you an antedated wire telling you to do it. *That will regularize the position.*'

What did one do at Corps H.Q.? My first job was the colouring of seven secret maps with eight different inks for the great offensive which should succeed the offensive after the next offensive which should follow the Arras battle now being staged. They lay in the confidential box in G office. That confidential box! I still see the drafts of the screeds which once a week the Corps Commander would write to Army in his fine cursive hand. I can still read the invariable opening sentence: 'Though I am not alarmed at the difficulties of defending my line, still I would draw the Army Commander's attention to the paucity of Divisions on my Corps front wherewith to carry out the scheme'; and so on for six or eight foolscap pages. I used to examine them with awe and reverence, along with the Order of Battle, the defence scheme, and all the other evidences of the seriousness of the war. The confidential box nearly ruined me: for, one day, the office being empty, I was called into another room and *forgot to lock it.* The Corps Commander, jangling in goose-neck spurs, came in a moment later and found it open. When I repeated the offence, I was warned that a similar delinquency would foretell my departure. True, if at high noon, a spy had succeeded in crossing the ground, slipped past the sentries, evaded the G office clerks, and reached the first floor, he might have been—encouraged by that correspondence. I was sorely to blame.

Those maps took some time to complete. I was rather a bungler and was always having to remove the colour for heavy tractors from the infantry pathways or converting pack animals to railway guns. This great task accomplished,

I was told to report on the Corps defences, a series of strong points some fifteen hundred yards behind the front line. It was, but for one area, a pleasant task in this February weather. The sun promised better things, and even so early there was a stir of life in the trees and grasses. The bad area was a marsh, where there was much wild duck: and here one was more likely to be taken for bird than man by enthusiastic gunners. Once as a duck clattered out of the reeds, I thanked God the New Army did not depend for its pay on its precision with the rifle. The bullet cut through an osier a yard from my shoulder.

A week, and I duly presented my report. It was, I still think, rather a good one, pointing out that the defences were antiquated. But no doubt it was filed; and a year later the Boche wiped my poor recommendations—if they were ever followed—out of existence, by pushing through as far west as Corps H.Q. itself.

After that, there seemed little to do except sit in O.P.'s with the artillery intelligence officer, a cheerful person whose chief interest, outside his motor bicycle, was the girl he had amused on his last leave, and the girl he was going to amuse on his next. We would sit comfortably on the second floor of a broken house, wherein a thick new brick and concrete tower lay cunningly masked by the shell of the building, and gaze out through a long slit upon the barren landscape, bashed and hummocked with mine craters, and beyond, a civilization knocked silly. Giants seemed to stalk through the sunlit haze. Occasionally a whorl of smoke would sweep into being and wither: the sound of the explosion reached our ears as the brown wreath drifted away. Sometimes a parapet sprouted with feathery wisps for a few seconds as a flight of rifle grenades burst. We would sit here and swop tales for hours. My companion had once taken his section to spend a week with a French battery. It was a quiet sector and the French refused to break the peace. They challenged the English section to shoot the

18-pounders against their own 75's and chose as their target an open field empty of life. The French possessed a long double saw which the English sergeant coveted. He stole it the first night. Nothing was said. The French stole it back on the second night. The English secured it again on the third; the French recovered it on the fourth. On the fifth the English got it once more, and on the last night the sergeant slept with his treasure clasped between his arms.

Perhaps I should have been dismissed earlier, for my division had already left the Corps area, but for the fact that the G.S.O. 3 departed for fourteen days as A.D.C. to the great on an Allied front; and on the day following his departure the G.S.O. 2 retired to hospital. My own small shabby person therefore occupied the office and spoke on terms of equality with Army and peremptorily to divisions. It was well it was a quiet sector. I enjoyed that spell of theatrical authority, and, waxing fat, indicated routes to batteries congregating on Arras, told divisions to report on new and curiously coloured rockets, talked picks, shovels, huts, and water-troughs with Q. Fortunately nothing happened. Two days after the return of the G.S.O. 2, a deep depression, with wind rising at times to gale force, advanced across our front.

That morning, we were rung up by our right division to say that a German had walked into their lines in the mist and been collared. Interrogated by battalion, brigade, and division, he had held his tongue. He was now being passed on to us to administer the rack and thumbscrew. I slipped down to I office to watch the process. The prisoner, a large sallow, unkempt man, shambled in. He was taciturn, evading questions with shakes of the head, leering at his interrogators. Suddenly the officer who was questioning, a little Anglo-Alsatian with the face and skin of a toad, spat out a sharp '*Achtung*', followed by a volley of threatening German. The prisoned jumped to attention, took his hands from his pockets, and stood rigid. Yes, he would tell all he knew. He was an officer's servant, had been going on leave, and getting out of the trench, had lost his way in the fog. He knew of nothing happening in his regiment's sector, nothing at all. Pressed, he reiterated his statements; and at last was let go. He was despatched to Army, who gleaned no further information. Then Army played the old trick; they shut the prisoner up with a 'camel'—an Alsatian camouflaged as a prisoner. At once the captive's tongue was loosed. That evening an excited voice at Army breathed his revelations down the telephone: a great attack was to be launched against the dominating feature of our line, at present held by a division brand-new from England; gas, fire, and two *sturm-divisionen* would be employed; five mines would be exploded and the date was fixed between 17th and 22nd March.

After that, there was no peace for anyone in the Corps area. Guns were switched to cover the danger point; batteries were loaned from the left to the right division. The heavies of the next Corps re-registered on our front. Finally, the last brigade of the regular division which had just been relieved, and though due for a rest before going in at Arras had not yet left the Corps area, were told to stand-by for counter-attacks.

The 17th passed in a fever of excitement: so did the 18th, 19th, and 20th. The 22nd came and I was given leave. By this time I had no faith in the prisoner, the *mouton*, or Intelligence. I went. Through my seven days, I read the communiqués with keen curiosity—and there was nothing in them. When I returned, the wind had subsided and calm reigned once more. The camp commandant exercised the ponies over the brushwood fences he had now completed. The Corps Commander stamped and jingled up and down the corridors, more like Job's war-horse than ever. The C.R.A. had taken up his permanent quarrel with G. The G.S.O. 2 murmured wearily into the phone: 'But you can't do it, old boy. It's not to be thought of.' The

G.S.O. 3 talked uninterruptedly of high policy. The A.Q.M.G. produced a colossal brochure: 'Lessons from a Visit to the French CCCLme Corps,' in which he deduced that their troops got out of their troubles by temperament, but failed to draw the obvious parallel that it was the British phlegm which pulled ours through.

My time with Corps was up. The division with prophetic eye to its probable casualties was calling in its loans. I was ordered to report at Arras. Before I could get a car, the attack opened. On the 11th of April I drove southwards.

XI

'Je n'ai pas vu que les bombarderies . . . aient acquis un pouce de territoire au Roi, et que loin de cela, elles lui ont consumé beaucoup de munitions inutilement, extrêmement fatigué et affaibli les troupes. . . .'

VAUBAN *to* LOUVOIS, 1691

THERE was a savage snap of cold as the car ran down the route nationale. Snow lay in white masses, threatening the cherry blossom. At the narrow gate to Arras I stopped the car. We were in a slow-moving, endless stream of traffic. 'In the caves of the Faubourg St. Sauveur,' rattled an A.P.M. in answer to my question: 'Go past the station, and don't hang about there; it's dangerous—*and put your tin hat on.* It's an order.' We slid down the streets of the romantic city. It was standing, but how it was shaken. Shop-fronts lay gaping, shutters torn down and swinging. Fronts of houses had fallen away, uncovering intimacies. A staircase hung poised; but none could reach the attics, for the bottom flight had been shattered to a heap of rubble. There was a thunder of gun-fire as we reached the station square; and the enemy was replying. Sharp noises slapped to and fro between streets. Our way became obscure. I dived out and ran into the station. A party of doleful men were struggling to mend the line. A shell fell just outside the vault and some of the roof fell tinkling down. I caught sight of a temporary bridge. In a few seconds the car was over it and had come to a square of trees between which lay rows of dead horses. The air moaned. We bundled out and made for a heap of chalk, marked DIV. H.Q.

'Who are you?' asked someone in red patches abruptly. 'Oh, yes, your battalion's done damn well this morning, fought its way into Monchy and out on to the other side. All right. Stand by for the time being. You'll find a bunk somewhere.' So I stood by. When one came to think of it, the greater part of life in these days was standing by. For two days I did as I'd been told, and held the telephone.

On the second day, I walked out on to the Cambrai Road. It was a cold, wet, yellow afternoon with hanging rags of fog. Through lakes of liquid mud traffic pushed slowly by, pack mules led by weary unshaven men who could scarcely prop up their red eyelids, horses splashed to the withers, ungroomed for days, an 8-inch howitzer, tractor-drawn, the grimy crew impervious to its racking noise, limbers, G.S. wagons, ambulances. Inextricable tangles reduced the columns to a standstill. Shells were falling sporadically near the maze of trenches known as the Harp, where the confusion was thickest. On the right of the road infantry were moving up, clean and fresh; on the left, infantry were coming back, dirty, unshaved, their tattered clothes white with chalk and grey with mud, their faces sallow with exhaustion. They shuffled blindly along in single file, their eyes on the ground. They pawed and staggered on the uneven pavé. They never turned when a hurrying ambulance hooted behind them, but lurched heavily to the side. They never looked up; they were too tired to face even this wan light. Each was a lonely secretive figure, its mind turned inward, desperately drawing the shrivelled soul back to life.

On my way back, I fell in with a subaltern of the 3rd D.G. He was leading two horses and behind him a trooper led another pair. From beneath mackintosh sheets, tossed over the saddles of the latter two, field boots dangled. The cavalryman saw my glance. 'It's been our first show for two years,' he said. 'We've lost an awful lot. I suppose you infantry have grown callous; besides, you get so many casualties, you can't bury your people. But this was our first show and we at least know where every officer is buried. These are two friends of mine I picked up by La

Bergère. Luckily, I caught a pair of loose animals.' Then with the sudden ferocity of a dead tired man: 'I'll shoot any A.P.M. who tries to stop me bringing them through Arras!'

Late that night we stood in the Grand Place, waiting for the buses to take us into reserve. A cold moon added a colder pallor to those lovely dead gables, windows, and arcades, 'relics of the Spanish domination', says the guide book. Evidence of another and more recent domination was offered by broken walls and pillars and by vast chasms in the cobbles. As I stamped my freezing feet against the stone, a voice at my elbow named me. It was Cuthbertson. He too was now attached to the staff, nominally as a Q learner, actually subbing as camp commandant for the A.D.C., another aspirant staff officer. 'It's a bloody job—hi! you fellows, that's not your lorry. Wait till you're told— And everyone curses you. It's like being governess to a lot of spoilt children. I'm sick of it. But the battalion's bloody now. There's no one left . . . here's our van.'

So we came to Lignereuil. The offices and stables were quartered on a handsome seventeenth-century château of grey stone, with marvellously wrought iron gates before it, and beyond a double avenue of limes thick now with young leaves. But even in this back area the hoof of war had stamped its print. The lime grove had been horse standings; the earth was black and the trees torn with ropes and teeth. The owner of the château had long since fled, taking his furniture with him.

An atmosphere of uneasiness and irritability hung over our headquarters. General Bruce-Williams believed in keeping his staff up to the mark and the two senior staff officers carried out his creed with Calvinistic thoroughness. The result was Genevan; absolute efficiency and complete unhappiness. Junior officers wore the faces of the hunted, as they crept out of the offices and fled with furtive hurrying steps from the building, gloomily shaking the fleas from their ears. The entrance of the burly figure of our general caused a minor stampede among the learners in Q office. In G there was comparative calm. The placidity of the G.S.O. 2 and 3 frequently averted the whip; and so long as we were busy being busy, we could rely on our obscurity for shelter, when the thunder roared.

We stayed there for five days, in which the only diversion was a lecture by the Corps Commander, General Maxse. 'Infantry, gentlemen,' he began, 'is a rectangular animal'; and then, delighted with his trope, proceeded to draw elaborations of a parallelogram on the blackboard. I glanced round the room. The rectangular animal sat with sullen face. Dim hopelessness settled on features as the Corps Commander warmed to his theme, a sullen resignation. They felt they had little enough time left to live: it was cruel to waste a spring afternoon listening to this high-falutin' chatter. In the group of Fusiliers there were only two familiar faces, Smith, now, after a course at home, commanding another battalion, and Vanneck. We met as the audience broke up. The 13th, as I had learned already from the strength returns, scarcely existed. Almost the only surviving officers of the Monchy show were the colonel, the adjutant, and those who had been left out: twelve officers had been hit and of these eight were dead. Nearly all the men of the old battalion had vanished, even the hitherto enchanted Ting had been wounded. Said Vanneck, 'We'll be for it again, I suppose, in a few days. I'm commanding Number Three now. You won't see anything of it in your cushy staff dugout.'

On the next day, pack on back, I was lorry-hopping back to Arras with the divisional traffic officer, a sober Australian farmer. Between bumps and wild slithers across the muddy road, he was telling me of a remote life on a Queensland sheep farm. Every three years he took a holiday, when he went to Thibet. 'I'd like to see just once more,' he said wistfully, 'those monks standing in a scarlet line at the edge of the precipice, blowing the great trumpets, as we struggle up the path.' Four days later, as he was opening out the traffic going forward on the narrow bridge by divisional headquarters, a shell tore his arm away. In a few minutes he was dead.

The headquarters of the division where I was to stay and gather information, was in a railway cutting beyond St. Laurent-Blangy, north of the Scarpe. It was a regular division, and its staff, which consisted only of the general, the G.S.O. 1 and the G.S.O. 3, worked with a quiet dexterity and the air of doing nothing. The general was a haggard, splenetic man who rarely spoke; but the G.S.O. 1 talked kindly and happily of cricket and fishing and reduced the war to a matter of bad weather outside. The junior took me up to the line and helped me to find an O.P. for the next show. Beyond a cutting lay a wide green tableland about two miles broad. For a modern battlefield it was singularly clean. Shells had pitted it lightly. Here and there lay a dead body nobody had troubled to bury, leaden-hued and puffy. A tornado swept to and fro over Athies, just above the river. Beyond it, Monchy hill was being conscientiously battered. On our left, the Point de Jour was plumed with grey smoke. Between all these eruptions it was like Hampstead Heath on the morrow of a Bank Holiday, a calm world of litter. The attack on the 9th had swept the enemy right over the brink of the plateau almost into the plain of Douai. Sightless, except for his aeroplanes, he was forced for the time being to shoot by the map.

I was taken to a machine-gun company in a position over the edge of the ridge. The front line lay just below us and then curled backwards. Low, the company commander, grinned when I was introduced. 'You've come at last?' and in answer to my puzzled look: 'We could have pushed through from here to the Rhine at any time on the first two days. They'd only a man and a dog holding the line. One battalion came through to here from the other side of Arras with three men killed—three men only; think of it. We've been told to sit tight here ever since. Now the old Hun's come back, and you'll have a damned tough time.' We were standing in a trench from which we looked eastward over a limitless flat plain. Peaceful villages lay here and there in their baskets of leaves; their churches thrust an evangelizing finger skyward. The Scarpe and the marshes round Plouvain were waters of gold. In the distance a bluish haze was said to mark Douai. It looked a promised land, only marred by the chalk tracery which lay in front of a brilliant wood on the skyline, the new big switch trenches flanking the Hindenburg Line.

'And that?' I asked, pointing to where heavy shells had been bursting ever since I arrived.

'Hyderabad redoubt,' answered my guide. 'They've plonked it steadily ever since we got it. There's a big dug-out in the middle with three entrances. It's always full of wounded, and all the doorways are smashed in at least once a day. . . . Well, so long. We're lent to you for part of the show. See you on the day.'

Our own division gradually took over in an atmosphere of jarred nerves and nagging temper. I sat timorously at the far end of the table with our machine-gun officer, a young regular from the 58th. The general was talking loudly about Winchester.

'Were you there?' I whispered to my neighbour.

'No, thank God,' he muttered.

'Same here. We're not of the elect. It may comfort you to reflect that the most important Wykehamist of the last two hundred years was an eighteenth-century bishop. They don't do things. They are.'

A slight mist had risen when I set out for the O.P. The night was full of the sound of moving men, the creak of leather, the rattle of entrenching-tool handles against the scabbard, the dull splash of water bottles. The trench was packed with men, some talking in low voices, some sleeping. A weary officer was sitting on guard over a flagon of rum. I pushed my way to Low's dugout where the signallers were already installed. 'Line's O.K.', said the signaller. He spoke into the mouthpiece: 'That you, chum? . . . Fine thanks. Cushy.' In an atmosphere of frowst and candle grease, Low was sleeping between his two gun crews. The men looked childishly young in the candle-light. There was a grave innocence in each simple pose. Presently they were roused and went off to man their guns on the roof. At 4.25, the bombardment crashed out. We swallowed a cup of tea and climbed into the cold murk. The infantry were not due to go over for twenty minutes, and the men in the trench were slowly filing past into the open. We leaned against the parapet and watched. There was nothing to see save a curtain of drifting smoke, patterned with arabesques of white, held there for a second by the flash of bursting shrapnel, with red and green S.O.S. lights and with yellow flares which spun and fell stifled in the whirling darkness. The noise was of an infernal orchestra, vibrating fortissimo, in which only the rhythmical smack of the field-guns behind us could be picked out. One gun firing directly over my head made my helmet ring at each discharge. Every now and again beneath the racking din one caught a whisper of humanity, a boot scraped on a duckboard. As zero hour approached the barrage sensibly thickened, grew faster, and as our watch hands crept over the actual minute, there was added the reckless clatter of the machine-gun barrage. The Germans too had started in answer to their front line's call. On all sides the earth rocked and shivered under crashing weights. A column of black smoke kept appearing twenty-five yards to our left, to be at once tossed away into the chaos; but I could not distinguish the explosion it betokened against the din. One seemed to lose all sense of personal being and to become as aloof as a cloud over the battlefield.

'Can't see anything,' shouted my companion in my ear. 'Let's have breakfast and come up again.'

In the dugout we bit through thick bread and bacon. Below ground, the noise became a uniform drumming.

'It looks like the Creation,' I said; 'In six days . . . I hope to God it hasn't taken them six minutes to get the front line. My battalion's in front.'

'Some of ours coming back, sir,' called a voice down the stairs.

A few trembling men, walking wounded, their rifles and equipment discarded, were scrambling painfully along the trench. 'Don't know at all, sir . . . they've gone forward . . . we was 'it in the Hyderabad before it started . . . crumped it fair cruel, Fritz did; didn't 'e, chum? Yes, thank yer, we can get along all right . . . glad to be out of it. . . .'

The blackness of the night was paling to a grey-brown wall. Small parties, ammunition carriers, appeared out of the ground and moved slowly away into the gloom. The machine guns behind us stopped chattering. The pace of the barrage had lessened. Suddenly above our heads there was a wild roar. We cowered automatically as a plane with black crosses on its wings rushed headlong down fifty feet above our heads. Behind, two British machines swept fiercely after it. They followed the bend of the hill-side out of our vision, but a wild boy in the machine-gun crew behind squealed. 'They've got him . . . got him . . . got the Fokker . . . there he is, down and out.' In a jiffy he was running over the brow of the hill. We watched his small figure, clad only in shirt, trousers and boots, twinkle out of sight.

The mist began to clear. Objects plotted themselves on to the blankness. A low ridge crept up; and for a moment a line of men stood shadowed on its edge. Then they stepped forward, and disappeared. Next, something more solid grew under our stare. A house? It moved. 'Tanks!' we shouted. That too nosed and dragged itself into the shimmering mirror of the mist. More news began to filter through: the first objective had been taken and the second was now occupied. The boy returned from the aeroplane with a superb chronometer and a large oil-balanced compass. 'Well, that's that,' said Low: 'I think we'll pack up and go home. Good luck. See you again sometime.' He nodded and led his nondescript crowd of hobbledehoys over the skyline.

The light was hardening now, and the mist giving way to the sun. The 5.9 which had been pounding away at our half acre had given up and turned to more active objects. The battle had surged forward a mile down to the foot of the slope, and for the time the bulk of the gun-fire was being devoted to the divisions on our flank. By the river, a kilted division was alternately capturing and being bumped out of a group of ruins known as the Chemical Works. A pall of smoke hung over it. On the left the village of Gavrelle showed itself in the eastern light to be a skull. Between these places on our divisional front, there lay the long slope dotted here and there with the wreckage of war, bodies, a couple of derelict tanks, the smashed Boche plane, equipment jettisoned by wounded men, a pile of Stokes mortar shells. Groups of men, reinforcements, machine-gun companies, ration and water parties, men with boxes of S.A.A. and bombs, threaded their way slowly forward, seeming to choose the most aimless of paths. Ahead, the line of the second objective, which the assault had carried, was fairly easily defined. There was no sign of life here. Occasionally a Lewis gun bickered; sometimes a wisp of smoke appeared and vanished. Twice, a man rose out of the earth, stretched himself, searched the ground for a few minutes, and disappeared. Shells dropped along a line of sliced trees, now pollarded. On the enemy side, far away over the plain, the same aimless activity was visible. Parties of men passed slowly to and fro. A wagon drove straight across the plain at a smart trot. A battalion, most oddly, marched and countermarched in column of companies for half an hour. Two guns below Vitry church flashed and flashed and flashed.

So the day wore through. At every other hour, it seemed, a voice from division announced a further attack on the Chemical Works by the Highlanders. Each time they won it, and each time they were driven out. Our line lay waiting for them to finish. There was no finish. Each time they went in, they killed everything that was on the ground, and each time, like dragon's teeth, the enemy sprang up again.

The light died away without any alteration in the landscape. It had been another failure. I rang up division and was told to report at the brigade headquarters half a mile back and offer my services. I found their dugout and went downstairs. There was a new general, a dark, calm man. Brodie told me to sit down and have a drink. The little chamber and the shaft were packed with men, and there was a continual going and coming. I sat down and drifted off to sleep. When I woke, it was late at night. Brodie said: 'All right. We don't need you. You'd better say we kept you.' I wandered back through the darkness to the railway cutting, reported and crept into my bivvy. Next morning, over breakfast, the D.M.G.O. said to me: 'You escaped last night. They were asking for you all over the place.'

'What for?' I asked listlessly. 'I was at Sixty-third Brigade. I was told to go there.'

'The Owner wanted you to go and find the front line for him. As you weren't here, he sent me.'

'Did you find it?'

'Good God, no. I sat in a broken-down tank half the night, while the Boche put gas shells all round us. You've no idea how uncomfortable a tank is, and how difficult it is to sleep in a gas-mask. . . . I'm keeping out of the way. You'd better, too.'

It was good advice, but unfortunately not to be compassed. We were both caught by our high-stomached leader: and after poor C. had been thoroughly tumbled in the mud and stamped on, the bulky figure stormed at me.

'Well, sir,' I objected, after I had been cursed for not coming back in time to be sent out again; 'if the battalion commanders can't tell you where their line is, I don't see how I can. I can only tell you what I saw from the O.P.' I thought of Sam Weller's reply to Sergeant Buzfus, but forebore to quote it.

'Did you see any flares?'

'Yes, sir, and reported them; in the trenches in I. 7, a.'

'Which trench?'

'The forward one, sir. Three flares.'

'How many trenches are there?'

'Two, sir, so far as I could see.'

'As far as you could see!' he snorted. 'Look at these.' He waved his hand at a blackboard covered with aeroplane photographs. 'Now, you see there are three trenches. In which were those flares?'

'I should say . . . ' I began cautiously. Witnesses cross-examined by Sir Edward Carson must have felt very much as I did.

'No, you shouldn't,' snapped my interrogator. 'I want a definite answer. In which of those trenches did you see flares?'

'I think . . .' I began feebly. The general's tremendous forehead, furrowed as a bull's, contracted furiously. For a moment, I thought he would gore me.

'You're not to think,' he bellowed. 'You've got to be sure. *I* can think.'

'You see,' he said, when he had rolled me over four or five times and left me trembling, 'you're no good to me. Why, I know more about this ground than you do, and I've never seen it.'

'If I could have those photos, sir,' I began timidly.

'You can't. You've got to use your wits.'

I crept away, full of a strong hatred. The unreasonableness of the man was an affront. As I stood on the edge of the cutting, a Scots officer, wearing the red and blue G.H.Q. brassard, accosted me. 'Can you show me the way to Athies?' he asked: 'I've got a Russian war correspondent here, who wants to see something of the battle.' For the moment I lost my manners and frankly gaped. The Russian war correspondent was the oddest figure that was ever seen in this nightmare landscape. He was very short, with a pale, fat, nervous face, from which Dundreary whiskers waved in the breeze. A large pair of iron spectacles bridged his nose. A cape with a hood, cut from one of those peculiarly hairy Austrian materials, fell round his plump figure, which was increased by the gas-mask lashed to his chest. Knickerbockers, thin stockings, and—on my word of honour—elastic-side boots finished his lower end, while the whole was crowned by an ill-balanced tin hat. 'There—down there,' was all I could ejaculate, waving my hand towards the place where three heavy German shells had just fallen, spouting up clouds of pink dust. I watched them bobbing over the ground, until they disappeared from view. They never came back, and to this day I am not sure whether I did not meet a phlizz.

Though the battle had died down for the moment on this sector, it was to be resumed. The battalions had lost heavily on 23rd. During the twenty minutes bombardment before the attack started, the enemy had dealt with them truly. The 13th had lost the C.O. and the second-in-command, and few other battalions had any senior officers left. On the day before the next attack, I was collared by the G.S.O. 1, Col. Dill, to bear him company to the front line brigade headquarters. It was a fine morning; and the Boche was using it. We ducked and fled through a covey of whizz-bangs which suddenly cracked about us, and took refuge in what must have been the Hell bunker of the

Arras links. At one point we dropped into a tiny dugout, where my companion was to give the final instructions to the commanding officers of one of the assault brigades. One major, one captain and two second lieutenants listened with gloomy faces to his unemotional lecture. Just as we were leaving, the major, a plump little man, whose eyes belied his fierce moustache, looked up and stammered through trembling lips: 'Look here, you don't expect us to do this? You know we've hardly got an officer left. Two battalions are commanded by junior officers; and the men—what there are left—are badly shaken.' There was a moment's pause. My companion viewed the pleader coldly. 'Those are your orders,' he said in a harsh voice. 'Obey them.'

The brigade headquarters was in a dugout below an old gun-pit, one of a pair of wrecked monoliths, the only features on the bare slope down to the line, twelve hundred yards away. Every now and then the enemy tossed a shell over it to remind the earth-dwellers that they were mortal. As, after a long conference, we emerged from the noisome atmosphere of tobacco and cooking into the clear air, my companion handed me a couple of maps, very white and about the size of a table-cloth. 'Carry these,' he said, 'and walk fifty yards behind me. It's better that you should get hit than me.' And with that he set off up the hill at a rare pace. I obeyed and rejoined him beyond the skyline. We did not converse on our way back.

That evening just before dinner Cuthbertson came hurrying over the edge of the cutting. He was wearing a soldier's jacket, webbing, and a tin hat: he was very hot and red. 'He's sending me up to command the Thirteenth,' he spluttered: 'I don't know where they are or anything about them. I've been beating the country all day trying to get fresh meat for the mess. I've been strafed because there's nothing but bully in the rations. Where's G office?'

He was not wanted after all. There had just joined us

from the base an elderly colonel who was told to take over the battalion. I was detailed to lead him up the line after he had dined. The flood of 'notions' ran at the other end of the table.

'Ha!' exploded the general. 'What's your school, Campion? We're all Wykehamists here. Best school in the world.'

'Don't agree with you at all, sir,' replied my neighbour. 'I was at Eton.' The general frowned. The newcomer had lost caste. He was a dear old gentleman who had no right or need to be here, instead of attending to his legislative duties at Westminster. Nothing but a strong sense of duty had brought him: and as I helped him up for the twentieth time after he had fallen with a meek 'damn' over a telephone wire or into a shell hole, I sincerely hoped that someone at Battalion would look after him as faithfully as I was doing.

Having disposed of him, I betook myself to the O.P. The telephone dugout was full of infantry, swart burly primitives from the Fens, blackly unshaved. They rumbled to each other and scratched their hairy chests. In the hot air the stench was overwhelming. I climbed back into the trench and waited a lonely hour in the mist. Once more the night was full of the sounds of an army moving: the shuffle of feet and the click and wheeze of accoutrements filled the small space the fog left me. Shrill impatient voices, called now and again, urging tired men forward. Boxes rattled and bumped against one another as a carrying party came to a sudden halt. Once the motor of a tank purred through the blackness, and a chink of light gleamed as the crew asked their way. Now and again came the slap-thud of a solitary field-gun. At last the men in the dugout passed up the steps and moved sturdily away. They joked and swore in the same monotone, as they pulled at their straps and heaved their shoulders. They had no illusions left.

The attack was to be launched at streak of dawn, 4.25;

and at that moment a wild racket was once more loosed into the void. Once more the curtain of darkness was changed to a whirling screen in which flaming clusters, red, orange and gold, dropped and died; and dun smoke, illuminated by explosions, drifted away greyish white. Once more red and green rockets called frantically for aid. Once more eyes stared into this impenetrable cataract, vainly trying to pick out familiar outlines. The enemy's barrage joined the din. Black columns of smoke stormed up in the foreground. And through it all came wave on wave of the malicious chitter of machine guns.

Slowly the darkness grew to grey, to opal, to gold; and the mist began to burn away. Shapes loomed up. Distances were deceptive in the haze. The round top of Greenland Hill came into outline. It was bare of life. A dark patch to the left became Square Wood. A contact plane hovering in the centre fired white Very-lights. Some red flares blossomed, like Chinese lanterns at a fête, on the edge of the Chemical Works.

As the day cleared, gunner officers and their linesmen began to come into the trench. Our shelling died down, but the enemy was shivering his old front line with vicious concentration. To the north, we could see men coming up and down the road from Gavrelle. Who they were no one could tell. We thought they were both English and German, but which was escorting which?

The story of this attack will no doubt appear in the military history of the war, elucidated by diagrams. To the watchers on the hill-side it was only a confused medley, in which English and Germans appeared most disconcertingly going to and fro, oblivious of each other. Even later it was only possible to glean that one brigade had lost direction, and coming up behind the flank of the other after the position had been taken, had swept on, carrying away with it the better part of two companies of the 13th; that some reached Square Wood, a mile past the objective, and that perhaps a dozen in all returned. This is part of history, but all we were able to see were some of the ingredients.

Questioning the countryside, I caught in my glass a grey ant crawling over the edge of the railway cutting, followed by another, and then more. They hurried into a road behind a shallow bank and lay down. The sun polished their steel helmets into a row of little shining discs. More and more were now coming out of the cutting. I pinched the elbow of the gunner beside me.

'See that? It's a counter-attack massing.'

'Not on my line,' he returned. 'Besides, they're out of range of field guns.'

I tumbled impetuously down the stairs and called division. A quiet voice in the distance assured me that the heavies would deal with what I had seen. When I looked again, the assembled ants had moved. They came crawling over the top of Greenland Hill in three lines, about six hundred strong. They were just starting down the forward slope when something flashed in front of them. A column of bright terra-cotta smoke was flung upwards so high, that there shot into my memory the pictures of the djinns in an old copy of the *Arabian Nights*, and I half expected a leering hook-nosed face to look down from its summit. Another and another rose until an arcade of smoking pillars seemed to move across the hill-side. 'Six-inch How,' shouted my neighbour excitedly, 'firing one-o-six.'

Already the grey ants had thinned. The first line was hardly there. It merged with the second and mechanically the whole inclined southwards to avoid the shells. But the guns followed the movement and another line of smoking columns fountained into the air. At last, reduced to one line, the minute figures turned and stumbled back over the crest of the hill.

I was so absorbed by this spectacle that until it was over I hardly heard the F.O.O. at my side whooping sharp orders to his signallers. Turning, I saw another body of midgets coming over the plain to the left. All the field guns were firing now. In what seemed a few minutes this formation too was scattered. Small groups tried to escape by flinging away to the flank. 'One-o degrees more right, up fifty,' shouted my neighbour. A little puff of white smoke danced gallantly in the air. A few tiny figures shrank to dots. 'Got 'em,' he shouted; 'Repeat.' Other officers up and down the trench were excitedly calling similar orders. In ten minutes the counter-attack was broken, smashed, and tossed in the air like a handful of dust: and up here everyone was whooping, laughing, and holloing. We were a Roman audience at the Coliseum, bull-fighting fans at a *fiesta*, good citizens who brown a pack of grouse tearing down the October wind: we were in fact a group of young Englishmen who had just helped to knock out about a thousand Boche, and we were damned glad about it.

His counter-attacks broken, the enemy spent the day shelling what he could get at. One shuddered to think of flesh cringing beneath the huge shells which fell again and again along the battered line. Darkness came gently in. I turned as I crossed the skyline. Solitary shells were singing through the air. Dull crunches announced their arrival in the distance. A dump was burning in Plouvain, and against its light, black ghosts towered upwards.

* * *

A pendant to Arras. Four nights later Cuth and I were dining with the relics of the 13th at Izel-lez-Hameau. Of those officers who had marched south six months earlier, there were just three, John Marquard, now transport officer, Vanneck, and the quartermaster.

'Yes, poor old Leeson's gone,' sighed Fairburn, 'too old, y'know. He ought never to have gone up, but you know what these Catholic padres are. . . . Hand blown off and he died of shock.'

A lion-faced officer near me, named Waley, was talking

fast. 'I told 'em if they didn't get into our barrage, they'd never get through the wire; but they didn't keep up and that's how both of them were scuppered. I got my lot right under it. It was pretty good hell, but nothing to what we'd have got if we hadn't been across the wire and into that trench just as soon as the lift came. There were a damned lot of shorts and duds too. Billy got it in the leg there and they put a hole through my tin hat. We got the line all right. Most of the Fritzes hands-upped. Then the Lincolns came up on our right, and one of them shouted, "Come on, Fusiliers, you're always late." Before I could stop 'em half our lot were out of the trench. Then something burst close to me and knocked me over. When I came to, I could see a kind of cup-tie crowd going east, so I followed on after it until we came up against a wood. Square Wood it must have been. There were three Boche guns on the other side firing like blazes, and our own guns were shooting us up too. I slipped into a bit of a trench with a dozen men and waited. We were miles past the objective. Then a Fritz plane came over our heads, gunning and firing lights, and I thought it was about time to pack up. So I tore up my maps and we set off for home. It took hours to get back. I don't know how many of us crawled in—damn few. There was a party of forty Boche prisoners got caught in our barrage and knocked out.'

'Did you hear about old Fake!' said Vanneck. 'There was a bombing block holding us up. He got out of the trench, slung his rifle, walked up to the block, and said: "Here now, come on, you"; and twenty Huns gave themselves up.'

A boy at the other end of the table looked up. He had red-gold hair and the bitterest mouth I have ever seen. 'Talking of prisoners,' he broke in, 'do you remember a corporal with the Messina medal?'

'You mean a sergeant, who was killed at Pozières.'

'No. Never heard of him. This was a fellow in Number Two company.'

'Oh, yes; a dark stocky man.'

'He went off with an officer we'd caught. Presently I found him back in the trench. I knew he couldn't have got down to the cage and back; so I asked him what had happened. "Well, sir," he said, "it's a very hot day. We sat down in a shell hole and he gave me his watch and his field-glasses and his money. It's a very hot day and a long way down. So I shot him." '

'What did you do?'

'There wasn't any need to do anything,' said Vaughan with a curl of his thin lips; 'he was killed that afternoon.'

As we were leaving, the quartermaster said: 'You know Ardagh's on his way back? Fact. Think of it, age God knows what, and a femur smashed six months ago. What a tiger, eh?'

XII

' "*English waiters would be as good as any; only there's one thing they can't learn.*"
"*Ha! What's that?*" *Sir Henry demanded.*
"*That the customer is always right, of course. It's that terrible British sense of justice*".'

IMPERIAL HOTEL

I SHOULD like to deal faithfully with the next four months. There are, however, what Mr Saintsbury calls the peculiarities of the laws of libel. Discretion demands brevity. Within a fortnight of our coming out of the line, I was commanded to relieve Cuthbertson as substitute A.D.C. and camp commandant. I protested. 'You shut up and do as you're damn well told.' I obeyed.

The duties of this office are onerous and difficult. I still cannot understand how any but the elderly or mutilated voluntarily accept the appointment. It demands all the finesse and tact of the older type of diplomat (the Seton Merriman type, if it ever existed) to choose between the claims and temperaments of staff officers new to their tabs but keenly sensitive to their positions. To decide whether it is worth infuriating the D.A.A.G. by giving his billet to the A.D.M.S., or whether the exasperatingly tedious A.D.M.S. can be safely left to stew in his own juice; to decide whether the G.O.C. can be lodged in the cell contentedly occupied by his predecessor, or whether he will pull the whole château down in his fury, and vent his indignation all over your body; these are but two of the daily problems of the A.D.C. Not hard, you will say, when, as people were wont to tell you with virtuous blandness, there's a war on; but a forlorn and irritating task. One passed from composing the jealousies of the divisional

Follies, whose tiffs would have amazed the most turbulent of green-rooms, to flattering the band-sergeant, that the General's favourite music, *The Bing Boys* and a cornet solo, *The End of a Perfect Day*, should not fail to be given at mess. Scarcely a day passed without some trouble to be smoothed away, without some complaint preferred. Either the posts in the camp had not been whitewashed in the pure Aldershot manner, or the supply of bully was too much. Either the G.S.O. 1 was protesting against the infliction of a fine on his batman for dodging fatigues, or the A.A. & Q.M.G. assailed one because the Canteen Committee refused to buy shears for cutting the grass in front of the General's hut, while my old acquaintance, the Baron, persistent as a fly, attempted daily by craft, guile and flattery to jockey me out of a horse, which, quite erroneously, he thought he could ride. Small stuff, poor stuff; but part of the fabric of war. Crushed and harassed by these petulances, I grew grey and old. I find few entries in my diary during this period.

'7.6.17 We took over 51st division's billets. Everyone complained.

12.6.17 Hell of a row with A.A. & Q.M.G. over allocation of divisional funds.

15.6.17 Owner and Bungo both on leave. Thank God.'

As a matter of fact, at this time, it was as keen and efficient a divisional staff as might be found in France. 'Q' put in hours of unremarked toil to ensure that such life and death matters as water and rations for the front line were forthcoming at the correct time and place. And it was due to their efforts that at no time did the infantry go short, or receive bad quality. 'A' did twelve solid hours a day at his thankless task and was never too harassed to address you a slow smile and give helpful advice. A touchy man but kind. It was a good staff, and the Owner had 'the front line mind', not, as some generals, turning uneasily westward. But to the camp commandant these good features are rarely apparent. His business is with private sensibilities.

There were compensations for the irritations of this fatuous existence. There was a week in Arras, where, smoking a pipe beneath the chestnuts in the Place de la Préfecture, I mused on ancient walls—Arras was an echo of Oxford—and read Meredith, a queer choice, but Meredith's artificial world transported the reader from a reality thudding with gunfire. Arras was full of surprises, from the superb caricatures on the walls of the signal station, painted two years earlier by the French, and the burgundy which Claims would wheedle from ancient cellar-keeping concierges, left to guard their masters' mansions, down to the Field Cashier's office unexpectedly discovered shell-broken and full of blood and wounded men. And there was the dud which Persevering Percy, the H.V. gun, one night neatly inserted between the floor joists of our billet.

From Arras we moved northward with much hurrying to and fro. Let me noose a warm June morning in Hesdin and recapture the flavour of beer brought in misty bottles from the coolest *cave* and drunk beneath scented limes. Let me recall the drink composed by the A.P.M. of the Highland Division at Bomy, in which a battery of nine bottles took part. I accepted a second glass of this dangerous drink, and then wandering out into the *place* to wait for the car, fell asleep under the trees, where Henry VIII and Francis I had once signed a treaty. I slept a long afternoon and was wakened by my car-driver's hand on my shoulder. Another, and a grisly memory is of the moat of a château abandoned by its owner—said to be an eccentric English milord—in which fish lay packed flank to flank, unable to move: now and then one jumping above the other tarnished backs could not get back into the water, but lay gasping, supported by his fellows.

So in due course we came by easy stages to the Salient, or at least its chord. At divisional headquarters, I saw at first little beyond the familiar preparations for a new offensive, the railheads, the aerodromes, wagon parks, refilling points, camps of Nissen huts, canteens, cinemas, bath-houses with Foden lorries and Thresh disinfectors, Y.M.C.A.'s, the wretched dysentery compound with men bent and straining over biscuit tins, horse standings, dumps, casualty clearing-stations, railway guns, water-points, ammunition parks, balloons tugging at their windlasses, pigeons wheeling and rushing in a white cloud above their travelling loft; and, more than all, columns of dusty apathetic men, moving eastward: the insignia of a mechanical war without soul or ardour, and by now almost without faith.

We took over from a pair of Irish divisions; and the infantry reported that for dirt there was nothing to choose between Ulster and the South. But they had some virtues. In my attic, I was wakened at five one morning by the sound of pipes. It came from a rifle battalion marching out to a jig step. I ran to the window and leaned out into the cool air until that elfin music had gone over the hill and faded away. For a space, the world seemed to hold the echo of the dancing notes. Then they were gone; and the road, which should have sprung flowers to these enchanted pipes, lay as it always was with its dirty cobbles and drab, splashed trees.

Even six miles behind the front line, one was aware of the loaded atmosphere. As if attracted by the impending doom of many innocents, clouds drifted up and formed into vast pasteboard cumuli, dwarfing the line of observation balloons hanging between them and the ridge, a row of question marks. From these clouds, a German plane would suddenly sweep down, and in a few seconds a volcano of smoking gas, challenging even the clouds in size, would slowly fall, while the crews hanging from their parachutes drifted like dragon-flies down the breeze. One afternoon, four balloons were despatched in such fashion in less than a minute. The enemy flashed down, darted from hulk to hulk and was back in his thicket before the futile Archies strung their display across the empty sky.

The battle opened in mist and rumour. The rumours proved false, and the mist turned to drizzle, to rain, and then to a savage torrent, in which the sky competed with the guns, and conquered. The sullen gun-fire died away. *Le bon dieu Boche* had won again. The battlefield was said to be flooded. Wounded were drowning in shell holes. All fighting had ceased, while the infantry sat miserably casting one preference against the other, death by water or by fire. On the next morning, the trickling brook behind our huts had risen three feet and quadrupled its width, and its brown flood was reflected in the upper air.

While I stood watching the eddies, a breathless orderly told me that I was required by the General in person at nine o'clock. Glancing at my watch, I found it was already five minutes past. I scrambled into the General's hut, and finding the first room empty, rushed hastily across to the other door. I knocked: then flinging it open and saluting in the most rigid manner, I said: 'You wished to see me at nine, sir.' I caught a glimpse of a bulky figure in wide striped blue and white pyjamas and gumboots, gentling its hair at a mirror. With the roar of the wounded gorilla, the figure turned and swept down on me, shouting: 'What the devil d'ye mean by coming to see your General in his pyjamas?' I cowered out of the room, and waited in strong agitation for the Owner to appear. When he did, he gave me ten minutes of the best telling-off that I have ever had. I was the worst A.D.C., the worst camp commandant, the worst... I forget the complete catalogue; but he finished by cancelling my recommendations from brigade and corps; and I was to return to my battalion. I refrained from reminding him that the office I was now filling was not of my seeking; but interjected 'Very good, sir,' at the paragraphs.

'Very good, sir,' I said at last. 'I'll rejoin the battalion today.'

'No, you won't,' snapped the General. 'You'll wait till I've found another A.D.C.'

'Oh, very good, sir.' As I was turning, he relented a little. 'I will say, however, that you're a gentleman.' On which undeserved shaft I faded out.

Of course, he was perfectly right. As camp commandant I had been a hopeless failure, though less from incapacity than from a stubborn and childish resentment at being rushed into the job. I had not that 'understrapping virtue of discretion' which the successful must possess. I shot my mouth off too quickly and too often, and I knew it. This did not prevent me from being furiously angry at his removal of my previous recommendations. My anger quickly died away; and it was with the feelings of a free man that I rode over to the battalion transport lines that afternoon, and announced my impending return to the quartermaster.

'Good,' he said, 'good, Guy. . . . Tell you what, old chap . . . what about a spot?'

While we solemnly had one, he spoke sadly of everything Belgic. 'Why, they can even speak our language,' he said indignantly. A few days before, while ambling in stately fashion through Locre, saluting with grave elegance the ladies of the place, he had offered a 'Bon jour, ma petite,' to a small girl who was watching him with serious eyes. Swift as a bullet came the reply: 'Garn, fat arse.'

'Smith's coming back,' he announced presently. 'Ardagh's going. You remember hearing of a shell hitting battalion headquarters pill-box a few weeks back?'

'When Samuda' (the new second-in-command) 'was killed?'

'Yes. It nearly got the old man. It half stunned him, and he's been shaky ever since.'

'He won't go,' I said positively.

'He's protesting. But I'm afraid they'll make him. They say Smith will come back and take over command.'

Soon the whole division side-stepped a little northward, still employed on the right flank of the attack, either making small costly assaults with one or two battalions, or holding the line, which in the Salient was almost as ruinous as a direct attack. I had nearly a month to wait until my successor appeared, and during that time, I kept away from headquarters as much as possible. There was always a welcome to be found at the Veterinary Section run by Yates, a red-headed, slow-tongued Yorkshireman, a perfect warlock of animal diseases and wounds. Out of something that to the unskilled eye was a sack of bones only fit for the knackers, he could reconstruct a sound and willing animal. There was one old heavy draft, whose back had been pierced by an Archie nose-cap. When he arrived, he had been paralysed in the hindquarters. In a few weeks he was convalescent, staggering with a puzzled look round the paddock, chewing plantains and very willing to be the interesting patient to any callers.

Headquarters were now camped on the sides of the Scherpenberg, an outer bastion of the Monts Noirs, hirsute with scrub oak, and coifed with a windmill. Hither a subaltern might scramble on a warm afternoon and lying belly downwards in a thick rug of blaeberries, alternately cram his mouth with the black fruit and survey the panorama of war. Far away to the left, he could just make out the yellow sands of the coast-line and the white break of waves. From here full across the landscape ran a brown smudge, as if the artist had deliberately drawn a dirty thumb over the finished canvas. This was the devastated belt of the battle. At the edge, every now and then the flash of a gun. At one point the flashes were thicker and patterned. Someone was attacking or counter-attacking, and men were being blasted to fragments of flesh. It could have little importance for the watcher ten miles away, as little as for the driver of the lorries roaring on the road below, or for G.H.Q., or for God. The sun lit the bones of Ypres to whiteness. Further round, the edge of the scarred links called Observatory Ridge glittered dully. Beyond it, in the far distance, grew the red towers and chimneys of a thriving town, Tournai perhaps. At last, the view was blocked by Kemmel Hill with its girdle of feathery trees. The sky was embellished by a line of observation balloons. Sometimes one would almost imperceptibly change its shape and drop slowly in a mantle of smoke. As evening drew on, the diamond dust of flashes would thicken along the line; soon the horizon would be filled with twinkling points of light, with every now and again a paused flush, where something, a gunpit probably, had caught fire, fading reluctantly. Then as night hurried in, the sky was slashed by candescent beams, thrusting and stabbing to find the intruder. A series of heavy reverberations announced that the enemy bomber had completed his task.

In the end, a new camp commandant came from England, and I prepared to depart. By September 1917, none except perhaps the very young joined the infantry without knowing that his chance of life was at best about 4 to 1 on. At the same time these premonitions were beaten down by the happy sense that I was going home.

PART TWO

THE GROGNARDS

'*We are but soldiers for the working day.*'

HENRY V

XIII

CHORUS OF RUSTICS. '*What will Master Jack say? But here comes Master Jack!*'
(BAND AD LIB.—*See the Conquering Hero comes.*)
MASTER JACK. '*Home again after forty years at the Front!*
How the old place has changed.'

AUCTOR IGNOTUS

THEY were lying in Kemmel Shelters, preparing for the line. Smith had taken over command a few days earlier. 'Sit tight and look round,' he said. 'There'll be a job for you soon.' I looked round.

Ten months had made deep changes in the battalion. It was like an ancient garment which had been darned and redarned until, though it hangs in the same shape, few fragments of the original cloth remain. Here and there were patches of the first fabric. The transport, the stores, the orderly room still showed familiar faces. The R.S.M. still swelled his chest and roared, though in a voice hoarser than of old. There was the calm and capable C.S.M. of No. 2, Edmonds, with his quiet persistent cheerfulness. The quartermaster-sergeants were the same, but they had shed all their militarism. In the ranks appeared now and again a face one remembered, a Crossley, a Ting. But the change was more definite than the loss of familiar landmarks. The spring, which had driven the battalion, was worn. The last flickers of our early credulous idealism had died in the Arras battles. The men, though docile, willing, and biddable, were tired beyond hope. Indeed, they knew now too well to hope, though despair had not overthrown them. They lived from hand to mouth, expecting nothing, and so disappointed nowhere. They were no longer decoyed by the vociferous patriotism of the newspapers. They no longer believed in the purity of politicians or the sacrifices of profiteers. They were as fed up with England as they were with France and Belgium, 'fed up, f—— up, and far from home.' The best they could count on was a blighty good for a year; the next, a little breathing space to stretch their legs and fill their lungs with sweet air in some back area, a village with good estaminets. The worst—they knew so much now that they dare not envisage worse than they knew: yet they felt that worse did exist and might even now be ripening for them.

The officers in degree were as the men. Very few of the pre-Somme vintage remained; Vanneck, miraculously escaped, worn and bitter, Whitehead, with two long periods in hospital, Jerome and P. E. Lewis wounded and rejoined. The rest were either very young or had served in the ranks. Many were as worn as their men, suffering in turn irritation, fear, and cafard. Our speech has grown coarser; our humour threadbare, at best cruel, met by sardonic laughter. We are in truth *grognards*, who have known, not Marengo, Austerlitz, Wagram, and Borodino, but frustrated attack upon attack along one tract, fifty miles long, of man-stale earth; and we have learned to appreciate that grim jape: 'The first seven years will be the worst.' We have come to and passed our Silver Age; our Bronze has set in. 'Time hath worn us into slovenry.' Yet the Aidôs still lingers in certain hearts, and in the heart of the battalion as a whole, animating it through calamities and afflictions. We have not yet lost the saving virtues of irony and humility.

Just before dusk on the next evening, we stumbled up the frayed corduroy road towards Hollebeke. Though the battle had died down here, it was still close enough to the offensive and sufficiently unorganized for continuous harassing. Of its details I have but dim recollections, for the front line was unapproachable by daylight. The stagnant waters of the Comines Canal swayed iridescently fifty feet below our left flank. Battalion H.Q. was in a rickety, louse-infested dugout in the bank. In the wood behind, two companies sweltered and swore in the fly-blown cellars of the White Château, once the summer pleasaunce of old Leopold of Belgium, now a hummock of pink, white and gold masonry, intermittently grubbed up by shells. The duckboards stopped short at battalion headquarters, and between here and the front line lay half a mile of pocky expanse, bare save for the débris of battle.

Our visit to this sector is marked in my mind by one of those delicious strokes of official humour. Propaganda had decided that the Navy must see the war, and attached to us seven sailormen for a dose of stimulation. Smith cocked an eye at me, and said: 'Your job, I think.' Accordingly, as soon as night fell, I started out on the smudge of beaten slippery earth, which served as a track to the front line, followed by seven strange figures in battle bowlers and box respirators. It was pitch dark, and we were all in a muck of sweat by the time we reached the company headquarters, a small pill-box a few yards in rear of the shell-hole line, its floor covered with eighteen inches of brown, scummy water in which old ammo boxes bobbed for the occupants to put their feet on and attempt a theatrical dryness. At the moment of our arrival, the Boche opened a heavy minnie hate on the front line. Whines and crunches filled the darkness. I pushed our guests under the lee of the wall, and wondered what kind of disciplinary action would overtake me, if one of them got it in the neck. The strafe died down, and wounded began to appear. One of the sailors, a hospital ship attendant, turned to like an adept and trussed a fractured thigh. Then I hurried them back to the supports, wondering how Propaganda would look on this jaunt, if they could see it. Next morning, they lined up before departure and tendered their hearty thanks for so amusing an evening: in earnest of his gratitude, the youngest and smallest A.B. ducked out of the ranks and pressed into the colonel's hand a twist of navy tobacco wound in tarred string. Smith nearly wept at this display and made the dugout even fouler for the next days by smoking it continuously. The only creatures who did not suffer were the lice.

Subsequent to this episode, we were hurried to and fro for a week. Two days were spent in Rossignol Wood. It was past the season for nightingales; but the enemy consoled us with the twitter of gas shells. On one of these days, Smith and I visited Colonel Ardagh, a lonely pathetic figure waiting for authority to decide what to do with him. We felt that he grudged us our problematical future, and bade us good-bye with an envy he could not conceal. From here we were hastened up to Bois Confluent and then for three nights to the Spoil Bank, a vast drumlin of canal spoil, dried and friable, into which galleries had been driven. The roof was not considered safe, and we were bound to admit the consideration when the better part of a 4.2 came hissing and spitting down the air-vent into our chamber. These tunnels were glorified by the presence of General Cubitt, now commanding an infantry brigade, of which he was the pride and wonder. Said one subaltern: 'When we relieved in front of Messines, he waited on the road for us to come out. He hailed each of us, as we came along with our platoons, and sent us in to brigade headquarters. He kept us there talking and drinking until four o'clock in the morning. Of course, none of the platoon sergeants knew where they had to go, and the battalion was scattered half over the countryside. It took most of next day to collect it again.'

Now we retired once more, to Locrehof Farm; but as soon as we were settled we were rushed up to a dismal collection of huts, which did not belie the name of Clem Camp. All the time, we moved in fighting order. Rumours of battle assailed us again and again. One day we were to support another division; on the next we were going out to rest; on the third, 'you'll be for it in the morning.' It mattered very little. The world was dissolving in a cataract of noise, which flooded the æther day, and night. This was the period of 'army barrages'. Since it was no longer possible to make a surprise attack—indeed, the advance advertising for the 31st July had been more thorough than for one of C. B. Cochran's revues—it was thought possible to deceive him as to the exact place and time of the next assault by constant artillery bombardment. So during September and October, thrice a day for two hours, all the guns in the Second Army belched, roared, quavered, and cracked; the air moaned and echoed; and the enemy replied. It was said that the enemy were not a penny the worse for this fury; but everyone was enfeebled by that ceaseless pulsation.

After one night of Clem Camp, we retreated to Locrehof Farm, half a world back between Locre and Dranoutre. Even here, though eight miles separated us from the nearest Boche gun, shells landed occasionally at night. But the autumn sun still shone, and it was pleasant to lie stretched to its healing fingers.

Then, one morning, during orderly room, a signaller summarily called the adjutant to the telephone. The colonel returned to the disreputable and diminutive figure of Private Woon, whose scandalous condition of uncleanness had driven his company to rebellion.

'If you can't keep yourself clean, I shall have to try,' he said. 'Sergeant-Major, find a fatigue party from this man's company and have him scrubbed. Cold water, mind.'

'Very good—sir. Prisneranescor', ri' tur', quick mar'h.'

The adjutant poked his head in. 'Reconnoitring party for the line, C.O. and company commanders. Rendezvous brigade office, nine-forty-five.'

The five hurried away. I turned to the orderly room table and moodily began to work on some overdue return.

From outside came shouts of laughter as Pte. Woon underwent his purgation. The sun was shining. Below the window of the hut, the runners on duty stretched themselves, lazily as cats. A voice rose:

'I'm as ready as the next to go out when there's a proper message; but I don't want any funny work—leastways, not in these parts.'

'What d'ye mean—funny work?'

' 'Member when he sent Clover and Frank up to Number Three at Arras? 'is 'ighness's compliments and a slice of cake for Captain Vanneck, and both the poor bastards got it in the kidneys.'

'Ar!'

' "Get me some tea," he says. I got it for him and he fills it up with whisky, and as soon as he put 'is nose to it, he says, "Poo! that's chlorinated. I can't drink this," and he handed it back. *Chlorinated! I* drank it all right.'

Once more the telephone. Orders to take over the line tonight; fighting order, extra bandolier, two bombs per man: embus full fighting strength at 6.30: guides will meet companies; but no destination is given. We put our equipment morosely together. We were for it, all right.

Towards six o'clock, Whitehead and the other company commanders turned up, hot, dusty, and tired. 'Where's Smith?' I asked, as Tebbutt grinned at me over a cup of tea.

'God knows. Dead, I expect. You never saw such a hell of a place. The Somme was a picnic to it. It's the most bloody awful spot I was ever in. Barrages everywhere. We found the H.Q. we're supposed to take over from, crumped in, pill-box cracked like an egg-shell—all dead, Hampshires, I think they were. We couldn't get any information. The C.O. told us to come back as fast as we could, and the last I saw of him was hopping off with Hobbs into a barrage.'

The lorries turned up as the sun was sinking. The hills stood out blackly against the glowing sky, and the world westward seemed to offer us a farewell. My mind went back to a similar evening over a year ago. This time there was no singing, no gaiety. The men swung themselves clumsily over the backboards. A dogged resignation to fate was reflected in each awkward body. I glanced at the parade-state in my hand as I clambered up. We were, including officers and headquarters, 353 all told. From this too we had to detail a carrying party under a bright and tireless boy, named Milsom, to remain at brigade headquarters.

As usual the buses carried us at first in the opposite direction; but this well-worn device no longer deceived. We swung round through Dranoutre and passed beneath the arbours of Kemmel. Night had fallen before we reached the three trees, known, perhaps after some long vanished caravanserai, as Bus House. It was quiet, too quiet. There was a full moon, and a light mist. One shell whined slowly overhead and travelled from our hearing; a dull thump long after announced its arrival. Smith rose out of the darkness and grinned at me. 'Get headquarters and come along,' he said. 'We're late.' We passed the one pink pillar which still stood a monument to civilization by the canal bridge, and moved slowly up the plank road. Feet shuffled behind us on that solemn march, the weary footsteps of overburdened men going into the line, the pace set by the slowest and most reluctant walker. The night stayed uncannily silent. Once an Archie yelped a dozen quick shells. There were eddies of smoke on Hill 60, where gas shells were falling. At the corner of the Verbrandenmolen Road lay the putrid, swollen carcases of two huge grey hairies, impesting the air. We tramped up Morland Avenue and reached the nick in the sky. A group of figures detached themselves from crevices in the side and questioned us in whispers. It was curious that we all spoke in low voices, though we were still a long way from our destination. We moved over the crest. Before us lay a long slope, a desert all silvery in the moonlight. To right and left stood ghosts of woods, and beyond, a sullen ridge. Above its crest a rare light floated downwards. This was the Salient.

We went on until we came to a pill-box beside one torn and splintered trunk. The place was named Bodmin Copse, but the lonely defiant spike was sole witness that here had once swayed a leafy covert. For an hour or so I lingered in the trench. From the tarnished mist down the valley southward, a German gun flashed now and again. The cold was increasing. Shivering, I pushed my way into the crowded pill-box and found room to sit on a bench. Between my legs, I could see the adjutant's face; he looked flushed and ill. Presently a message came in that relief was complete.

XIV

'And I will make thee to pass with thine enemies into a land which thou knowest not; for a fire is kindled in mine anger which shall burn upon you.'

JEREMIAH

Two mornings later we sat on the Tower Hamlets Ridge and surveyed desolation. Many months hence, I was standing at this point with a major in the Bedfords. 'I was here in nineteen-fourteen,' he said; 'then you could not see half a mile for the woods.' It was scarcely credible. In nineteen-seventeen, it was as bare as a man's hand. It could not, one thought, have ever been otherwise. Could such destruction be wreaked? Were these puke acres ever grow fields of clover, beet or cabbage? Did a clear stream ever run through this squalmy glen? This, the map tells you, was once a magnate's estate. Now the lawns are bare of grass. The ornamental water has been replanned by more recent landscape gardeners; it is a quag of islands and stagnant pools, over which foul gases hang. The undergrowth has been tangled with more spiked and wiry bushes than ever nature grew. The woods are a quayside of naked spars. A tree hangs a maimed branch which creaks in the wind; another has been pruned to the roots: here a whole avenue has been sliced to extinction. The soil has been churned and furrowed until no two paces are level. In this belt, perhaps four miles wide, there are no seasons. The air grows colder or warmer; the days contract or lengthen: but the earth makes no response. To our eyes, its life has ceased. There is not a blade of grass, not a leaf. Only man, by his superior agility, has survived; but not often, if the sallow death-masks near the line—to bury them at this season demands greater leisure and fortitude than the infantry can command—are to be believed.

But this was no time to muse on scenery. The adjutant had withdrawn with a violent fever, handing over to me a mass of papers. I gathered them to my knees and began to puzzle out the situation.

Our headquarters was in a large and apparently solid concrete shelter at the crest of the ridge. It was visible from all sides, particularly from the enemy's. A passage ran from front to rear, off which lay two adjacent rooms, one the aid-post, presided over by our quiet, sardonic M.O., Mackwood; the other where the rest of us, signallers, runners, officers, three batsmen, lay crowded in the company of a strange and ancient sapper with two baskets of pigeons. No one knew how long he had been here. His beard was well sprouted. He had reached the stage when he would rather stay where he was than face the shelling outside. He had one of those long grave faces, which you will see in el Greco's Burial of the Conde de Orgaz. He was a Somersetshire man.

He was not to be blamed for his tremors. The enemy shelled the ridge without relief. Day and night, hour after hour, heavy explosions rocked our neighbourhood. Northward ran a trench. It was choked with dead. From the marks on the shoulders and collars, three divisions at least must have been here. They lay slung carelessly on top of each other, sprawled in obscene attitudes. As I walked along the edge with Smith, my eye caught something white and shining. I stooped. It was the last five joints of a spine. There was nothing else, no body, no flesh. This apparition overcame me. I turned away and choked back a sudden nausea: but Smith merely chuckled. Indeed the place overawed one. We descended to primal man. No washing or shaving here; and the demands of nature answered as quickly as possible in the handiest and deepest shell-hole.

The front line lay some four or five hundred yards eastward on the dip of the forward slope, facing marshy country studded with pill-boxes and bristling with torn wire. It was a broken curved line with one pill-box held by an officer and ten men, fifty yards forward. On the unsheltered plateau between the line and headquarters the constant shelling had sprinkled the ground with flecks of earth until it looked like a brown choppy sea heaving under rain. To the north lay that doleful highway, the Menin Road, cutting the skyline. Behind us, the Basse-villebeek, once no doubt a cheerful brook, but now a deep marsh sixty yards wide, was spanned by two duckboard foot-bridges across which the gun and machine-gun fire rarely ceased. Behind this again the slope ran up for a mile to Observatory Ridge, a rugous waste in which the only features, save the transparent woods, were bits of broken trench and a rare concrete shelter. Looking eastward over these the position seemed impregnable. The men who had stormed it must have been of heroic nature. But in reverse it was a treacherous place, a lonely peninsula to which, should the enemy carry the line, no supports would ever come. There was no telephone communication. Runners did most of the work, gallantly passing through shelling thick as a winter storm: they can never be praised too much. Pigeons were unreliable. We had a lamp which could flash a message to brigade, a mile and a half across the valley. But brigade could not reply. Each flash they made brought them a sharp rebuke of 5.9's.

That morning I was awakened by a direct hit on our roof, a solid bump which bowed the head and confused the ears; but the concrete withstood it. I looked later and found a small shallow saucer just over where I had been sitting. An hour later another shell hit the rear doorway, breaking the thinner stone, and a signaller went down with a scream. The shell had not hit him, but he was shattered and perforated by the concrete. He died in a few minutes. The day passed in a storm of shelling tossed to and fro over our position. During the night it grew quieter. The country faded out in mist.

Towards dawn, Bevan, our bluff little intelligence officer, went out with his gigantic ally, Private Digby, to explore No-Man's-Land. The mist was now thick and there was dead silence. Presently the shelling started again all over our tableland. We sat with heads bent, enduring it. Just as daylight was filtering through, a man came tumbling into the entrance. 'They're through—through on the left. The Boche are coming,' he gasped. The Colonel was on his feet in a second. 'Turn out. Get the S.O.S. away.'

'Lamp's no good, sir,' said the signaller at the door. 'Fog's too thick.'

'Pigeon!'

A note was scribbled, 'S.O.S., Marrow,' tucked under the pigeon's armpit and the bird thrown up into the air. We strung out in front of the pill-box. I recollect the difficulty of selecting a hole which was both deep and clean. Then there was a shout and a runner came breathlessly through the mist. 'Cap'n Whitehead sent me, sir. They got in—flammenwerfer—but the captain bombed them out. And there's a lot of casualties.'

Under cover of the hurly-burly of shelling on our plateau and the thick mist, the enemy had concentrated a number of trench-mortars against our segment of line. They pounded it lavishly for ten minutes. Then the defenders suddenly saw advancing towards them a wave of fire. The enemy were attacking under cover of flammenwerfer, hose pipes leading to petrol-tanks carried on the backs of men. When the nozzles were lighted, they threw out a roaring, hissing flame twenty to thirty feet long, swelling at the end to a whirling oily rose, six feet in diameter. Under the protection of these hideous weapons, the enemy surrounded the advance pill-box, stormed it and killed the garrison. Shorman, its commander, was last seen by Bevan and Digby, who were lying out in front, wounded and being carried away. Bevan himself had been shot in the stomach; but Digby, stayed with him and in the end managed to drag him back to our line. In the meantime, the enemy was consolidating the captured pill-box; but Whitehead and C.S.M. Edmonds, collecting a few men to carry for them, furiously assailed the place and bombed their way into it. Most of the occupants were killed, and six surrendered.

Then the stream of wounded began. Bevan was brought in, his face nigger black and his groaning lips blood-red from the fire. The doctor bound him up and gave him a shot of morphia. 'Give me a drink,' he groaned, 'give me a drink.' 'Not with that hole in your stomach,' I said gently. More and more men came in, with black faces, singed hair and eyebrows, and red swollen lips, were bound up and soothed as well as possible, and then sent or carried away.

In the meantime we were surprised that nothing had come of our S.O.S. Our artillery had maintained a stolid indifference to the appeal. We looked about, and to our mortification perceived our brave pigeon, which should have been on the Scherpenberg an hour past, solemnly walking round and round the pill-box, chuckling to itself.

'You'd better wring the wretched dove's neck,' said the colonel bitterly to the pigeon man.

'Oo, I couldn't do that, sir.' He explained in his soft, west-country accent that pigeons could not fly in fog.

'Then I don't see much good in your staying here,' retorted Smith.

'Nor do I, sir,' said the pigeoneer humbly; 'I'll be glad to go.'

That night we were relieved, but it was little enough relief for the companies. They trudged a mile back to Bodmin Copse and sheltered in broken trenches, embellished with a few small elephant splinter-proofs and blown-in funk-holes. For the next three days they endured all the tribulation of war. They were shelled steadily day and night. At every hour there were casualties. The ration dump was a nightmare. A shell pitched in the middle of one company's carrying party, killing and maiming a dozen. And there was sickness. Men came in, shaking with fever, to be despatched to hospital or the transport lines.

Ourselves at headquarters were fortunate. There was put at our disposal a tiny chamber next door to brigade headquarters in Canada Street Tunnels. It was perhaps ten by five, filled with fetid air, impregnated with the reek of burning fat from the Tommies' cookers, on which the men in the passage brewed endless tea. To me that cell has fixed itself as the portrait of any battalion headquarters in this dirty war. The walls were of pit props, covered with stained and ragged canvas. At the end a previous tenant had once pinned a Vie Parisienne picture of a naked girl. The pins had fallen out and it now hung awkwardly neglected, a great smudge of black across the face. Below a rough shelf was hooked a sheaf of pink telegraph forms, relics of earlier guests at this road-house. A two-tiered bunk of rabbit wire occupied a third of the room. There was one double stool and an upturned S.A.A. box. A narrow table ran along one wall. On it lay a *nature morte*, a scrawled map, a whisky flask, a packet of Goldflake, a steel helmet, a couple of Mills bombs, a half-pint enamelled mug full of thick tea, lighted by three inches of candle stuck in a bottle neck down which the grease of countless forerunners had spilled and congealed. Beneath the table a petrol tin of chlorinated water clanked when it was kicked. From nails hung two panoplies, tangles of equipment, helmets, haversacks, water-bottles and revolver cases. Outside in the darkness there was the never-ending tump-tump of pumps keeping the water back: and every now and then the muted explosion of a heavy shell near the top of the staircase. When a barrage was being fired one's brain was assailed by a series of countless small pressures. For the rest, it was waiting for something to occur, the next meal, the next orders, the end of the war, or the end of the world.

We had not long to wait. On the second day we received

orders to attack from our late position beside the Menin Road and to capture a group of pill-boxes to our immediate front. We were the right battalion of the attack. Our business was to protect the right flank of the 5th division, while our own right flank was to be kept safe from a peculiarly obnoxious group of dugouts a little further south by a raid on the part of the 60th. We were promised relief on the night after the attack.

By now our 353 had dwindled by a third. No. 2 company, which had borne the brunt of the flammenwerfer attack, was reduced to seventeen. We reclaimed our carrying party from brigade, though they were as tired as the men who had been in the line and had had a number of casualties. For our staff captain with admirable forethought was provisioning the front line with enough rations and water for twenty-four hours, and the carrying party had been making several journeys each night from Bodmin Copse to a broken pill-box at the edge of the Menin Road to make this ready. Even with this reinforcement we could only raise three companies of about seventy men apiece and a battalion headquarters of seventeen.

'Is three officers enough for a company?' I asked the colonel.

'Yes. Send Knappett from Number Two down to the transport lines.'

'And Milsom? He's had a pretty tough time on the carrying party.'

'He can go too.'

That evening the sacking in front of the door was pulled aside and a pale face looked through. It was that of R——, an officer who had joined us after the Somme and gone home sick before the Ancre. He had recently rejoined. He was regarded with suspicion as a line-dodger and a lead-swinger. Smith had given instructions to the M.O. that R—— should not be permitted to go down except on serious well-diagnosed grounds.

'What do you want?' I asked.

'I'm going down to the transport lines. I'm not well.'

'Are you, indeed? What's the matter?'

'My bowels haven't moved for four days.'

'Nor have mine. It seems quite natural to this neighbourhood. You'd better rejoin your company.'

'But the M.O.'s sent me down. I've a chit from him.'

'Show me. . . . Whose signature is this? This isn't Mackwood's.'

'No. I couldn't find our doctor so I went over to the R.B.'s.'

I felt furiously angry. The man had deliberately dodged the M.O. who knew him and had got his paper from another who did not. Had I been more experienced I should have sent him to our own man to be vetted. As it was I told him coldly to go away.

Smith listened to my story and his face turned very grim. 'I'll deal with him when we get out of this show. But Number One will be short of an officer. Keep back Milsom.'

After that, time lay down. The minutes dropped into a stagnant pool from which there was no outfall. The hands lingered over the divisions on the watch. We looked round to see whether we had collected all our goods. We ate a meal unwillingly, to break the monotony, and made poor jokes. Above us we could hear the rumble of gun-fire, like the tide coming in on a distant shore. It rained, too, to add to the misery of the companies.

It was nine o'clock before we loaded ourselves, myself with an additional haversack of papers, maps, notebooks, and telegraph forms. There was a shuffling of feet in the passage. Our fat little Lewis-gun sergeant, Battersby, reported, 'Headquarters all ready, sir.'

The rain had stopped. The night was chilly and damp as we nosed into the darkness. Light clouds covered the moon. We pushed along quickly as far as Bodmin Copse and saw by the empty shelters that the companies had gone on. Shells were dropping haphazardly about the waste land, a spiral of smoke spreading upwards to a mad ghost. Our pace declined as the track ended. We felt our way between the hummocks. There came a faint hail. Figures stumbled towards us. It was Mackwood and his aid-post orderlies, who had missed the path. As we turned down towards Dumbarton Wood, there came a threatening whisper through the air, growing louder and louder to a roar. 'It's on top of us,' I thought, and dived. I felt the head of the man behind me hit my boots, saw a shoot of black soot ten feet away and heard a crash. The air was full of flying pieces and the stink of explosives. Something whirled near me and banged me over the kidneys. I jumped, but it was only a huge clod of dried earth. We scrambled up and hurried on.

By now we could see the far edge of the naked wood. The track led under banks beside holes of stinking water; roots clutched at our feet. On the other side lay the foot-bridge, and as we went forward we could see a fury of shells falling about it. Two guns were firing alternate rounds with instantaneous fuse at a rate of about four rounds a minute each. Smith was leading, and as we drew near to the spot—for this was the only way across the morass—there seemed to be no hope of getting through. Smith's figure trudged steadily forward. We were very close now. A shell burst and the boy behind me gave a sharp exclamation. 'Hit?' I asked; 'can you walk?' 'Yes, sir, only me arm's gone.' 'Give me your rifle,' I jerked in a desperate voice, 'and come on.' It looked as if this was going to be the end of us. We plunged forward and down the bank on to the foot-bridge. The miracle, for miracle it surely was, had happened; that had been the last shell. Many men after a period of war took to themselves some mascot on which they pinned the little faith left in them, a guardian ju-ju, a mystic rite, to omit which spelled disaster. This solid three-cornered miracle gave me mine. From that moment, the colonel became the talisman which could soothe frayed nerves and call up new strength.

When we climbed the other side and reached headquarters, a riot of shelling was covering the plateau. No. 1 company, which had taken the southern track, was passing. The lion-headed Waley was leading them; tall Allen brought up the rear. I murmured a deeply-wished 'good luck' to Milsom. The Rifle Brigade whom we were relieving was lending us one of their companies as a reserve, to make up our strength a little in case——. Anything might happen in this unholy place.

Some time later No. 3, the other attacking company, passed. Of the support company, No. 4, there was no news. It was commanded by a young but very senior captain, named S——, a couple of months out from England for the first time. We waited. I went outside. There was nothing to be seen but shells bursting along the edge of the ridge. We had been allotted a wireless for this show. The mast was standing at the back of the pill-box, held up by four halyards, and the sapper in charge was tinkering at it. A gunner subaltern and his orderly came out of the night. 'I'm detailed to you for tomorrow, though God knows what I can do,' he grumbled.

It was now nearly three o'clock. The R.B. headquarters had gone, but our last company had not turned up. I sent off two runners, Morgan and Gillions, to beat the woods, and reported to Smith. My batman, Johns, handed me a mug of tea. A note came from Whitehead in the front line. 'Nos. 1 and 3 relief complete. Where is No. 4?' Smith leapt to his feet and ran out of the dugout. I grabbed his helmet and gas-mask and ran after him. With some difficulty I persuaded him to put them on as he ran up and down the ridge peering into the night. Shells were falling all round us but they did not seem to matter. Pieces came winging viciously past us, slapping against some half-destroyed concrete walls. At last when we were at the pitch of despair we saw a long line of men slowly struggling up the bank. I rushed over and met young Jerome at the head of the missing company. 'Where in hell have you been?' I demanded angrily. Jerome was as furious as I. His shrill cockney voice swung up. 'Where? Nearly up to Passchendael, I think. That bloody fool, S——, lost his bloody way and took us somewhere up north. It wasn't till we'd crossed the Menin Road, I found he didn't know where he was. So I about turned the company and came straight here. God damn him. Lead on, sergeant.' The company limped wearily past. They had been walking over shell holes for six hours and they were dead beat with the weight of the Lewis guns and their drums, the bombs and the extra bandoliers and their two days' rations. S—— came haltingly past in the rear, as beaten as his men.

We settled down to wait. There was still an hour and a half before zero. The pigeons rustled and cooed in their baskets. The runners were drinking tea. Our signal officer, Daniels, known familiarly as Dozy, was busy over the lamp with four or five experts. The gunner officer had gone to sleep. He slept on and off until he left us. The wireless mechanic was crouching in a corner. 'Is your machine ready?' I asked.

'Not yet,' he answered.

'Get on with it, then.' I sat down and my head began to nod. Suddenly I heard the colonel's voice say: 'Have you got your connection yet?'

'No.'

'Why not?'

'They're shelling.'

I listened. The guns had switched away from our quarter.

'Go and put it right,' said the colonel. The man hesitated and glared. Smith sat up straight. 'If you don't go at once, I'll have you thrown out by the runners. You should have been in touch an hour ago.'

The man stumbled clumsily into the darkness. Three minutes later there was a blinding crash over our heads. The candles swept out. From the door came a careless voice: 'They've got that wireless cove all right, and blown his aerial to shivers.'

Smith shrugged his shoulders. 'If he'd done it when you told him, he'd be alive now,' he said to me.

It was now five-thirty, and the Boche had started laying about him. Shelling grew fiercer and fiercer. Zero was 6, and as the moment arrived, our own guns joined in the storm. The noise tore out of the abyss, flooded and overwhelmed us. One could just catch the maniac rattle of machine guns. The two assault companies had started at zero plus 3. And now there was nothing to do but wait. The intolerable barrage went on and on and on. Direct hits fell on us. The air eddied violently under contending explosions. About 6.45, Waley tumbled into the pill-box, panting and swearing hard. A piece of shell had pierced his shoulder and nicked the top of his lung. 'We couldn't get there,' he snorted; 'the bloody barrage fell behind the objective. We've got within fifty yards, but the company's finished. Allen's in charge. Milsom was killed as we started.' Mackwood dressed him and we tucked him in a corner. Confirmation came later. The raiding party covering our right flank had been stopped on their own parapet. Our right company, which was to wheel outwards and form three posts, did their job, but the frontal assault was stopped short of the objective. Allen, the remaining subaltern, with the fourteen men out of the seventy who had started to cross those two hundred yards, went to ground where they were. The West Kent's company immediately on the left had got no further than ourselves. It was the usual sacrifice flank attack, with small gains and heavy casualties. The battalion dug in and stuck there.

During that morning gallant pairs of stretcher bearers sometimes staggered through the storm with a groaning burden. The wounded were bound up, doped and laid down, until the passage was filled with maimed and semi-conscious soldiers. None could be got away. The enemy guns concentrated on the line of the Bassevillebeek and the wood to prevent supports coming through. The shelling never ceased. The bursts at the edge of Dumbarton Lakes looked like woodmen's fires of autumn leaves. Glanville looked in for a moment, grinned and went back to his Stokes guns. The colonel led me over to the company of the 10th who were holding the gap between ourselves and the battalion on our right. Their tiny hovel was filled to the brim; one dodged in hastily hoping that nothing would push one forward from behind.

We had been promised relief that night; but no orders came. We spelled out a question on the Lucas lamp. Brigade ignored us. The shelling went on. Gradually one grew inured to the crashing. I humped my shoulders and read and re-read 'The 2nd Army Appreciation of Recent Operations.' At the fourth perusal, I began to understand it and to get interested.

In the early afternoon the shelling grew lighter. About three o'clock a runner from brigade came staggering in. I tore open the brown envelope, which a glance assured me did not contain relief orders. 'On visiting your horse-lines today, I found that the grease-traps were not in good condition. For information and necessary action, please. A.B. Area Sanitary Officer.' It was too grim and too old-fashioned a jest. The brigade runner was thirstily swallowing a mug of tea. 'What time did you start?' I asked him. 'Ten o'clock, sir. I've had to lie up several times on the way.' He had spent five hours crossing two miles of country to carry this triviality.

The shelling was beginning to die down. The sun was shining over the forlorn countryside. We sent off our walking wounded, and delivered as many lying-down cases as they could take to the Field Ambulance orderlies. Waley was given another shot of morphia and laid on a stretcher. The orderlies raised him shoulder high. 'Christ!' he shouted; 'I'm not going down on this thing. It isn't *safe*!' and slid off into my arms. 'All right. Walk, if you must,' said Mackwood. We watched him stagger away on the arm of the R.A.M.C. man. 'He's quite safe,' Mackwood remarked; 'he'll be asleep before he's gone half a mile.' Even so, we had been unable to evacuate all the cases. The passage was filled with a dozen badly wounded, drugged men.

Twilight began to gather. An aeroplane was floating slowly up the line above our heads. We looked northwards. Far away against the indigo sky, a light shot up, breaking at its acme into three hanging balls, red-green-red. It was the English S.O.S. Another rose nearer, and then other like rockets began to rise closer and closer, swinging outwards in the western evening wind. The barrage was already rumbling and tumbling in a wild rhythm, and as each successive front flung up its appeal, more guns opened to swell the racket. Nothing was happening on our front. 'Wind up,' shrugged Smith; 'we'll wait until the front line asks.' Our front remained unalarmed; but a rocket went up on our left, and then was taken up on our right to be passed southward. Soon all the artillery was firing; and the enemy nervously replying. The hurricane swept down on us once more. We went inside our shelter, and drank our twentieth or thirtieth cup of tea. No one was eating; but there was a continual boiling of tea all day.

About nine that night we received a message that we should not be relieved for another twenty-four hours, and that the remainder of the Rifle Brigade would be sent to fill up the gaps in our front line. While we were waiting for them, a fatigue party from another battalion arrived with water. The officer was drawn and haggard. He had started with twenty men and eight had been hit on the way. The survivors stood round him, silent and dazed. They were muddy from head to foot. I told him to go on to the support company, as we had no one who could carry the tins forward. He protested that his orders were to deliver to our battalion headquarters only. I was on the point of reiterating the order when I noticed the state of one of the cans. It had been perforated by a shell splinter and only held about a pint. On examination, we found that of the twenty-four cans, there were only four sound ones; all the rest had been pierced by fragments of shell and were as good as empty. Since the front line still had their reserve supply to draw on, I sent the party thankfully homewards.

About two o'clock in the morning, the leading files of the riflemen began to arrive. Though they had merely held the line or stayed in support, they had suffered as severely as ourselves; 130 represented the full strength of three companies. Even their leader, Nothard, another of these staunch South Africans of unconquerable spirit, seemed dismayed. He asked us to provide his men with bombs, and then went forward to reconnoitre the position he was to take over. We sat down again. The shelling on the ridge had died down. We could hear the mumble of voices and the chink of accoutrements as the men were served out with bombs.

There came one shattering clang. In the infinitesimal fraction of a second, I saw the pigeoneer, his hands fluttering, his face like a martyr's in the fire, leap upward to the ceiling, and young Morgan, the runner, pitching forward on top of me. The candles shot up and died. I remember running trembling hands over my belly and legs, automatically searching for a wound. A complete silence fell. Then from the passage came one sigh, the simultaneous passing of life from the dozen wounded men lying there. Another silence, in which the pigeons began to coo and flutter; and at that, there broke out from the aid-post a high shrilling. One of the orderlies had been half scythed

PP—G*

in two by a piece of shell which had cleft him through the buttocks.

The candles were relit by our shaking hands. The shell had fallen directly on the bomb boxes by the door, exploding the contents, smashing the stone and burying a number of those standing by. For a space of time, we were all partially stunned and frozen by the shock. As we slowly recovered, one of the Rifle Brigade officers shot into the chamber and squatted down in front of Smith, shouting incoherently. His hair was grey-white, powdered with concrete, and stood on end. His face muscles leaped up and down as he gabbled. He was followed by a sergeant, who sank down beside him, and began shouting in his ear: ' 'E's gone, poor old Mack's gone, 'e's buried under the blasted concrete. D'ye 'ear?' repeating it again and again while tears trickled out of his eyes; but the officer had been deafened by the explosion and took no notice. With eyes staring, he kept on chattering and waving his hands. We got them out at last and sent them back. Mackwood had given the poor aid-post boy a heavy dose of morphia, and the cries sank to groans and whimpers. He died half an hour later. The Rifle Brigade, without their bombs, went forward.

Somehow the pill-box was cleared and the night ended. A bright uncompassionate day came in. The area round the dugout was a shambles. The most conspicuous body was the one mixed up with the crushed wireless set; the head, one shoulder and an arm had been sliced clean away, leaving a raw trunk.

'Afflictions,' says Sir Thomas Browne, 'induce callosities.' The day passed, leaving scarcely a trace on our memories. Most of us were too numbed and lethargic to care whether rain or shells fell. Two of the mess servants and Crosby, a kindly, elderly subaltern, suddenly appeared at noon bringing us cooked food and whisky from the transport lines. They had come eight miles and voluntarily risked their lives to comfort us. But we did not want food, and when we looked at the whisky bottle, we had drunk but two fingers.

The battle died down. There was only an obstinate shelling of picked spots. We sent away our wounded. Night fell, and soon afterwards, in the midst of the army barrage, the East Lancashires arrived to take over. We fled away before midnight, with orders to rendezvous at Shrapnel Corner, an unknown place of unhealthy name, where lorries would pick us up. We sped across the ridge and down the bank. The enemy was dropping 5.9's about the Bassevillebeek, but not on the foot-bridges, fortunately, for the duckboards were crowded with dazed and desperate men from our own and the 5th Division; they were tumbling over one another in their anxiety to escape from the pit. As I followed the colonel, I tripped over his heel and plunged off the boards into the morass up to my waist. 'Oh, help me,' I wailed. ' 'Ere you are, mate,' said a figure above me, and held out an iron arm. I staggered up on to the boards, fell against my rescuer, and threw him in on the opposite side. To my eternal dishonour, I did not wait to pull him out, but left him to his friends and fled after Smith, who had not observed my misfortune. I ran through the wood; but when I reached the other side, I could not find him. Thinking that I had passed him among the trees, I turned back and waited. At last out of the darkness came Morgan and the two remaining aid-post orderlies, who assured me that Smith had long departed. We set out for brigade to report the completion of relief. Its report centre was alleged to have moved to Tor Top. Here we fought our way down a precipitous stairway, full of men, into a room, where a tired brigade-major told me I should have gone to Canada Street. 'You had better go through the tunnel,' he said kindly. For hours, as it seemed, we pushed our way along this tunnel. It was packed with men pale, unshaven, feverish-eyed and husky, eating, unlacing boots with stiff mud-caked fingers, some naked rubbing themselves over with their shirts. At brigade H.Q. at the end, I reported relief complete. 'Smith came in two hours ago,' yawned the staff captain; 'I say, you'd better hurry, or you'll miss the last bus.'

We stumbled out on to Morland Avenue. I had now some vague idea where Shrapnel Corner was situated. The night was cold and lightish. In the fresh air, I was suddenly possessed by a new feeling of personal liberty and an absurd exaltation. I strode rapidly along beside my three tired and laden boys. In a mile, I was carrying a rifle and half the aid-post equipment. We came to a lonely sentry-box in which the ancient night watchman sat, warming his hands over a brazier.

'Do you know where Shrapnel Corner is?'

'Well, sir, there's a good many of them about in these parts. There's one there, now.' He waved a hand eastwards where Hill 60 was going up in smoke.

'Not mine, anyhow,' I rejoined. I was determined that even if we were to walk all night, it would be in a westerly direction.

At last we found it. 'You're just in time,' said a voice; 'jump in and we'll run you down to Beggars' Rest.'

At five in the morning we rolled into a shabby camp of worn tents and old gun-pits. There was a pan of hot rum and lemon warming by a fire; and a new flea-bag waiting for me. I felt very grateful and strangely happy. I slid in, drank my night-cap and fell into an unwakeable sleep.

* * *

When I woke, it was raining: and it rained for the next six days. The men lay miserably under rotting canvas, from which the camouflage paint had long been washed away, and cursed. There was little we could do for them, except distribute pay and bring up the canteen. Mackwood and I spent our afternoons collecting empty shell boxes from abandoned battery positions. In the evenings round a blazing fire in our elephant shelter, friends would collect, drink rum and reconstruct the last week. Freddy Hart, who had commanded No. 3 company in the battle, had had his whole headquarters killed round him in a shell hole by one of our own 4.5 Hows. Whitehead recalled how in the early hours before the attack he had heard a voice up the trench shouting, ' "Over the top! Over the top! We're coming over for you." The man had somehow got at the rum and was drunk. I said to someone, "Keep that man quiet." And presently the noise stopped. When I went along next day, I found him, quite quiet. Someone had stuck a bayonet into him.'

During these days Smith was very gloomy. He was ill and in pain. The battalion was now a shred. Of the 350 who had gone up on 27th September, only eight had come out. 'We no longer exist,' he said once or twice. He was worried also about two officers. The first was the lead-swinger, by whose evasion a reliable boy had been killed. The other was the incompetent company commander, S——. He had sat all the day of 4th in the pill-box, rolling a bomb to and fro between his hands. Suddenly the pin had slipped, and Whitehead had just had time to lob it out of the door before it exploded. Lastly, he had handed over one of our precious Lewis guns to the incoming battalion. 'They said they were one short,' he had explained, 'so it saved our men carrying it back.'

After six days we were sent in again, to the forward edge of Shrewsbury Forest. The weather was boisterous, and the earth a slimy eruption, over which one slithered, fell and crawled. We were so weak that we could only muster 113 all told, one company and a skeleton headquarters. The latter lay a long way back in Hedge Street Tunnels, a Dedalian plague-pit, built round a central crypt, from which ran dark shallow drives and stinking holes, filled with refuse and ordurous relics of human occupation. It was a windy spot, on the crest of Observatory Ridge, and the enemy shelled it industriously and implacably. The short hundred yards to brigade headquarters in a similar pit was covered as rapidly as the mud would permit. Many peaceable wayfarers were slaughtered daily hereabouts, and the dead of many different units lay by the roadside. They remained a long time without burial, for who was going to risk lives for such a task? The weather was no longer hot, and the dead would keep. They lay out there at the side of the track in the drizzle, yellow or grey or blue with blood dried black on their skins and clothes; sometimes a shell would hasten the indignity of slow decomposition. They were certainly not worth another life. Each day the necessity of economizing men became the first problem for a battalion headquarters. Here in the Salient where a battalion never went into an attack without having from fifty to eighty per cent casualties, where holding the line was scarcely easier, where ration carriers and digging parties were knocked out far behind the line, and when these losses were never made completely good, and what was made up, was inferior material, a kernel of the best (so far as might be) must always be husbanded. We were now glad to send officers and men away on courses, not for their education (the front line was the only true school), but to rest them. We took as few as we possibly could do with into the line, when it was only a matter of holding it. The wisdom of this policy became evident, as, from the safety of a doorway, one looked across the treeless acres of Armagh Wood and watched an area shoot of 5.9 and 8-inch howitzers falling about four miserable field-guns, axle deep in mud, four lonely widows peering through their veils of camouflage.

But no man in all these armies could by any act of faith save one life. From the line came those tired desperate voices: ‘ ’E cawn’t do it, Ser’eant; ’e’s finished’: ‘The platoon’s all in, old boy; we’ll only make a balls of it’: ‘I’ve only sixty men left in the company, sir; it's too few for the job': 'My battalion's been in the line for ten days, general; it's had 80 per cent casualties. We no longer exist'; 'Unless my brigade's relieved, I'll not answer for the consequences.' Those desperate voices never carried to England, or, if they did, they were drowned by the full-fed bawling of such safe patriots as Lord Northcliffe and Mr. Punch. When, a month later, Lord Lansdowne issued his peace letter, to be abolished in a howl of civilian execration, the army shrugged its shoulders and said: 'Poor old buffer; decent of him, but what did he expect with this gang in charge . . . ?'

On our third evening in Hedge Street we welcomed a very young, very fair and very shy subaltern from the Royal Sussex, who were to relieve us next day. His battalion had preceded us at Tower Hamlets and had suffered a like experience. Late that evening a 6-inch How-battery commander came in to ask for accommodation and stayed to dinner. He was a pale bald man with a neat fair moustache. He thumped the table and recited Kipling for our entertainment. On the next day I showed our incoming tenant from the Sussex over his noxious habitation. As we bade him good-bye, he shyly put a small paper-covered book into my hand. *The Harbingers*, ran the title, 'Poems by E. C. Blunden.' It went into my kit along with the battered Shakespeare, the torn *Evan Harrington*, and Sir Thomas Browne.

We trod lightly over the planks of Morland Avenue, grateful for our deliverance. The enemy was diverting himself elsewhere, on Hill 60 and Zillebeke. We snuffed the damp autumn wind and looked with glad eyes at the mottled sunset and the black line of the Monts Noirs, crowned with trees and windmills. Once more our feet were free and our minds unshackled. The lorries at Bus House were no longer tumbrils. As we slid and rattled towards Locre, we allowed ourselves to notice and marvel at the rich phenomena of the war. Half a mile short of our destination, the lorry shot across the road, hit the hedge and then canted sideways into the ditch.

'Mother told you ridin' on buses was dangerous,' said a voice behind.

XV

'Christians have handsomely glossed the deformity of death by careful consideration of the body.'

HYDRIOTAPHIA

WE spent a week at Birr Barracks. It was a week of casualty lists, of refitting, of despatching the kits of dead and wounded. The German planes visited the railhead half a mile away punctually at 7 p.m. each night and dropped a cargo of bombs. As I was usually taking a bath at this moment, I found their assiduity inconvenient, more especially since the visitors usually overpassed their target and swung their explosives in our direction. The week was chiefly notable for a dinner to the survivors of the original battalion, followed by a private show of the divisional Follies. We mustered perhaps a hundred, and the greater part of these were from the transport and the stores. Unfortunately, I arrived late, at the moment when the so-called milk punch was being served, the recipe for which hell broth had been deeply cogitated by Fairburn and the quartermaster-sergeants. A mug was pressed on me, half full of a curious, sweet but not unpleasant sediment which, having had nothing to eat, I rashly spooned into my mouth. From this moment reason declined and I was later led nearly snoring to bed by the dear and wholly reliable George Knappett.

The colonel solved his problem of the fainéant and the incompetent. Both appeared before the divisional commander. There was no court-martial. Their commissions were removed on his report and they left us to be drafted into the ranks at the base. It may have been cruel; but it was a necessity. The lives of others depended on it.

Now we moved back to the country, to Strazeele and its neighbourhood, scattered in farms over half a county. We were inspected and re-inspected. There was held amid curses from John Marquard the fourth or fifth divisional horse show of the year. It took place in pouring rain, and the brakesmen carried pots of paint ready to retouch points where the drops had flecked the spotless limbers. There was a tump-line and shoe-pack competition in which the prize was carried off by a team led by Ting, now a corporal wearing the Military Medal. Drafts came, which included Private Woon, more dishevelled than ever. 'I did think we'd really lost him at last,' wailed Vanneck. There was Whitehead's twenty-first birthday party, which the quartermaster and I attended. As arm in arm we solemnly walked out two miles home, a volley of yells rent the air. It was a midnight hare-and-hounds chase. 'Yes,' said Fairburn, shaking his head, 'I was afraid that punch 'ud be too strong.' 'What's your recipe?' 'Heat the rum, light it with a match, and then cool with more rum.'

News came from Italy of Caporetto, or as one of our brigadiers put it: 'The Ice-creamos have cut their stick.' There were rumours that we were to relieve Rome. Like all rumours they ended when we found ourselves at the beginning of winter floundering in a shell-hole line north of the Comines Canal. It was a sombre place, suited to a sombre time, when doubts already born began to thrive and swell.

We had a new M.O. now. Mackwood had left us for England and a rest, well deserved after cruel labours: we missed his thin face and his shy sardonic wit. In compensation we received a sturdy round-faced American doctor from Baltimore, of a humour and an ingenuousness to smooth our currish insularity. As yet he did not know the ways of the army. During our time in support, we had to find a daily working party of four hundred. On the day after Toulson's arrival the normal sick parade of perhaps a dozen was suitably gratified by being marked 'Excused duty', instead of the harsh 'M & D' of Mackwood. Too jubilant to keep the news to themselves, they commended this new curious M.O. to their friends. On the second day, two dozen doleful invalids presented themselves at the aid-post and were also excused duty. By the third morning the glad story had spread: a sick parade of fifty queued up. Individuals produced genealogical trees of ancient and malignant complaints and gained a sympathetic hearing. At this point, authority surmised the truth and began to ask questions. 'But you can't send men up the line in the state they say they're in; they'll die,' the doctor persisted. 'You try tomorrow, doc, and we'll see,' replied Smith: 'have you met that old scoundrel Carrick?' 'Lemme see. Would he be the man with the weak heart, or piles?' 'Both, probably,' said Smith: 'I suppose you took his word?' 'P'raps I did. D'you mean these boys have been guying me? All right, sir.'

The hundred odd which seethed round the aid-post on the next day were surprised and shocked to find that the M.O.'s bowels had dried up during the night. Instead of the kindly audience to which the old hands were now accustomed, a steely blue eye pinned them down. The aid-post lists came in with only one abbreviation, M & D. The working parties paraded with full numbers, voluble and objurgatory.

'If any arms or legs drop off during the day, you surely will not blame me,' remarked Toulson at lunch.

'If any do,' I answered, 'you can hang them in the aid-post as a souvenir.'

Sick parade dropped to the normal figure on the following morning. Another episode was closed.

It was a strange line in which we found ourselves, approached by a long communication trench through Battle Wood. At the end lay the railway from Ypres to Comines: but in deference to our use of the line, expresses had ceased to run. Beneath it lay headquarters and the right company in some stout concrete shelters. A scattered fringe of posts ran from the canal north-eastwards in a wide arc, some in pill-boxes, with the entrance facing eastward, others in short trench lengths. The left company dwelt on a hill towards Belgian Wood. It was unapproachable by day, though Smith once crawled the last two hundred yards to Vanneck's pill-box at noon and received the upbraidings of both the company commanders and ourselves when it became known. It was at once a good and a bad area. There was comparatively little shelling, but the conditions under which the men in the line existed were subhuman. In the left post, for instance, five or six men lay in a short trench, perhaps twenty-foot long, with no shelter save a couple of pieces of corrugated iron. They could not move by day, and during our second tour, it snowed. The next post was in a tiny pill-box at the edge of a ragged wood. The enemy lay just beyond the crest, and on two occasions they made playful snatches at the garrison; and once unfortunately they collared two unlucky men who were wiring by themselves in the freezing dawn. Visiting the place in the grey light, one would find the group standing-to in attitudes of defiance, their backs to the wall in the best romantic manner, while its commander kept up a running chatter of learned comment. This charming person was, I fancy, a scholar of Balliol, one of the many strange characters who had been co-opted into the army. At nineteen he was already the typical professor of farce, spectacled, ruffle-headed and absent-minded, the most delightful companion in a library, the most maddening in a pill-box. His leisure hours in rest were spent hurrying from church to church in the Second Army area, copying down the Latin inscriptions—I forget the technical name for them—which, when the correct formula had been found, spell out the name of the patron and the date of the tablet's erection. It was pleasant to watch him, in the midst of a crowd of people singing *All that I want is somebody to love me*, puzzling feverishly over his most recent trouvaille.

A black-browed Irishman, MacCarthy, was our new I.O., reputed to be a Sinn Feiner and to hold a commission in the I.R.A. Whatever the truth of this, he possessed a stolid cheerfulness. About four on a black cold morning we would go out after a tot of rum, and as soon as MacCarthy had been a little sick, an early morning habit, would grope our way over the frosty duckboards to the left company. The day was coming in as we hurried back over the brow of the hill down to our fastness in the railway line.

A further refinement of the war was the situation of a listening set in a little pill-box fifty yards down the railway. It was manned by a strange, vilely polyglot assembly, commanded by a ruffian said to be of Spanish-Roumanian birth and to speak seventeen languages. We used to bribe them to tell us what they picked up and no doubt they pulled our legs. The enemy at first seemed to talk about nothing but the failure of rations to arrive and to grouse in High Dutch on the quality of the soup. But just before Christmas, a voice was reported to have said: 'Success to our new offensive!' to which the reply was: 'Bailleul on New Year's Day!' That must have been the last message we were given, for the same night the Hispano-Roumanian got fighting tight, drew his revolver, and held up one of our ration parties. He had to be clouted on the head, handcuffed, and carried down the long miles of Oaf Alley on a stretcher by growling bearers.

By this time telephone conversation had become a nightmare. The art of circumlocution has never been more deftly practised. So our disgust and dismay were explosive when a newly-joined gunner liaison officer called up his battery and blandly remarked: 'I shan't shoot yet as the infantry will be relieving in an hour's time.' No doubt our fears were as exaggerated as the rumoured strength of the enemy's listening sets. The companies went out by a long and complicated alternative route and throughout the anxious hours the normally used Oaf Alley remained as peaceful as a country lane in Berkshire.

Christmas came and went under a foot of snow. We played snowballs, fed cigarettes—apparently without harming it—to a disgustingly odorous goat which had found a home in our camp at Vierstraat, lorry-hopped into Locre, where the nuns at the hospice gave us boiling baths in vast receptacles, and afterwards drank hot Malaga (such a thing is youth) in a neighbouring estaminet. The eight days in reserve were spent at Murrumbidgee camp at La Clytte, a collection of mean structures obviously erected by some pre-Crimean sapper. The huts were windowless; the stoves threw out a feeble heat within a narrow circumference. There was a filthy frozen bath-house which a miserable fatigue party was commissioned to work for the benefit of the division. We were visited here, not to our delight, by the divisional commander; and an hour or so later by a huge formation of Boche planes, which in place of bombs dropped showers of leaflets in praise of peace. This was an unusual incident. The droppings hitherto had been of a heavier and less pacific nature. A spell in support where the working parties were ceaseless (it was only by special pleading that Christmas Day was exempt), and a spell at Murrumbidgee were sufficient to assure us that on the whole the front line was the cushiest spot at this season.

Our second departure from Murrumbidgee gave the Practical Joke echelon the opportunity for one more of its morbid strokes of humour. Paternal authority decreed that on our next relief we should not march but be conveyed by light railway as far as the Spoil Bank, leaving only the towpath and the long Oaf Alley for the men to walk up. The idea was excellent; and though we had to parade half an hour before our usual time, we accepted the suggestion with less than the usual amount of grumbling.

We found our station—was it Euston?—and with difficulty entrained. No spacious allowance had been made for luggage, the Lewis guns, the rations and all the other impedimenta of a week's rustication. The trucks were open; there were no racks. Still we squeezed on board, and amid cheers the cobby little engine took the strain. It was 1.45 in the afternoon. In contrast to its broad-gauge relatives, this train was stimulatingly incautious. Soon we were whirling round a curve reminiscent of the more nightmarish defiles of switchbacks. As we tore down the gradient on to an embankment, the truck in front of mine suddenly lurched from side to side, shedding caps, steel helmets, and bags of rations into the meadow below. For a moment, disaster overlooked us; then the engine stopped. We got out and discovered that the track had been so badly torn up by the bogeys that further progress was impossible. The driver assured us that we could eaily get another train at the next station. Where was that? Willesden Junction. Of course, we agreed; all expresses stopped at Willesden. The junction was marked by a lonely shack half a mile ahead. After half an hour's fruitless communication through a refractory telephone, we were finally promised a train: and sure enough, at 3.30, a train slowly clanked in. But whereas our first conveyance had been designed to accommodate a battalion, the newcomer's trucks were only about two-thirds of the original's size. Twenty pushing, swearing, bawling minutes passed before by sheer pressure we had nailed the last man on board; they were so tightly packed that an unbridled movement threatened to burst the sides. Smith and I, still outside, found there was no room for ourselves. We discovered at the back of the engine a projecting iron plate below the smoke stack, facing the front truck, and perched ourselves on it. The train jogged off. The mist, which had been falling in swathes as the sun faded, now closed on us in winter darkness. Beneath a shower of sparks we clung precariously to our platform, hopefully assuring one another that we should soon be there, and that the time was only 4.30. Very slowly the engine panted and struggled up a gradient, a hill so immense that I began to think we must have passed out of the county, for no such incline could be recalled. At last it achieved the summit, and with a prolonged whoop and a veritable Brock's Benefit of sparks, sprang forward into the darkness, galloping down the other side in a series of uneven jerks on four stiff legs. We swayed, we rocked, we were pitched about on our tray, which we gripped with desperate tenacity. Suddenly there was a grinding of brakes; wheels screamed; trucks banged and clattered; and with one dull thud, we stopped dead. We shot from our perch, and exploring into the darkness, found our engine embraced head-on with another; both were off the line. A subaltern standing by exclaimed mournfully: 'We've been four hours putting this blasted kettle back on the rails, and now you've knocked it off again.' He belonged to the Lincolnshires, whom authority had also engaged to convey home. We found their colonel, who had no more idea where he was than we had. The night had thickened to a frozen density, and the ground on both sides of the track was a wilderness of watery shell holes. Somebody found a telephone; somehow touch was made with the local Sir Sam Fay and it was at last arranged that engines should come from Euston and Carlisle to haul the trains apart, leaving our first engines locked in their death grip athwart the line. All that was left for us to do was to exchange trains. Nightmares set in about this period of the evening. Let me hope that Uncle Toby's recording angel was on duty that night; for the fog and the darkness grew phosphorescent under the blasphemy of some eight hundred men; but in the end the miracle was accomplished. Towards ten o'clock we pulled into Spoil Bank; and the relief usually complete by six in the evening was consummated at 1.30 a.m. The anger of our hosts, I am glad to say, melted into laughter in the face of our pathetic narrative; and they departed thankful that they could reasonably conjecture the hour when their own legs would carry them safely to their beds.

During this period of hibernation war became more and more a matter of housewifery. Salvage was the fashionable winter amusement. The order had gone forth that no man was to return from the front line without some derelict article, a hat, a bomb or two, a barbed-wire picket, a Lewis-gun drum. Some units affected to despise this domesticity, boldly returning nil reports. Not so ourselves, Smith saw in this last brain-wave an idea which might be turned to our own profit. This area was strewn with dead. The dead had haversacks. The haversacks had socks. A unit was still judged by the number of men who developed trench feet during the winter. Defeating this disease was a matter of dry socks. The allowance was two pairs per man, both of which were usually wet through in the course of a couple of days. Now, thanks to salvage, we acquired some thousands of pairs of unauthorized socks. The colonel himself took the lead. Pipe in mouth he might be seen hopping, carrion-crow-wise, from body to body in the appropriately named Opaque Wood, returning home towards lunch time with his runner, their arms full of necessaries for the battalion. Occasionally I accompanied him on these jaunts: but my stomach was too queasy. Smith's mind was actively interested in all phenomena. He was as interested in a dead as in a living man, wanted to know just why the corpse lay in that position, speculated on the caprice which had left a head and a leg with no body to join them. Though I could look on bodies unmoved, I could not abide bare fresh bones: and after a morning in which the colonel tried vainly to interest me in a complete jaw without skull or cervicle, and with the teeth still flecked with blood, I excused myself from further operations.

So salvage occupied us and gained us certain high marks with Q. It was easy game. No one who has not seen a modern battlefield has any conception of the débris with which it is covered. A couple of years after the war a distinguished old gentleman who had been visiting the battlefields told me he had picked up two rifles in the neighbourhood of Courcelette. He was surprised that anyone should have been so careless as to leave such things behind. I tried to enlighten him by describing the litter on these Yprian fields in 1917, the ancient belts of wire nearly obliterated, with here and there a peering stump waving a malignant claw, the rifles with their bayonets rusted to the muzzle, the bunches of discarded equipment, the shovels, water-bottles and tin hats, maps stamped and ground into brown mud, the cotton bandoliers of S.A.A., boxes of bombs, of Very-lights, odd rounds of Stokes shells, flares, entrenching tool handles, stretchers, petrol tins for water, odd pieces of clothing, tins of bully, ground-sheets, buckets of Lewis-gun magazines, occasionally a gun itself, not to speak of the nearly obliterated relics of an earlier civilization; and this débris, often driven into or overthrown with earth, filthy with mud. It was one vast dump of discarded war material. Smith with homely truth observed: 'You can tell a shell hole by its contents, two Mills bombs and a lump of faeces.'

Our last tour in this sector was gladdened by the sight of Gwinnell. He had come to France from the training school at Bath, where he was an instructor, as part of a committee investigating the newest methods of warfare. Having found our pin-point, he deserted his committee for a week-end in trenches. Perhaps the familiar chatter of a battalion intoxicated him. Before we left he had thrown good sense to the winds and got himself posted to us once more.

We were relieved about the middle of January by a battalion of Australians: at least, they arrived, lounged about in the trench, talking in their thin wire-drawn voices, until we chose to evacuate the line. They were very patient with us. Their adjutant even permitted information to be conveyed to him, though with an obvious air of disbelief in its truth or utility. We crept away feeling like ancient landowners bought out by the new race of bustling plutocrats. But we lost this feeling as we passed over the crest of the hill. A traversing gun burst a couple either side of the slender breastwork. Then out of the fog rang the sinister howl of a klaxon. Gas alarm! I put my hand to my chest! I had left my gas-mask behind in the dugout. Smith heard my exclamation and chuckled. Nevertheless, he doubled his pace; and we beat it down to Spoil Bank at a rate that made the best-trained groan. Of course the gas alarm was a wash-out.

The next day we were on lorries, going back for a good rest. We drove through country long unfamiliar to us, Bailleul, Hazebrouck, Wallon Cappel. That night we found ourselves at Campagne. As I looked out of the window of the mess at a grey apple-orchard, I said to Smith: 'Do you remember? Number One slept in this field in August nineteen-fifteen two years and a half ago. There isn't much left of us now.' And I suddenly perceived that I was looking back on people who had grown so old and altered so much that one was a dream and the other reality, but which was which it was impossible to determine.

Two days later I was lying miserably in bed. On our last tour the Boche had dropped half a dozen mustard-gas shells round headquarters. I had heard them, but since I had smelt nothing had neglected to put on my gas-mask as the signallers in the next compartment had done. Now my eyes had begun to run, and as soon as I opened them fountains of water gushed down my cheeks. I tried reading with one eye closed, and when that became impossible, opening the other. Doc Toulson washed them and washed them. It was no use. The flood continued.

Smith decreed ten days' leave, which I thankfully accepted. That night I boarded an empty cattle train at Arques. By five in the morning when I reached Boulogne I was shivering from head to foot and full of griping pains.

XVI

'Then said Diffidence: "Take them into the castle-yard tomorrow and show them the bones and skulls of those thou hast already despatched: and make them believe, ere a week come to an end, thou wilt tear them also in pieces, as thou hast done their fellows before them.'

THE PILGRIM'S PROGRESS

By the time my leave had elapsed, the great re-shuffling of the British Army had begun. It was a matter of some pride that none of the battalions in our brigade were to be despatched. But the reorganization of an infantry brigade on a three instead of a four battalion basis implied the transfer of one battalion, and we were annoyed that it was ourselves who were elected for removal to a formation foreign to us, which we naturally despised and in which we had to learn all over again the idiosyncrasies of our commander. We were heartened by the arrival of some two hundred officers and men from our 20th battalion.

Of our new brigade only one battalion had survived, the other newcomer besides ourselves being a regular battalion. From our humble point of view we had always looked upon the regulars as corps d'élite, paragons of smartness and efficiency. This one was a shocker. On the morning after my return two of us watched pass a filthy unwashed limber drawn by two ungroomed mules with a dirty rider and an unshaven brakesman. Our own transport, like that of every other unit in the division, was spotless: I shudder to think of the amount of money we spent on paint and polish. 'What on earth's that?' I asked. 'That's our new regular battalion,' Freddy Hart replied: 'Fact. Very regular. Regular C.O., second-in-command, adjutant, quartermaster.' 'I'll bet their own division was glad to lose them.' 'I'll bet the Owner will startle them a bit.'

In mid-February we started back to the line, a fine battalion stronger than it had ever been, nominally indeed over strength, though, with men on command, on leave, on courses, and detached elsewhere, we should probably muster about a hundred and fifty per company in trenches, a vast number compared with the miserable fragment which had attacked in October. We set out on a damp blustering morning, our reinforced band blowing vigorously. Curs from wayside houses joined us, until we had a score or so in company. At Ebblinghem station we parted from them, a whirl of fighting bodies, last seen as a furry ball falling headlong into a dyke of water. Our train bore us so slowly that every now and then a freezing soldier would drop on to the track and run easily beside it to the accompaniment of his friends' encouragement and the adjutant's abominable oaths. One night was passed in a camp at Dickebusch. The next afternoon saw us picking our way across the confluent acne of the waste land under the walls of Ypres. Night found us with a company holding an uneasy group of shell holes between the Polygonbeek and the Reutelbeek, a wet and windy spot, and the others scattered in various shelters over a square mile of dead lava. The area still advertised the expense of the last offensive. A cluster of tanks was slowly disintegrating round Clapham Junction. What had been six bright bays and their drivers dissolved in a stinking opalescent pool at the edge of Sanctuary Wood. The stare of the horses' eyes was furious in their dead agony. Here and there in thickets of wire lay pease-porridge sacks, once living men. Headquarters was lodged in some new underground concrete chambers in Glencorse Wood. The builders and decorators were still at work, but the plumbers had obviously downed tools. We were glad to escape the advancing water at the end of five days and retire to drier if less commodious pill-boxes at Stirling Castle.

The main problem at present was the absorption of the new officers, N.C.O.'s, and men. The newcomers were nearly as strong as ourselves, and though they were willing enough to conform to our tenets and customs, they were naturally reluctant to part with those of their disbanded battalion. All tried honestly to achieve a common basis, but at first the process was slow. Some things we did they considered silly: some they believed in we thought rank heresy.

I had now been adjutant for four months and had blazed a track through the rank growth of returns, formulae, pro-formas, pamphlets, affidavits, army forms, with which superior formations bombarded us. It seemed that as soon as an idea crystallized in some warm office it became incumbent upon its happy projector to advertise it to the world. Certainly the winter of 1917–18 was more prolific of paper than any other period earlier or later. Among many others, there was issued, I think about this time, that singularly infuriating fantasy entitled: 'Am I being offensive enough? Notes for subordinate commanders. Not to be taken into the front line.' The owner of the happy wit which devised this title would doubtless have been gratified by the reception accorded to his phrase. 'You are,' said platoon and company commanders with one voice. 'Bloody offensive.' Gradually it was borne in upon us that a strong wind was blowing in the west: gusts of it whistled down to the front line. Wire, wire, wire was megaphoned from on high.

These tempestuous adjurations were not confined to the General Staff. Q, harassed by the voice of criticism in England that the army was shamefully overfed, took steps to placate our supporters at home by decreeing an economy campaign. 'EAT LESS AND SAVE SHIPPING,' read a pathetic notice board in the reserve camp. The legend was received with derisive hoots, and recoined by the vulgar to a more plausible assonance. Simultaneously the Quartermaster's stores became the scene of many curious minor industries, fat boiling and solder melting. Fairburn presided over these frugal activities, conscientiously fulminatory, and for many weeks was able proudly to display us as the most thrifty battalion in the division. The war had indeed gone far beyond mere matters of fighting. It had become an organized industry, a job of routine work to be filled day in, day out, *ohne Hast, ohne Rast.* This atmosphere had infected the front line. Men did not live as boldly as they had lived even at the end of 1916. In our young days, we had discouraged sporadic rifle fire at night. We had thought it a sign of nervousness. But with advancing years the precept had gone bad. The 1918 soldier preferred not to shoot, for fear, as he put it, of 'drawing fire'. Gwinnell at Campagne had been enthusiastic over the spotless barrels of his company's rifles. 'Perhaps,' answered Tebbutt Whitehead cynically, 'it's because they never fire them.' It was too true. Gwinnell remedied it by seeing that every man fired ten rounds a day.

The private soldier was not to be blamed. He had realized that with the almost complete dehumanizing of war, the matter of his individual efficiency was of the last importance. This mechanization had relieved him as much as it added to his dangers. He knew that if the guns failed he would be swept out of existence. He had become so steeped in the pickle of war that he could scarcely imagine another existence: the only change possible to him was 'casualty—g.s.w.' In evidence of this, one remarked that we no longer troubled to build the long communication trenches or breastworks of 1915 and 1916, but except within a few hundred yards of the line, moved freely in the open.

If the spirit of mechanism had affected the psychology of the fighting soldier, it had also affected that of the staff.

Officers of the higher formations no longer went to and fro about the battlefields. When the 2nd Worcestershires made their famous counter-attack at Gheluvelt on 31st October, 1914, 2nd Divisional Headquarters lay at Hooge Château, four thousand yards away. When we attacked at Gheluvelt in October, 1917, our Divisional H.Q. lay on the Scherpenberg, as the crow flies near ten miles away, and more by road. Had they been nearer, they would not have been more useful: once an attack was mounted, it was impossible to control it. Its fate rested on the skill with which it had been prepared; if the time-table went awry, there was no opportunity for sudden improvizations.

The weather cleared at the end of February as we went back to reserve near Café Belge. Spring started early. Under a fine warm sun we sat about on the doorsteps of the Nissen huts. Above our heads, an observation balloon, 'old cock and balls', swayed gently. An H.V. gun sniped at him from the distance; a cloud of brown smoke would suddenly appear in the air, followed by a scream and a detonation. If it was close, old cock and balls would climb a hundred feet higher until his pursuer had changed his elevation, then cannily descend again. Two hundred yards beyond the camp a 16-inch railway gun was towed backwards and forwards by its little engine. The enemy were always searching for it. Shells would come yelling down over our heads and fall about the Dickebusch Road. We would laugh heartily at the traffic scurrying away during these performances.

There were departures in these days. Jerome transferred to the R.F.C. At the same time an order came down that any infantry officer with two years or more service in France might be exchanged to England for six months. Vanneck went, I was aware that I could apply to go too. As I read the order I felt Smith's eye on me, and wondered if he would ask me if I would like to be transferred; because just then I had an overwhelming impulse to say out loud:

'I don't want to go to England at all.' By some route far too difficult to follow, I had unconsciously identified myself with the battalion. It had become my home and nothing short of its disbandment would induce me to leave it. A year earlier I should have thought myself a fool for this mysticism. Now I knew that I was right.

Or was I? In meditation since that time another question has been propounded. Was it not perhaps a subtler, even a vile, attraction? For long watching my colonel, I believe—I do not think falsely—that he enjoyed the war, even in its most terrifying aspects. The worst the trial to be faced the more perfect became the balance of his nervous system and the greater the increase of his physical and moral power. This quiet level-headed man was lifted to a higher plane, bewitched by apparitions. He seemed to be nourished by them, while to myself they brought only shrivelling fear.

And yet, in spite of it, there grew a compelling fascination. I do not think I exaggerate: for in that fascination lies War's power. Once you have lain in her arms you can admit no other mistress. You may loathe, you may execrate, but you cannot deny her. No lover can offer you defter caresses, more exquisite tortures, such breaking delights. No wine gives fiercer intoxication, no drug more vivid exaltation. Every writer of imagination who has set down in honesty his experience has confessed it. Even those who hate her most are prisoners to her spell. They rise from her embraces, pillaged, soiled, it may be ashamed; but they are still hers. 'J'avais beau me débarbouiller et me laver les mains en la quittant, son odeur restait en moi.'

* * *

Orders came for us to take over another sector. 'Not Tower Hamlets,' we exclaimed. Tower Hamlets in sooth. The sinister ridge held for those who recalled it in October a host of apprehensions. 'This bloody place will be the death of us,' I murmured to Smith. He smiled and quoted his favourite tale of the moment. 'We said, "Jump, Bill, we've got a blanket." And Bill jumped. We 'adn't got no blanket. Laugh! 'Aven't laughed so much since farver died.'

On the night before we went up, Marshall, one of the new entry, brewed a punch. Bacchus alone knows what went into it, all the flowers of Hymettus, all the grapes of the Aube, and other incomparable nectars. It was smooth, it was soft, it was golden. Three-cornered Sarah was cold tea in comparison. It would have carried peace and goodwill into the heart of Germany.

On 4th March we took over our old sector, and in addition an acre of shell holes north of the Menin Road. Our premonitions were almost immediately justified. There was some talk of a raid, a horrid word, now only mentioned as a calamity. George Knappett nosed about in shell holes and began to make plans. We did not know whether to be pleased or sorry when an ominous note cancelling all projects arrived in company with another more disturbing. The inevitable prisoner had given away that a strong attack was maturing from Polderhoek to Gheluvelt and would fall on us in a day or so. Our grins stiffened. Next day our guns fired three twenty-minutes' 'counter preparations' as the phrase of the day had it. To our ears, still echoing with the ruthless hurricane of the autumn, they seemed singularly thin. 'Wouldn't stop two mules and a limber,' grunted an old hand. These morning and evening commentaries on the situation had been uttered daily since we returned and we were fed up with them. That evening the warning message was reiterated. Our American doctor beamed all over at the sight of our serious faces. 'Waal, maybe I'll get some wo-ik instead of lancing these boys' boils. I tell you I'm tired of sitting on my butt getting calloused.'

Next morning broke brightly. The enemy started about 6.30 with field guns on the front line, sweeping back to the supports. About three hours later they warmed up and began to plug the whole ridge, including the support line and the line of battalion H.Q. about two hundred yards behind. They mixed heavier stuff with it, 5.9's which came whooping over our heads and luckily for us plunged over the edge of the bank into the Bassevillebeek. Wounded men began to drift back to the aid-post, and the doctor soon had his hands full. There was a pause about one o'clock. I suppose, like the Spartan soldiers, the Germans broke off for lunch. Half an hour later they were at it again. It was curiously unconcentrated shelling, seeming to sweep and search rather than to attack points which they knew and could see. The two front line companies reported that they were being knocked about but could see no signs of an attack preparing. All the same, the shelling was getting heavier, and as the sun began to fall, there came a definite impression that this was not a knockabout sketch but real business. The valley behind us and the long slope up to Tor Top was empty. The western sky above the ridge was glowing peace. Our guns were firing very rarely. An English biplane slowly cruised up and down the line behind our heads. Smith clambered on to the roof of the signal station and stood there looking anxiously eastward. The shelling had now become fiercer and fiercer, and, as it were at the crest of the wave, Smith nodded to me. The S.O.S. rocket went floating up. Fifteen seconds later there was a roar over our heads as of a flight of rocs, and a vast billow of smoke and flame broke along the German front. Our gunners had been standing-to for hours, waiting for the signal. When it came they put down the most devastating defensive barrage. It lasted for half an hour, a seething splashing turmoil. In the dusk we could see the violet flame of a 6-inch Stokes repeated time and time again as it twanged its bombs over. Before the noise died down the enemy had stopped shelling. Smith climbed from his watch-tower and held out his hands. They were cut and bleeding from six or seven tiny wounds, where pieces had grazed them. At the same moment a runner from No. 3, who were north of the road, shoved a scrap of paper into my hand. It was from a sergeant, asking for as many stretchers as possible since there were only a few men left to carry on. Two officers were dead and two wounded. Bower, the company commander, had been killed, and a newly-joined subaltern from a Highland regiment, who by some whim of circumstance had been sent to us kilts, bonnet and all. He was killed, his man said, shooting over the parapet, uttering wild furious cries. In all we had a hundred and forty-five killed and wounded. All the evening stretchers were coming down. Marshall, the concocter of the famous punch, was among them with a piece of shell in the knee. Said Toulson as he bound him up, 'I'm not going to send you down, Marshall, until you tell me how you make it.' 'Oh, doc,' groaned the victim, 'ask my batman: he knows.' 'And,' the doc said later, 'half an hour after I'd sent that boy down, his batman come too, wounded *and* unconscious. Oh boy, I could cry with mortification.'

It was never known for certain whether the enemy had tried to come over opposite the left company. Some said yes; some, no. Probably he had not. We were merely smothered while a more spectacular but less bloody encounter was taking place on our left, which did not end until dawn. But the loss of nearly a hundred and fifty officers and men gave us an inkling of what would happen if the now freely advertised Spring offensive should be rung up on our sector. The position was naked except for half a dozen small pill-boxes, and the way to it such that no supports could possibly reach it without the loss of half their strength. An afternoon later we buried our dead in a wide common trench at the edge of the ridge.

The pioneers sent up a huge wooden cross. Would this monument last until the ridge was free?

When, in a couple of days, we went back into support at Stirling Castle, we had another example of how nibby-gibby the position was. One fine night we were sitting in our pill-box singing, a habit we had acquired from our American, when a strange hubbub made itself felt. Going into the trench we found a gas shell shoot in full progress on the approaches. The front line was fed by two duck-board tracks on either side of us, which passed through Inverness Copse and Dumbarton Wood up to the edge of the plateau. Along both these tracks mustard-gas shells were being poured as fast as the enemy guns could loose them, as well as across the chord of the woods, and less heavily on our own trench. It was a true box barrage. The horizon was filled with the shimmer of gun-fire; the air echoed with the far-away beat of guns firing and with the eerie flight of the shells, which exploded with a faint plop. The air became impregnated with the savour of garlic. Every now and then the uncertain whistle peculiar to gas shells, coming close, made us duck below the parapet. The front line was not being troubled; but the performance was weird and disturbing. It might, we thought, be a rehearsal for the big show. After forty or fifty minutes it died away. Just at the end one shell fell a few yards from where we stood in the mouth of a little shelter, which housed our runners. Ten minutes later six blind, burnt, poisoned boys—'the best of our flights'—were being led away, among them Smith's own particular bodyguard, Hobbs, one of our few remaining originals. One died within the next few days, and none returned to us. On the next morning we investigated the result. The lines of the bombardment were clearly indicated by smashed duck-boards and yellow-stained shell holes. We could see quite plainly that the chances of any battalion reaching the front line with sufficient men to be of use were less than thin.

Though it is said that the High Command knew all about the German preparations, at least so far as regards the venue, we humble units were not in their confidence. Here in the north the necessity of alertness had been so constantly impressed on us that we heard with immense relief the news of the attack starting at the southern end of the line. The earliest messages were cheerful; and, knowing what it had cost us to drive our attack even the few miles outward from Ypres last autumn, we were inclined to believe the Germans would be held. We went into trenches on the night of the 21st, a night of shame for myself; for in a fit of hubris I had neglected to consult the map and led three companies to the wrong rendezvous for the Lewis-gun limbers. Blushing hotly, I had to amend my error by guiding a profane and sweating mob over half a mile of shell holes to the right place. I registered a mental oath of future discretion.

This last tour on Tower Hamlets was utterly peaceful. It was as if both sides, recognizing that the issue was being fought out elsewhere, had relaxed into oblivion of one another. There was little shelling, though the 6-inch Stokes artist claimed to have sunk a large German pill-box under the mud by bursting a shell on its roof. It was not until the morning of 23rd that we grasped how serious the situation was. Though the communiqués were still cheerful, the contrary evidence was overwhelming. Instead of the usual portmanteau of chits, ordinances, regulations, and what-not, from G.H.Q., Army, Corps, Division, Brigade, and all their attached echelons, there was nothing. The great idea, as the Poet Laureate has it, was dust. We sat in the March sunlight and wondered how soon we should be involved. It was German weather all right.

Two nights later, our old friends of the Rifle Brigade, or rather half a battalion of them, relieved us. The move was sudden, but not surprising. We were sped to a camp new to us, Manawatu, by Shrapnel Corner, facing the sullen ramparts of Ypres. Were these too going to be abandoned? By now the walls scarcely cared who occupied them.

The straits to which the army was reduced may be exemplified by the relief of the Rifle Brigade, who had taken over a two-battalion front, on the following night. The newcomers, so Nothard said, were a regiment of yeomanry and a battalion of cyclists. The only experience of the former had been grave-digging after Messines. 'They arrived—would you believe it—with two blankets per man, full kit, and spurs! They fell about, cursed and shouted until I thought the old Boche would wake up any minute. Then the yeoboy C.O. was affronted because the cyclist C.O., being the senior, had command. He thought the cavalry ought to take precedence. So he refused to share the dugout and sulked by himself in another pill-box. There was a runner perpetually going to and fro across the ten yards' interval with messages from one to the other. The push-bike merchant was only a little less at sea. He asked us if we were leaving our mess cook. When we looked surprised, he said he had always understood that cooks were trench stores. God knows what will happen to them.'

For twenty-four hours we stayed idle. Then at 8 p.m. on 26th, orders began to shoal. At 1 a.m. we were still packing, with an enemy H.V. gun firing woolly bears over the camp. They could be seen black against the night before the sound of the crash came. At eight in the morning we were mustered on the road to Vierstraat for a convoy of lorries. The day was fortunately thick. Otherwise we should not have escaped in silence. We passed our Divisional Headquarters and were enraptured to observe a Nissen hut on end. A shell in the night had burst under its edge and heaved it over. For hours we drove down unfamiliar tracks. Here and there we recognized villages of days to us long dead. That night we sheltered at Borre. On the next afternoon we marched over our shoulders to Caestre. Our orders were less spacious than usual; the next square only on the board was indicated, and no further, though we knew we were to entrain and guessed that our destination lay somewhere in the south. We halted at the roadside by the station with other battalions. Engines were busy and there was a great going and coming from the yard. Presently a motor-car swept out of the enclosure. As it reached us I recognized the pennon fluttering above the bonnet, caught a glimpse of a sad bearded face, and saluted. But the men lying against the bank did not move. Two days—three days—perhaps in a few hours if the Boche planes were lucky, they knew that many of them would have done with kings and all the futility of nationality. They watched the car disappear in the dust with indifferent eyes. Soon there were sharp orders ringing out, and we fell in. As we wheeled into the station, one of the 60th caught my arm. 'Did you see? Did you see?' he exclaimed furiously. 'He shook hands with the bloody R.T.O. And we . . . ' His anger choked him. 'It doesn't matter,' I returned. 'Nothing matters now.'

We clambered into the horse wagons. We had been warned that German planes had been raiding the line and so we perched men with Lewis guns in the look-out hutches at the end of the roofs. Someone drew attention to the last truck, which displayed a number of brand new shrapnel holes. 'They say he's plonking St. Pol hard. He put a big 'un into a train load of Aussies last night.'

Our truck was luxurious. It had a table and benches, and the floor was covered with comparatively clean straw. The night was cold and we lay snuggled closely against each other. Once when the train paused I slid back the door to a crack. There were flat meadows and a line of ungainly elms beyond. Overhead the stars glittered coldly. It was so quiet that a man might catch the sound of the firmament slowly wheeling. The peace of the countryside swam up and clouded round me. Whatever the next days might bring forth, the curse of the threatening Salient was lifted at last.

XVII

'BRUTUS. *Come, poor remains of friends, rest on this rock.*
CLITUS. *Statilius show'd the torch light, but, my lord,*
He came not back : he is or ta'en or slain.
BRUTUS. *Sit thee down, Clitus : slaying is the word.*
It is a deed in fashion.'

JULIUS CAESAR

IT was a whole new bright world into which we woke. Outside Mondicourt station, from which the R.T.O., fearful of bombs, hastily shooed us, there were trees in bud; there were clean fields; there were birds, fluttering and chirruping. The country through which we marched had been but lightly grazed. The dozen cool miles to Toutencourt seemed but a stride.

At Toutencourt we were rejoined for a few hours by our old R.S.M., Key. He was going home. But somehow, he had been held up at Boulogne on March 21st, and put in charge of a section of the rest camp. It was, I am sure, the first time in his life he had ever been excited; and the excitement of those queer days was still on him. 'You never saw such b——s,' he stammered. 'There'd be a notice put up in the morning that all men for the 3rd and 18th Divisions would parade at 12, and for the 36th and 56th at 5. When the time came, there wasn't a man of those divisions to be found. Oh no, they all belonged to the 37th and 47th. And next day when the parade was for the 37th and 47th, they all belonged to the 3rd and 18th. They tore the badges off their jackets and lay doggo.'

He went to England in a day or two; and in his place we secured the R.S.M. of the 20th, Armour, as fine a soldier as ever I have seen. A tall, lean, trim-waisted martial figure with a long Scots jaw and a fair moustache, he was always the cleanest thing in the battalion. Not only the cleanest, but the most efficient; for he knew everything about the army and the war that was worth knowing. He had been out since August, 1914, and had won the Military Cross at High Wood. He rarely smoked and never drank. He had a number of personal gods, in particular the 2nd Argyles, though he was from the Scottish Rifles himself. His account of that battalion at Loos was epic. 'Sirr,' he would say, 'you never saw men fight like it before, and you never will again. They went over like madmen, and after they were broken, men would come back to us—we had taken over their line—and say, "Ha'e ye a bomb, Jock?" and go in again. One private ran across No-Man's-Land with an apron full of bombs, drew the pin of one, slung the whole lot into the trench and jumped in on top of them. Another stopped to pick up a wounded officer. As he did so, he shook his fist at the enemy and a bullet came through his elbow. He brought his officer in, mortally wounded. He stood, with his own wound undressed, so that the dying man could grip his ankles as long as he was conscious. Then he went back to the German trenches with a pocket full of bombs, drawing the safety pins with his teeth and throwing with his unwounded arm, until he was killed.'

Toutencourt confirmed certain lurking intuitions that all was not as right as those gay communiqués would have us think. Offices and billets so hurriedly abandoned that no one had troubled to remove the signboards from the houses were a matter for humorous comment. Not so the swish of shells and solid crumps about three in the morning. I would not believe my ears until others mentioned the same phenomenon. Where was the line? On our last information, no nearer than Bapaume.

We had no time to inquire. Officers were summoned to a conference at Souastre. The name seemed of happy augury. We remembered it from 1915 as a rather grand village. Our transport had by miraculous forced marches caught us up. The ponies were fresh. Ginger, the pretty chestnut with no markings save the tiniest star, the protagonist of Leader's lapse two years before, had descended to me. As ever, she insisted on leading the cavalcade. As Gwinnell and I cantered across the meadows by Bus, we were astonished to see black earth being thrown skyward and to hear the crash of a 5.9. Melancholy men were digging trenches in an uninterested fashion.

At Souastre, we were told that in two nights' time we should take over a line, a rather vague line, sketchily indicated, near Bucquoy. Bucquoy, we recalled as a cluster of roofs and trees peering over the top of a ridge. Strange as it may seem, there was an atmosphere of buoyancy about the conference. The escape from Ypres had had a tonic effect. I even laughed at a sally of the Divisional Commander's and was rewarded by a good-humoured poke in the ribs. I felt like Cardinal Newman when he was kissed by Manning. It was the first time in many months that the Owner had deigned to recognize my existence.

While the hasty conference was in progress, the battalion was already moving. We found them in a large building called Rossignol Farm, by Coigneux. On our way, we crossed the first serious evidence of how badly hit the army was. It was a matter of atmosphere rather than obtruding fact. We had often seen roads packed with stationary transport interspersed with worn infantry: but at those times there had been an alertness and an order even in disorder. Now the drivers seemed listless, unwilling to help themselves, until shouted on by impatient officers and N.C.O.'s. The road was ankle deep in creamy March mud, through which laboured small infantry drafts led by worried subalterns. The privates were nearly all children, tired, hardly able to drag their laden shoulders after their aching legs. Here and there an exhausted boy trudged along with tears coursing down his face.

Rossignol Farm was a large empty barrack of a place on a hill-top. At orderly room that afternoon there appeared on the crime sheet the complete list of names of a new draft which had come in two days before. 'Eating iron rations without permission,' read the charge. Smith walked quickly down the rank. They were all boys, ignorant and frightened. He gave them a lecture. Sentence, 'Pay for loss of goods,' and that was all. Not quite; for the next morning one was found missing. A month later he was picked up by the military police twenty miles behind the line. It was, according to the manual, desertion in the face of the enemy: and yet—we had lost our rigour of 1915. The charge could not be slipped on one side. The F.G.C.M. took place. But somehow the prosecutor, Hart, now assistant adjutant, was nothing better than prisoner's friend. The sentence was trifling.

On the next afternoon we started to relieve a Yorkshire battalion. 'In front of Bucquoy,' was all the information we were given. Between Bayencourt and Funky Villas (we had already caught up with the old names) the sky soused us. Night was coming down as we plodded up the road into Gommecourt Wood. Looking up the valley, we pointed out old landmarks to each other, Hannescamps, the broken poteau, Monchy. Ahead lay La Brayelle Farm, Essarts ('Do you remember the pip-squeak battery?'), and that half-credited place where bands used to play, Bucquoy. The Lewis-gun limbers were emptied in the dark. We moved on stiffly across country and waited for an interminable period at the edge of a park of tall trees among which shells were falling. At last guides arrived. The companies dispersed into the murk. The guide for headquarters did not seem very confident, but we plunged trustfully on through misty obscurity. The dark mass over the skyline proved to be Bucquoy. Soon we were walking between abandoned but hardly damaged houses. We bade good-bye to Toulson at the door of a stately mansion with the roof in poor repair. Each minute was outraged by an explosion, followed by the clatter of tiles and rafters. We traversed a crossroad, the target. The overburdened men behind us lagged; but there was no bank to lie on. Another shell burst close by and our second-in-command stumbled and grunted. 'It's all right,' he gasped; 'got me in the knee, but nothing broken.' Without stopping we accepted his assurances. At the end of the village, we turned into a hollow road, whereupon our guide announced that he had lost his way. It did not look a happy place to linger in; the crump holes were far too fresh and too numerous. We plodded feverishly to and fro; the neighbourhood seemed absolutely deserted. A man was found—who knew nothing. We cast back, and quartered the ground, and after twenty minutes' random essaying tumbled on to the Koyli headquarters. While we waited for relief complete, these Koylis told us what they knew, and talked of their recent experiences. 'You can't trust anyone,' said the adjutant bitterly. 'Two days ago we were in a magnificent position, place we could have held until the end of the world. Then we suddenly found the companies coming back. Some blasted brass hat had come along and given the order to retire. By the time we had stopped the retreat the Boche had nipped into our old line and the brass hat had disappeared. So here we are in the blue again about a hundred times worse off. Well, it's yours for keeps now. Take my tip; if you see any brass hats knocking around, shoot 'em.'

They went away at last and I spent the rest of the night walking from one end of our extended line to the other. It was fine to be out on grass again. Every step was a delirious pleasure. The jump of turf under my feet was rapturous, a forgotten treasure to be snatched up again. Fitful shells, both English and German, seemed to add to my feeling of elation. I was only stopped walking into Germany by an alert post at a trench block. I came in after dawn and promptly fell asleep. When I woke, I was told that the protecting post had been attacked half an hour later and done in. It was only by the efforts of our gigantic bombing sergeant, Bowden, and a new officer named Davis, that the place had been recaptured. This affray cost No. 2 company fourteen men.

In daylight, the position proved to be much shakier than it had appeared by night. The trenches were cut deeply into chalk, an old German switch line running east and west, built, I suppose, in late 1916, and never occupied, with a few deep dugouts and good wire to the front. It had a fair command of the valley to the south, but not to the south-east or east. The battalion was strung out across the southern side of Bucquoy, extended over a mile of these trenches. P. E. Lewis's company, on the right, was divided from the other three by a wide plank road, supporting a light railway line which ran straight into the enemy's country. The other three companies, with battalion H.Q. in the middle, were triangled over the point of a hillock on the south-east corner of the village. No. 2 were pushed out beyond the main line, to hold the trench blocks facing east. The division on the left lay behind our flank and extended northwards. Diagrammatically the line was the bottom stroke of an up-ended letter T. In defiance of all the rules laid down by F.S.R. and other authorities that a salient should be held all round by one unit, the apex of this one was the dividing line between battalions, brigades, divisions and, for all I know, between corps. In the agitation of the retreat, the higher command appeared to have abandoned even the most rudimentary principles.

Nevertheless it soon became apparent that the enemy was as ignorant of our whereabouts as we of his. On our first two mornings, he bobbed up rabbitwise all over the valley. Many of our men who had not dared to show a head in the Ypres sector were leaning over the parapet, shooting at distant figures. Now and again a German field gun drove them down for a few minutes; but they were soon at it again. It was the first bit of shooting many of them had had, and a relief after the wearisome waiting and watching an uninhabited dead countryside. During the next nights, our patrols picked up a number of wanderers. Gwinnell and the unconquerable Crossley, exploring the light railway, ran into a couple who tried to bolt. Crossley shot one and Gwinnell brought off a perfect Twickenham ankle tackle. Two or three times lost ration parties were piloted in. 'Another little lot, sir,' a voice would shout down the dug-out stairs: 'ration party again. Number One says the coffee's all right but the soup's bad.' Some stained and uncouth men would stumble down the stairs and stand blinking in the candle-light. They rarely had a word of English or French, and after a brief examination by George Knappett would be sent off to where Silesian, Ukrainian or Polish could be understood.

The position, we found, could not be improved. We had not enough men to hold the line and find our own supports, but the brigadier did not move the support battalion any closer to us. The colonel shifted battalion headquarters into a little isolated orchard behind the right company, where the Germans had built two dugouts. Since our first morning the line had been peaceful, but there were a number of small disquieting symptoms. One evening, as we were looking southwards towards Puisieux, a crumpled village in the middle distance, we could see a number of men digging furiously on the skyline. Presently up the ridge road, perfectly silhouetted against the light, came a team of horses dragging a heavy howitzer. With the utmost sangfroid, the gun was unhooked and left standing on the skyline until the emplacement was ready. We pointed it out to our gunner liaison officer, who shrugged his shoulders and said that our divisional artillery could not reach the place. Heavies? He smiled. 'There aren't any heavies behind us. There's one battery of 60-pounders away on the right and that's all.' Again, one morning four Boche planes came calmly over. The few English machines beat it for home. I didn't blame them; they knew their own business and they probably were not fighting machines. The four Germans sailed up over Bucquoy, wing tip to wing tip. When they seemed to be nearly overhead, I caught the sun flash on four objects swinging down and away. A second later four bombs crashed into the village. Two or three times our line was registered very conscientiously with the assistance of an aeroplane. On the afternoon of April 4th the enemy suddenly set about two left companies with field guns and howitzers, and taking them in enfilade knocked their trenches about badly. At the end of two hours Gwinnell's three junior officers and nine men had been killed or wounded.

That afternoon we were warned that the brigade on our right would attack down the valley between Gommecourt and Hebuterne at 5.30 on the following morning. Our own business was to form the *claque* on the left flank and offer ourselves as a distraction to the now obviously massing German guns.

At 5.30 a.m., the curtain went up. The field-gun barrage —rather weak it seemed to our connoisseur ears—duly attracted the enemy. Large shells came tearing out of the mist hanging about the valley and burst over the ridge behind. After a chilly hour, we began to wake up to the fact that the shelling, instead of dying down in proper fashion, was actually thickening up. Soon the whole of our line and our little orchard were being rocked to and fro by violent explosions. This unpleasant retaliation for business that was being carried out a mile away was unusual and puzzling. It should have switched elsewhere; it went on. After two hours a message from Lewis told us that the valley was full of Boche and that an attack seemed probable. In ten minutes the Lewis guns were bickering all along our line. At the awkward open flank on the left, the enemy tried to rush the two trench blocks; and at the southern one he got in and drove the garrison a hundred yards up the trench. But once more Bowden, with Sykes, the company commander, bombed their way back, and the Boche bolted, leaving several dead, including an officer. By ten o'clock the battalion was contentedly shaking its ears.

It was just after all the companies had reported the enemy beaten off, that Smith, who had been nosing about in the fog, suddenly appeared. 'Do you know anything about the people on our left? Because I've just met a flock of them going back like smoke to Essarts. I tried to stop them, but they just shouted at me and went on. I rather think the Boche is through.'

'That means . . . they're right in behind us.'

'Yes. I'll go over to the headquarters on the left and see their C.O.' He hurried away. The shelling had started again, the mist seemed thicker, and we waited shivering in the dripping air. If the Boche had broken in on the other side of the salient, he would be coming through the orchards on our side of the village almost at once. There were very few men at headquarters, half a dozen signallers, a few batmen, a runner or two. We lined them up on the shallow road which ran up to the village. Then a man who was running across the front was shot at close range, and a German machine gun began to clatter close by. It was clear that if the left companies stayed any longer on their knoll beyond the village they would be completely cut off in the next half-hour. I scribbled a message warning them of the situation and telling them that if there were no longer any English troops on their left, they must withdraw westwards down the front line and take up a position on the road our headquarters was now holding. It was an unorthodox and dangerous manœuvre, but only thus could we span the base of the triangle of which one side had disappeared. The two boys with the message trotted off across the meadow. As I watched them, I wondered whether they would get through. The shells were light stuff, but there seemed to be plenty of them; and the wide plank road at the bottom of the village was a nasty place to cross. Then Smith reappeared. I told him what I had done and was grateful when he said, 'That's quite right. . . . They don't know anything about anything at that battalion headquarters,' he went on; 'they were either asleep or having breakfast. They don't know anything about their line. But they've got no battalion left. They didn't know until I told them that their front line's scuppered and the supports have bolted. I ran into Gibbons and told him to bring his carrying party down here. Get his men strung out up the road. There's a Stokes gun in the village that'll hold on for a bit.' As we learned later, the colonel of the battalion on the left attempted to recover his lost line by counter-attacking with his headquarters through the middle of the village. It was a forlorn hope. The little contingent was shot down before they knew what they were attacking.

Presently sections began to come back. 'You'd better shift headquarters over to that trench.' Smith nodded at a broken line about three hundred yards back. 'Come on.'

I freely confess I despaired as I trudged slowly with my haversacks over that heavy furlong and a half. Shells seemed to be falling all about us. Every second a new serpent of grey smoke stated out of the ground with a ringing clang. Things seemed to hurl themselves over one's shoulder and burst at one's feet. Pieces of steel hissed past and nose-caps slapped into the soil. I offered up thanksgiving in my mind that the ground was soft and the shells were half buried before they exploded. 'That's the place,' said Smith, pointing to a spot where a 4.2 had just burst. The orderlies and I slid into a narrow shaft. It had begun to rain.

In the meantime two of the companies had retired and were forming up on the line. Only No. 1 had not yet appeared. When Gwinnell received my message he had dashed over to No. 3 behind him and was assured by one of their officers who was pottering about by a derelict tank that they saw no reason to retire. No. 3 had a joint post with the next battalion in the lee of this tank. (This was actually about half a platoon of the battalion whose men Smith had seen going down the road to Essarts an hour earlier. It knew nothing of what was happening to its main body, any more than No. 3 did; neither that its front line had been overrun nor that its supports had already retired.) Gwinnell decided to stay where he was. As he and Crossley sprawled across the parapet, they presently saw a line of grey infantry moving through the wood behind them. 'Fritzes,' said Crossley. 'Prisoners going back,' answered Gwinnell. As more and more passed through the next battalion's line, he felt a spasm of uneasiness. After all, he had been warned by my message that the enemy were through behind our backs and he had stayed here for more than another hour. Once more he went over to No. 3 and was horrified to find their trenches empty. At the joint post by the tank there was no one. Finding their flank bare, they had retired without informing him. He ran back and gave the order to go back. The enemy had started shelling his line again. A fragment hit him in the shoulder. He found he could walk, but his voice had completely failed. He started to go back. While the company was retiring the Germans attacked again. A heavy shell blew in the entrance to the forward signal station, and a few men who were frantically trying to dig out their entombed friends, were surrounded and captured.

Meanwhile, weakening but conscious, Gwinnell was trying to direct his platoon's retirement. 'Only,' as he explained later, 'my voice wouldn't carry. When I shouted, "Pick up those drums," or, "Bring the water along," the stupid fellows looked at each other and asked "Wot's 'e say? Wot's 'e bloody saying?" ' He found himself alone in a small enclosure. A body of Germans pushed through the further hedge. 'Hands *oop*! Hands *oop*!' they called. Gwinnell flung himself through a thicket and managed to totter across the fields and up to the aid-post.

It was now two o'clock in the afternoon. Rain thinned to mist and then thickened back to rain. A new battalion from the division on our flank came up into the gap, which still existed on our left, and attempted a counter-attack. Two of our companies tried to conform, but the men were dead beat. The enemy, invisible in the orchards and houses, swept the open plateau with machine-gun fire. The counter-attack moved a few yards forward and faded away. Late that afternoon, our brigade sent up a company of Bedfords, who took over the left end of our line.

We stayed here for two days longer. It rained, and a damp fog hung over the tree-tops and hedges. There began the cold calculation of casualties; it reached nearly 250. A few we guessed to be prisoners, but very few. Among other things our ration dump had fallen into the enemy's hands; but by some unexplained stratagem Fairburn magicked a fresh supply. We had lost, too, a large number of Lewis-gun drums. Two abandoned tanks became an admirable ordnance stores.

On the seventh day, we were relieved and moved into dugouts half a mile back. We were worn and rather hopeless. A mocking chorus of gas shells added to our depression. We were a ragged band of scarecrows. We had not washed or shaved since we left Rossignol Farm. Our garments were plastered and stained with mud. Many had painful feet swollen by exposure to the chill mud. There were a few cases of trench foot, but the regulars who held the line on our right had over two hundred. 'They've sacked the colonel, the second-in-command, the adjutant, the R.S.M.; and the quartermaster's died of broken heart,' was the news John Marquard brought up with the rations.

High authority was demanding heads on chargers for the loss of the village. There were reports of a hot quarrel between the Owner and the commander of the division on the left, a saucy catchword artist. After mutual recrimination, the matter fizzled out. It had been a bad, muddled business without a single brightness to redeem it. We felt we had been badly let down, and the feeling was not even dissipated by the award of a D.S.O. to Smith.

On our ninth evening we went out of trenches into old gun-pits on the outskirts of Hebuterne. There were hot meals again and our mail came up. On that day, the Germans delivered their second stroke, in the north. Down here, there was an air of a return to 'normalcy'. Not quite perhaps. Baths were taken in a Fonquevillers beset by 5.9's: and the following night we were hurried back, this time into Gommecourt Park, a spiky knoll of hacked and haggard trees, of vast chalky craters and of a ramifying subterrane. The map showed a village, but that had long since disappeared. Our spirits were recovering. Daniels, our signal officer, unearthed a buried cable which ran into the front line, and bid fare to out-rage Homer in his exposition of this—to us tedious—theme. The doctor stuck his nose in the air, and crooned:

> '*There's a girl in the heart of Maryland*
> *With a heart that belongs to me;*'

breaking off to remark: 'Say, boys, when the old Boche got through the other afternoon, I began to wonder whether he'd shoot me for a spy. This funny old hat Gen'ral Pershing fitted us out in don't somehow look the real thing. . . . What I'd give to be home naow, riding down Charles Street Bully-vard, Baltimore, in an automobile with a pretty girl under my arm.' George Knappett conscientiously drew a map showing the exact locality where a German had been caught on the previous night. I stared unseeing at a pro-forma: my eyes were beginning to give way again. Round the corner, I could hear the batmen in husky argument.

' 'E's not a bad little chap,' said a voice.

'Little, all right,' replied my own batman Johns; 'why 'e don't come even as high as my Tich even.' (I mutely thanked him for the comparison.)

The voice of the mess cook took up the discourse.

'That there young Knappett, y'know, 'e's too regimental, making us all come up for the rum every night. Now young Brenchley, 'e knows 'ow to treat us. The other night, when the Sar'nt wants us all one by one, 'e says—didn't 'e, Johns?—"All right, sar'nt," 'e says; "I can trust the servants." See. Trusts us, 'e does. 'Member when we was on the Menin Road, old Nobby an' me was lyin' in a shell-'ole. 'E comes over the top. " 'Ow are yer gettin' on," 'e says; "would yer like a drop of rum?" Would we like a drop of rum! And 'e brings it over 'isself. O, 'e's my ideel of an orficer, 'e is.'

Time dripped away, and at last, relieved, we were marched back through familiar unchanged villages. The Bois de Warnimont, a long wood of beech trees, flaming in their spring foliage, sheltered us. Green light slanted down upon our tents. It was a trifle damp perhaps, but there were estaminets in Authie down the hill, and the divisional concert party had recovered some of their earlier fire. 'O-o-o, it's a lovely war,' appealed to our ironic mood.

My eyes were again streaming with tears. In desperation, I allowed myself to be evacuated, as the phrase runs, to C.C.S. at Frévent. The locum-tenens washed his hands of me. 'I can't help you. You'll have to go to the base.' The base, from all I had heard, was no place for me. I sneaked out, shot on to a passing lorry, and by perseverance made my way back to the Bois de Warnimont. Toulson made me a patch, which was changed from eye to eye, until after ten day's wretchedness, they dried up.

Our respite was short. In the last week of April we were moving into the line again. We sat in support in the Gommecourt Z and wondered at the courage of the troops who two years before had tried to cross the wide lawn between the lines, now as verdurous as the rectory cricket pitch, and storm through the thick girdle of wire to the intricate grid of trenches beyond.

XVIII

'that old common arbitrator, Time,
Will one day end it.'

TROILUS AND CRESSIDA

WE stayed for nearly a month in this neighbourhood, moving from Rettemoy Farm to Pigeon Wood, to Souastre and back again to the camouflaged trench—front, support, reserve, front. We had a friendly feeling for this part of the world, if one felt any friendliness at all left for France. We were the oldest inhabitants. Places we knew as distant Jerusalems were now revealed as merely other slums. Still we were not a little astonished to see how small the damage was which the artilleries of France and England, for all their high explosive, had inflicted on the groves and meadows in these parts. True, Rettemoy Farm was a ruddy ruin, patchwork over a fetid bed; but the stately elms still shaded a carriage drive, and at the same time sheltered us from the enemy's view, if not from his touch. Pigeon Wood, although frequently scented with chemical perfumes, was genuinely bosky; even blossoms dared to deck the shrubs, and a few bold starlings did their best to understudy the legendary pigeons. We found, too, the battery position from which the lightning had so frequently smitten us in the 'crool' winter of 1915 (all war winters, one recalls, were 'crool'). No wonder he had never been silenced. Six magnificent chambers with swing doors lay beneath a long mound of unspotted turf. Behind lay a trench covered with wire netting and disguised with leaves and bunches of grass. Below, at the foot of twenty-stepped shafts, timbered dug-outs stood off from a central corridor. Even in 1918 aeroplane photographs failed to reveal it. We offered our thanks to these admirable engineers for so secure a retreat, which now sheltered a battalion head-quarters and a support company. We lay behind the bank, divested of jackets, bathed in the glory of sunlight. The line could be surveyed from here, and at any unusual manifestation of war, a row of heads would pop over the edge to watch.

The battle had died down, but every now and then there was a harsh revival. One afternoon the upper air vibrated with the flight of shells and there was a great humming. It was the noise of a gas shoot on Fonquevillers. That night the roads were blocked with blinded men going back and ambulances. Perhaps it was in return for this atrocity that on another evening a 60-pounder battery did its best to overawe a group of German dugouts in a prehistoric wood, Le Bois des Rossignols. The battery was firing a compound known as Thermite. Smith and I watched shell after shell burst among the broken stumps at an unexampled speed. Sheets of fire, great Jovian thunderbolts, fifteen or twenty feet long, hurled down on their prey with an almost human decision and cruelty. Flames shot and rolled over the bristling hillock with ever-increasing frenzy, until for us it become too abominable to watch.

Even our reserve billets were not the peaceful sanctuary of former days. A long range, high-velocity gun exercised its humour upon Souastre with a diabolical uncertainty of time and object. It was shooting one day as I passed the entrance to the pioneers' shop. Corporal Tunnacliffe drew his section smartly to attention. An awkward angular man, Tunnacliffe, invariably sucking a straw, one of our originals in No. 1, whom it had been impossible to coerce until an outlet for his genius was found among the tools of his trade. Two hundred yards further down, I heard the crash and a cry. By the time I returned, another of the old crowd was being carried out.

About this time, there came a letter from Colonel

Ardagh. He was wounded once more and in a base hospital. He had been commanding a laundry-cum-brewery at Poperinghe. When the northern retreat started, he was ordered to evacuate his stronghold. This he had refused to do. Dismissing his workers, he had remained defiantly in position. No one had ever visited him, and rations had been hard to come by; but he and his batman clung on, regardless of shells and hunger. 'The great virtue of all this was that no one ever visited me, not a single Staff Officer.' Then one morning something came through the wall and staved in two of his ribs. But he hoped to be fit soon and most certainly was not going back to England. Months later a caller at the mess said: 'I saw your old colonel the other day. He was commanding a train and giving away clean clothes to the troops. Marvellous old man.' We echoed his approbation.

In May, with the unexpectedness with which all good gifts should occur, we were offered a holiday. Lorries met us in morning mist and carried us away to Louvencourt. Our rejoicings were cut short by peremptory orders to man the Army line a mile beyond the village. It was supposed to be a time test. We settled into a magnificently carved trench, indented with large square machine-gun emplacements, and sat there waiting. Presently a galaxy of red tabs fluttered across the field. The Corps Commander with a swollen staff passed slowly along our line, offering trifling criticism. On reaching No. 4 company, he was shocked to perceive a Lewis gun not resting in the emplacement, but half hidden in sprouting corn a dozen yards away. 'Why aren't you in the place built for you, my man?' asked Uncle Harper, delighted to have found something to talk about. The dark lance-corporal in charge of the gun looked up at the radiant figure above him. 'It's this way, you see, sir. That place is all very nice to look at, built by somebody up at Army, I shouldn't be surprised'—a wealth of contempt dwelled in the word 'Army'—'but no one oo's ever 'andled a Lewis gun 'ud go into a place like that. Now, in the line, we . . .' The General was defeated. He turned on his heel and abruptly left us. 'You know,' murmured an exquisite Staff Officer in the rear, 'he really ought not to talk to the Corps Commander like that.'

A week later we moved another mile back to Vauchelles, and here, Blake rejoined us as second-in-command. What was more, he arranged to bring over Jim Driscoll to fight an exhibition round with our young champion, Dale. The great boxer came, to my eyes an elderly man. But as soon as he stripped, we could see the lines of a master. Our hard-fighting boy, who had won the divisional welterweights, melted to a child in his hands. Wherever he led, the older man was not. Amidst roars of applause and laughter, Driscoll danced and buffooned about the ring, swirling round the amateur, the peer of Nijinski. Later, in the mess, he complained of the treatment accorded to the gymnasium instructors at the base, many of whom were as famous as himself. He told us that during the black days in March, they had been armed with rifles and ordered to foot-slog towards the line. As a result, half of them had broken down; pleurisy had been his share. We sympathized with him on his experience.

At Vauchelles, our Bedfordshire battalion was disbanded to make room for a battalion of territorials. With them they brought a strange assortment of vehicles, acquired during long months in France. By this date, there was not a unit in France which had not some addition to the authorized equipment of transport. The supplements to the paraphernalia of a battalion, water cans, pioneer stores, bomb buckets, rifle-grenade cups, had been numerous and heavy, but appeals for transport to carry these things had been rejected. We had in the end furnished ourselves with all kinds of tall country traps, small wagons, gigs, and what-nots. Their appearance had mightily distressed the divisional commander and he had forbidden their existence. In defiance of the order, for a time we had kept them. It was no unusual sight during a move to find some comical vehicle touring the backwaters in its efforts to escape the Owner's eye. Recently the order had been reaffirmed, and periodical raids were made on transport lines by the Q staff. However, the old soldier is not by such means circumvented. Mysterious visits would be paid by a man with a couple of mules to innocent ordnance workshops, to return with half a limber. A limber left momentarily by a driver from another division (always another division; to plunder one's own was not only unfriendly but too risky) would be found with the rear half missing. By ingenious artistry, the winnings were quickly disguised. As for animals—if a battalion transport could not 'find' a pair of mules, or a horse in France in 1918, it was too virginal to keep even what it had been born with. Occasionally, there was a detection. But no one could look at Marquard's candid face and believe him guilty of anything worse than giving shelter to a lost animal. Poor John, he loved his beasts and his men with a serious affection. When in this month Jude returned to us to take over the transport, John had to go back to a company. In signing the order, I had a premonition that I was writing my name at the foot of a friend's death-warrant.

About this time, we received a warning that we were to go further southwards to a place named Bougainville. We discovered it somewhere to the south-west of Amiens. The move was to be by bus. My affliction had beset me again. The patch roved from one eye to the other one and back again. I carved a box respirator in fragments to procure the goggles. Towards dark the brigade transport faded away in a column of dust. At a respectful distance behind crawled three strange vehicles from another age, two gigs and an ancient solid-wheeled tumbril beneath a cape-cart hood, from the shadow of which jutted a whip and a pipe. It was the territorials' spare transport.

Through the night lordly chars-à-bancs raced the infantry over white roads, churned to whirling clouds of dust. In the early morning, a motley band of figures, befloured in front from head to boot-tip, marched into billets. Bougainville was comparatively innocent of war. Estaminets had not yet been drunk to their last bottle and replenished with ersatz compounds. The four days here were in the nature of a beanfeast. It is regrettable to add that there were many lapses from grace. Ting, whom a long spell in the arid Salient had heaved to a corporalcy, retired once more to private life. There was a long and intricate detective romance in which the R.S.M. and the transport officer took the leading parts, concluding in the arrest of some forty innocents from the horse lines. The four days were sufficient to ensure a permanent breach between ourselves and our allies.

At the end of that time we were moved still further south. The transit to our new habitation was a small matter of perhaps a dozen miles. We would have marched it cheerfully; but our allies prayed to be allowed the courtesy of transporting us. We rose early and marched four miles in the opposite direction from that we should go. We then climbed on to a very large number of extravagantly rickety camions, and set off down the road for Amiens. There was a great show of marshalling and dragooning by a handsome officer in a furred pelisse, who spun to and fro in a midget car between and around our heavy lorries. At each mile we halted for four or five minutes to readjust the necessary twenty metres between the vehicles. In the suburbs of Amiens a halt more prolonged than the others enabled us to eat our sandwich ration. An hour wandered by, a second, even more heavy-footed. We heard that one lorry had broken down in an impassable defile, and until it was shifted we must wait.

The French M.T. officer shattered to and fro in his perambulator. He was raging to the point of tears, crying curses on those who had betrayed him in the eyes of *l'armée britannique*. He was pursued by cheers or cat-calls according to our individual sense of humour. It was almost nightfall before we climbed a long steep hill, crowned by a village, to be met by Freddy Hart, reporting really adequate billets, and the fact that the secret caravan, which had been seen slinking away some nights before, had got stuck between two lines of transport and guns in a neighbouring village and had there been surprised by the Divisional Commander. The echoes of this discovery rang for many days. Our duplicate numbers 7 and 8 wagons took to the woods.

A sedate village was Le Bosquel, looking down upon the enchanting valley of the Noye. We had been brought there because the French believed an attack on the Hangard–Montdidier line was imminent. For their reasons, we did not care very much. Here was a good, new, and unexplored territory. Our instructions to reconnoitre the Noye crossings were a pleasure to carry out. Everyone who could borrow a horse rode the river bank day after day.

We would ride down to where the abundant Noye moves richly through its marshes between aisles of poplar and birch. Turning Polly and Ginger loose into a field of clover—not for years had they enjoyed such luscious feeds—we would sit upon the bank, speculating on what the future held. I have seen the place many times since. As the train rushes towards Paris, ten minutes after you have left the spire of Amiens Cathedral cleaving the sky in one pure thrust, you will come to Ailly-sur-Noye, a plain white-stuccoed village. If you glance down into the valley below, you may between the poplars catch the ghosts of horses and of a group of English officers who watch the stream flow by with tired eyes.

The north of France is habited to war, and the French army keeps its habits ever present in the minds of *les civils*. There was no tenderness for the non-combatant section of the population. Ailly-sur-Noye and the other villages up and down the bank still sheltered a fraction of their inhabitants, though the support line ran just the other side of the river; and guns, ingeniously and expensively camouflaged, hid in fields where old men toiled. These fields were striated with wheel tracks and bridle paths cutting clean across standing corn and flowering clover. Such spoliation by ourselves, who often had the greatest difficulty in renting ground even for training, would have been followed by courts of inquiry and ended in heavy penalties. The French soldiers, too, seemed lighter-hearted than ours. The divisional signs on the camions were gaily decorative, though the framework was often so dilapidated that one wondered if they would bear another load. The woods were full of *chasseurs alpins*, living in holes cleverly hollowed beneath trees. The trunks were often decked with frivolous pictures. Smith as he cantered past smacked the portrait of a buxom Parisienne torn from *La Vie*, and was applauded with shouts of mirth and windings on a curved hunting horn.

Behind in Le Bosquel, our doctor was improving his French under the instruction of our hostess. 'My, she's a fine girl. No, I don't want to come riding, and I don't want any help. Just lemme go on learning French.'

It could not last. One morning we were sent six miles or so north to make room for the Foreign Legion. They arrived and in no way fell short of expectation. They were true desperadoes, bearded and lean, who sauntered in with their rifles slung across their backs, their hands in their pockets, and an impudence worthy of their reputation. We had great difficulty in uprooting the M.O. His last quarter of an hour was spent in walking savagely up and down the garden, repeating in a defiant voice: 'Je vous aime. . . . Say, come here, one of you boys, and tell the mam'zelle what I mean.'

We were split up, with a half battalion in Dury and the rest at Hébécourt. The doctor did his best to soothe his torn heart by teaching us baseball. He was in very low spirits. 'Oh, I'd like to be sitting at a ball game, with me little straw hat on the back of me head, me coat over me arm, and a bag of peanuts between me feet, whistling *Arabee*.'

The colonel made what he called liaison with the gunners, returning after midnight to sit on my bed and get me to decipher from his notebook exactly what he had backed his pony to do. '6 to 4, Polly contra mundum,' was one such entry. Sometimes our billets would be claimed by French gunner officers. A little whisky usually smoothed the way to a complete understanding. A vast defence scheme running to some twenty folios with appendices was concocted by myself against any emergency on any of the six divisional fronts on which we might be deployed. A few officers penetrated into Amiens and reported the city not worth a visit, being filled with lean cats and Australian deserters. From the two companies in Dury we received the most vivid reports. The place was a French corps headquarters, at which a terrific long range gun used to fire. The officers of the corps staff had apparently imported a bevy of guardian angels, who in the intervals of consoling the staff were not averse to accepting consolation from foreign settlers. Incidents after Crébillon fils took place in the dugouts whither the world retired when the big gun fired, or even when it did not. 'You've no idea what a long time it takes to brush this chalk off a black silk dress,' remarked one nineteen-year-old swashbuckler, and, cocking his hat to a still more desperate angle, swaggered off. 'You be careful,' I called after him; 'you'll be getting us turned off.'

He probably was not; for in a few days the French

decided that there would be no battle on this front. We marched reluctantly away, under a sullen sky, to Namps-au-Mont, and on the next day we entrained. It was the usual casual journey. We lingered for an hour at the edge of Amiens race-course and wondered if the Boche would repeat his efforts to knock out the grand stand during our engine's relapse. Another night and we were back in Souastre. It was the 24th June.

The next two months passed as May had. We took over the same group of sectors, Bucquoy right, centre, left, the same support points, and every twelfth day came back to Souastre. The same things occurred which had been happening for years. There was now no novelty in any phenomena. Selected points received their daily dozen from the enemy. Our artillery replied. The Germans sometimes tried to use our own shrapnel from captured 18-pounders on us, but they were sorry performers. The H.V. gun continued to shell Souastre. The horse-lines belonging to an unfortunate Hussar regiment behind were stampeded; the division profited by their misfortunes. The German planes came swinging over each night. Once they dropped a bomb on an orchard in Souastre. It was said to be bigger than anything we had ever seen. We strolled round after breakfast. The vast crater into which a cottage could be dropped surprised even us. 'Any casualties?' we asked. 'Four of my cooks,' said the Rifle Brigade quartermaster gruffly; 'I haven't found them yet. They're under the earth.' We shrugged our shoulders. 'Bad luck,' we said conventionally. Nothing was really bad luck, and death was mechanical. The war, so far as we were concerned, would go on without end. We only half believed in the Americans, much to Toulson's disgust; and our first specimen, a very young New Yorker, whose clumsiness was such that he could not be trusted to carry a revolver, confirmed our suspicions of their innocence. On the other hand, our next, a couple of sergeants, were real huskies, large square solid men from the Middle West who refused to be surprised at anything, and earned the approval of a cynical company commander.

But it looks as if we shall be here until the world collapses. For at long last the sappers are constructing deep dugouts on our front. 'G.H.Q. will hear of concrete in another year or two,' says Whitehead disgustedly.

How much longer will this go on, we asked in our hearts. Another year? another two years? Though we had survived the enemy's last forward move, were we ourselves strong enough to attack? Compared with even a year ago everyone was less eager. Compared with two years ago, the battalion was unrecognizable. We had reached the borders of *accedie*. We had drunk our fill of propaganda, and our stomachs rebelled from it. In this penny world, what hopes? There was a country called England somewhere. It had once possessed beauties, perhaps more beautiful in dreams than in reality. I put in for a month's special leave at the end of July on the grounds of three years' foreign service. It was granted from the 23rd August. The news of the attack in front of Amiens came, a surprising breeze in these doldrums. On the night of 19th August, we retired to the Z. 'Any news?' we asked the Middlesex, who relieved us. 'None,' they replied. My leave warrant felt very cosy in my pocket as we walked through Pigeon Wood. A runner was waiting at the Z with an enormous packet marked VERY SECRET. It contained instructions for an attack in two days' time, on the morning of the 21st. Not that so bald a statement does justice to the folios of instruction. Never before had we seen the preparations so carefully worked out to the smallest minutiae. Everything was here—if events followed the programme. It was a colossal show, in which we were only cast for a minor role, to support the Middlesex to the other side of Bucquoy. All the same, my leave warrant turned a trifle cold against my breast.

Through the next day I wrote savagely and stubbornly, marking sheets, marking maps, sending last-minute instructions. The typewriter of the faithful orderly room staff never stopped. Our old friend, Macdonald, commanding the 4.5 How battery, sat in our arbour and told stories. 'What's that decoration you wear?' I asked him. It was a flamboyant harmony of pink and green. 'L'ordre du Mérite Agricole,' he grinned. 'I got it at Bullecourt, for digging the regalia of the Mayor of Arras out of my gun-pits.' He winked and raised his glass. 'It's the best-deserved decoration in the army—barring present company. It's about all I'll get. I'm not very popular just now. The French Mission say I've been deliberately shooting at a crucifix. . . . Well, Smith, see you in the morning.'

We moved up after dusk, and as soon as we had crossed Pigeon Wood, we became aware that we were in the midst of an invisible army. We blundered into a gun with its team. All round us where that afternoon had beeen lawn, bare but for the intersecting trenches, now stood batteries in thick masses, almost wheel to wheel it seemed. A tank, then several more came nosing by. A column of infantry, with the emblems of another division, crossed our path. The company dugout in the front line, which was to be battalion H.Q. for this show, was surrounded by recumbent soldiers. All the space between the trenches was occupied. Shelling had died away almost to silence. By 4.40, when the light was beginning to filter through, there was a thick mist. Packs of men crouching in the grass could just be seen on their knees, ready to move. The hands crept over the watch face. 4.45. Now! Like the attack of the orchestra on the 3rd Brandenburg Concerto, the guns of the corps on the right started. A second later those on the left. Then our own let loose their flood of steel, poured it above our heads. A few lights flickered up; a few enemy guns dropped shells: but they were scarcely noticed. The companies moved forward. In an hour they were in the place we had evacuated on April 5th; and the infantry of the next division in support were puzzling their way through the mist into an unknown land. The battalion was recalled to assemble behind our old front line. As I went up the road, a wild shell fell fifty yards behind me. Gripping my leave warrant, I hurried on. Hallam and Ginger were standing at the crossroads. Freddy Hart was waiting to take over. I bade good-bye to Whitehead and Marquard, and trotted off. Miracles were already apparent. Here were heavies, rattling along behind tractors, A.S.C. wagons, a supply tank with tins of water, all passing forward. And above all, here was a light railway already magically repaired, with an engine panting past, where yesterday a man showed himself at his own risk.

I slept in Jude's tent on the edge of Fonquevillers. All through the night, shells came tearing down out of the distance, great big bad ones. As I trotted off next morning, something spurted out of the ground by the roadside with a strident clang. Ginger shied and set off towards railhead at a stretched gallop. I let her have her head.

XIX

'Un nuage passe,
Il fait noir comme en un four.
Un nuage passe,
Tiens! le petit jour!'
VERLAINE

THAT leave was different from the others. I spent it in Ireland. The month was an interlude wholly unconnected with the war—or rather with our war. Our war only showed itself in Col. Lynch uttering passionate and unavailing crusading speeches at the corner of Amiens Street to apathetic or jeering audiences; in the scarlet face of Sir John French, an overblown peony in the centre of a bouquet of feminine beauty; in the conversation of those cunning persons who knew just where a mountain of butter or a river of treacle might be discovered at normal prices; and in the inevitable Irish anecdote, which, thank God, finds no market across St. George's Channel. But the local war, the Irish war, could be felt gathering below the surface, waiting to erupt. In the cove below the house, rifles had been landed two years before, and in spite of the punishment for Easter Week, 1916, had not been forgotten. I was asked to wear uniform in the city, and to take no notice if I was spat at.

The quietness of the country, a quiet unbroken by restless gun-fire, unravished by the cobblestone-cracking lorry convoys, unperturbed by the beat and hum of aeroplane engines, gathered me in its bosom, rocking the mind to rest.

And there were all sorts of forgotten things in this Cockaigne, heather in bloom, a wall covered with figs and apricots; in the city, Monet and Manet in the dark little house in Harcourt Street; the conversation of the aged but virile provost, a child from a larger epoch, telling tales of his retorts to royalty, over a glass of real vintage port.

The battalion was in action three times that month. The daily communiqués were now giving the numbers of the divisions engaged, and each morning I snatched the paper to run my eye down the report and then turn automatically to the casualty lists; but these were always a month behind time. Whitehead scribbled me a letter. The battalion had done damned well at Achiet-le-Grand. Blake, who had commanded for this action, had been recommended for the D.S.O.; the writer said nothing of his own. But there had been a lot of casualties, well over 200, and John Marquard was dead, and MacCarthy. I laid down the letter. It was a lie, a lie, my mind protested again and again. Such protest was useless.

The sea at Folkestone prophesied a filthy crossing, and in a fit of abstraction I had allowed myself to be caught for boat's adjutant. My excuses that I should be incapable by sickness were brutally thrust aside with a 'So will everyone else be.' When the boat was started, a friend and I raided the bar; there was nothing left but half a bottle of brandy and half a bottle of gin. 'Purely medicinal,' said my friend. They proved so. While staff captains and bishops lined the rail, I watched them from the height of alcoholic contempt and talked to the sergeant-major of the boat, who seemed to be the only other unmoved person.

A prodigious and wearisome journey followed on the next day. We started at eight in the morning; by nightfall we had just reached Doullens. These journeys had ceased to be romantic. The whole countryside was soiled. The railway track was littered with bully-beef tins, bottles and broken biscuit. Darkness fell. As we climbed to Arras, the horizon produced its familiar display of gun flicker. At midnight we toiled into Achiet-le-Grand. The battalion was at Warlencourt-Eaucourt. I shivered out the darkness in an empty marquee, and with morning walked the five miles down to the camp. Once more there had been too many changes. The battalion had had two fights since Achiet. One of our baby officers, a child whom we old-young men had tried to protect by leaving out in every action and sending on all available courses, had been killed at Trescault. Another babe had gone home with both arms smashed. Another hundred and fifty men had been lost since Achiet. Our strength was being replenished by drafts, but drafts of the lowest category. 'Fourteen weeks' service,' said P. E. in a low voice. 'Never fired a rifle or thrown a bomb. The show the company did at Trescault was a nightmare. I hounded one lot up to the bomb blocks with an entrenching tool handle, and then the leading man slipped down a dugout shaft and I had to drive 'em up again. And they get the real men killed. My God, if they can't send out better than this we'd better call it a draw.'

There had been other departures. Our father confessor, the quartermaster, after four years' service with the battalion, had suddenly applied to go home. It was a blow. No one could adequately fill the gap left by his stalwart figure. And at the same time, Toulson had been recalled to the American Army. We missed his fresh transatlantic comments on our islander taboos. Graves, our new M.O., a skeleton of a man with a passion for playing the flute, entertained us with wild tales of fourteen months in the Struma Valley with an infantry brigade, of which the average age was fifty-one and which was forbidden to march more than eight miles a day. It was known as the Too-too-late or Win-the-war Brigade. I hope that some day its history will be written. Then, too, my batman had been wounded when the enemy suddenly blasted our advance echelon at Hermies.

Le temps s'en va, le temps s'en va, ma dame.
Las! le temps non, mais nous, nous en allons.

'Your first job,' said Smith, 'is to sit down and compose stories for decorations. Have a drink and let your imagination rip.' During the last twelve months, it had become obvious that the award of decorations was chiefly a matter of penmanship. A barren statement of facts was invariably passed over. As someone had said, scanning the plethoric list in Army Orders of ribbons given to the Australians: 'With so many heroes, I can't think why the war is still going on.' There had been a wry jest about one colonel in the division, whose recommendation for a D.S.O. had been so florid that Corps had sent back to say that the leader of this counter-attack must have the V.C. and asked for the necessary corroborative evidence of eye-witnesses; which had not been forthcoming. Caution, as well as imagination, was therefore desirable. One had no scruples about it. All the men in the line who were decorated had done deeds which in South Africa or on the Indian frontier would have seemed superhuman, but in France were a job of ordinary routine. What might have settled this invidious practice of writing up reports would have been an award such as the French gave, the Medaille Militaire or the Croix de Guerre, to a whole battalion, entitling the men to wear the *fourragère*, the knot and cordon round the shoulder in the ribbon's colour. Such not being our English habit I wrought and sweated over the bald narratives of heroism, turned in by unimaginative platoon commanders, supplying what I hoped was the necessary trickery of epithet and local colour to catch the eye of the A.G.'s branch.

It was the end of September, though by the rusty field you might tell nothing of the season. Here and there a leaf tumbled from a branch in which life had not quite died. The Butte de Warlencourt gleamed frostily down on our column as we marched out. There was already winter chill in the air. By now we knew we had the enemy weakening, though by no means overthrown. At a dinner given by Blake to celebrate his promotion to the command of our regular battalion, we had debated and concluded that with luck we might be facing the line of the Meuse before winter drew down. Another year at least we gave it, and agreed that not with our tired men would the Meuse be crossed.

Those last months hang cloudily in my mind. The richness of detail which make the early years vivid is lacking. Individuals have lost their sharp outline. Probably I was more fatigued than I knew. The next six weeks remain in my memory a mere set of disconnected pictures with periods of complete blankness. There are the names of places in the itinerary which summon up no more explicit detail than the corner of a shed and an icy wind. There is a hill-side of rank grass, a beard covering old deep scars. From its brow is a view of a distant green land beyond the Scheldt Canal with unfouled turf and bonny dark woods.

There follow three days of attack (8th, 9th, 10th October), and the sight of men walking and falling in alternate groups up a slope towards a line of wood and a barton called Hurtebise Farm, of a small party lying round a strong point while a tank crawls towards it. There is a memory of a group of us sitting back to back shivering and nodding with sleep at three o'clock in the morning, waiting for attack orders, in a shelter from which we have dragged three bodies in field grey. And of the next morning at Ligny, with the battalion silhouetted above a ridge and then dodging forward in a spatter of bullets across a patch of cabbage; of a line of railway being methodically blown into clouds of pink smoke, while the territorials who have passed through us, try to work their way forward against a sweeping flail of machine guns, invisible in the roofs of a distant town. A man of the support company in the dip of ground behind us has found a rickety chair. He sits on it proudly in the middle of a jesting platoon, until a Boche field gun suddenly drops a scurry of shells on the place. The party scatters laughing, while the buffoon hurries after them with the chair still clapped to him. There runs for a second the flash of a troop of cavalry, tearing up the road to Caudry, the horrid chuckle of firearms, the check, and the riderless horses galloping back. 'The bloody fools,' remarks the twenty-year-old veteran at my elbow. And there is a 'still' of the grey puzzled face of a boy, in the arms of two pals, who has been shot through the testicles, the scrotum swollen to the size of a polo ball. In the distance roll vast clouds of smoke from burning Cambrai.

There is Caudry, captured next morning, a gaunt town, pillaged so thoroughly that even the covers of the chairs have been ripped out. There are houses defiled by the retreating enemy. We wonder, having no knowledge of the agony of defeat, that such hatred should still exist, and that it should find expression in so childish an offence. 'Quaint old Boche,' says Tebbutt Whitehead. The clang of the shell, bursting terrifically by the goods yard offers an amendment to the epithet.

There are shabby days at the end of October, with night marches in sooty mist, with orders given in hurried voices in the dark against a frieze of humid ground-sheets and glimmering helmets, with the hubbub of wild shelling above the mutter of a river. One bright patch is a New Zealand headquarters, filled with quiet athletic men, who talk in serious confidence of a country which they will make the new England, the new Attica, while shells fall round the crazy house, hit the roof, and tumble some cheerful, swearing wounded out of the attics. That was the dawn of the attack on Ghissignies, when the companies with their right flank exposed worked their way two miles across country as bare as the Plain, forded a river, and wriggled in the teeth of machine gun fire on to a crossroads and into an orchard beyond the village. The platoon in the orchard was wiped out to a man by machine guns, but the rest held on to their objective for two days, deluged with gas shells, before they were relieved.

The cinematograph flicks past quickly. We had little understanding of the pictures. There was always the dreaded casualty list at the end of each block of days: twelve officers, one hundred and four N.C.O.'s and men; six and a hundred and two. We have sent back burial parties each time we have been relieved, to find our dead and to build the last dugouts for those who will never again feel rain or fear. Crossley is dead, almost the last of the first No. 1 company. P. E. is gone, so are both the Daniels, Dozy and Danny, all wounded. We are now only a shredded rag. The divisional commander inspects us. Very soberly he tells us that we are the making of our brigade. 'In the two years I have known you, you have never failed me or let me down.' As I glance at the rigid figures and stiff faces, I know it is no more than what is due to such a valour and endurance; but at the general's serious praise I have to blink to keep the tears back.

No; we did not perceive the significance of these flurried days. Smith went on leave. We sat in Beaurain and wondered how soon it would be before the H.V. gun, which pursued its occupation relentlessly by day and by night, would hit the barn in which the stub of a battalion—it was no more—was housed. Most of the shells fell in an orchard beside our cottage, and twice I fled from my tent in the small hours when the hedge thirty yards away was smashed. Then one morning our new brigadier blew in; the familiar word applies to his cheerful presence. 'Look here, you fellows.' He sat down and we listened to a quite incredible promise. 'The division will attack in three days' time, right into the Mormal Forest, and we are promised from above that it is the last attack we shall ever be asked to make.' We looked at him stupidly. He was quite serious. Then solemnly we all had a drink.

The preparations for this attack were voluminous. Even Keeble, our transport officer, was drawn away from crooning over a recent triumph. 'He came into my lines and asked if we'd seen or found a dark bay charger. I told him no. He went away quite happily, and there was the blasted nag being groomed before his eyes! . . . All right, you shall have the pack animals up in the front line.' The committee over the attack sat in our tiny room. We were the last battalion to go through, 'to the line of exploitation.' It was miles away, through enclosed country and forest, and all we had left was some two hundred and fifty soldiers. 'We'd better make it a two-company battalion and trust in God,' said Tebbutt, staring at a vast rhomboid of woodland on the map, a perfect tartan of rides. Crash! The H.C. fiend dropped one across the road. A small chunk slapped between our heads through the map. 'After that, I think we're safe,' said someone.

On the evening of 3rd November, the brigade gathered in the Ferme Bernier by Salesches. The other battalions were nearly as weak as ourselves. At 5.30 in the morning we were all awake and taking a stirrup cup of sherry with our tea. The guns had opened. By the time we moved off the barrage had thinned out to one round a gun a minute. We went through the line of batteries lying out in the open in field-day formation. Ghissignies was being visited by half a gale of shells and machine-gun bullets. One shell spread-eagled on the church roof like a cock-pheasant bustling into a spinney. Tiles were flying about and bits of brick. A few men were wounded as we came through and sheltered under a bank.

Presently we were moving over a broad smiling plain. On our left we could see through the poplars the rosy bastions of Le Quesnoy, the fortress which Vauban had beseeched Louvois to let him build for the sake of its beauty. A brigade of New Zealanders was now sitting round it like hungry dogs, waiting for its surrender. We laughed as two gunner officers were chased down the road by machine-gun bullets from its walls. A German gun suddenly went mad and fired wildly up and down the field on our line. In ten minutes we had plunged into orchards all golden in the November sunshine, and hedged fields.

We reached a farm, as huge as a convent, at the end of a wood. Outside, a small group of Germans were putting up a stout fight against a company of Blake's battalion and two of our platoons. Inside, the mess-cook was saying: 'Shall we be here long, sir? So as I could get you a bit of dinner.' Blake joined us in a cup of sherry. A gunner, muddy and cheerful, arrived out of nowhere. 'Anything I can do for you? I've got a couple of guns outside.' There was a stir at the gateway. Two teams of German battery horses, ridden by grave, plump children in steel helmets three heads too large for them, were being conducted into the yard by a grinning Fusilier. 'What'll you take for those?' exclaimed the gunner: 'I'll give you . . .' 'We want a limber,' I answered quickly. 'I'll give you a limber and two pairs of mules. Will that do? Done! Those are mine, sonny. Lead 'em back to C. 123, *and don't talk to anyone on the road*.' The German boys put their whips across their horses, and followed stolidly after their English guide.

The pocket of Germans had surrendered during the bidding, and we moved on into Jolimetz. The attack was a little behind time. Our two companies were invisible among the orchards. As we passed Blake at Jolimetz château a car with a staff officer from Army drove up. 'It *is* the end of the war,' said Whitehead.

We pushed on through hedges and over tiny streams. A few tired shells came very gently whimpering from far away. Across the orchards, we broke out on to a straight line of pavé at the edge of the forest. At each entrance to the wood lay in a puddle of blood a heap of carcases of horses with here and there the body of a driver, the teams which had vainly come up to recover the guns and been smashed by bombs from our aeroplanes. The wood was very silent. The last flush of November sunlight was fading rapidly. The thin platoons passed down the Laie de la Musique. Once there was a rattle of machine guns which abruptly stopped. An officer came limping back with a bullet wound in his calf. 'We got that team all right,' he said. The battalion on the right met our companies at a crossroad. It was now pitch dark. The New Zealanders had been held up, and there was no one on the left flank. It was decided to wait till morning. One platoon had disappeared. Patrols were thrown out northwards, and met nothing. The cookers and water carts came up. At 2 a.m. a patrol pushing forward discovered the missing platoon on the objective. The enemy had melted away in the darkness. Once we heard the irregular beat of a German aeroplane overhead. There were four stunning crashes. They were the last explosions we were to hear. At 5.30 next morning the 1st Norfolks passed through our line and went on towards the watery horizon.

That day we went back to Louvignies, whose roofs the war had only playfully cracked. It was cold; it was wet. The difficulties of supply had become almost paralysing. Food was scarce; and there were no amenities. We buried those who had died at Ghissignies. The faces of the section killed in the orchard had been mutilated by the enemy. The instrument, a knife lashed to a stick, was found beside a corpse, the eyes of which had been gouged out. A large draft joined us, boys, combed-out miners, and a few old soldiers. The news of the impending Armistice was accepted with a shrug.

On 11th November we marched back fifteen miles to Bethencourt. A blanket of fog covered the countryside. At eleven o'clock we slung on our packs and tramped on along the muddy pavé. The band played, but there was very little singing. 'Before a man comes to be wise, he is half dead with Catarrhes and aches, with sore eyes, and a worn-out body.' We were very old, very tired, and now very wise. We took over our billets and listlessly devoured a meal. In an effort to cure our apathy, the little American doctor from Vermont who had joined us a fortnight earlier broke his invincible teetotalism, drank half a bottle of whisky, and danced a cachucha. We looked at his antics with dull eyes and at last put him to bed.

XX

'All, all of a piece throughout:
Thy chace had a beast in view:—
Thy wars brought nothing about;—
Thy lovers were all untrue:—
'Tis well an old age is out,
And time to begin anew.'

DRYDEN

SINCE March 1st, we had lost over forty officers and well over a thousand men; but war had not quite let us go. An epidemic of influenza fell upon us. Half the transport men were down with it, and in a week we learned that death had overtaken our good Corporal Andrews and with him our young boxer, Dale. The pity of it was painful enough for laughter.

Three dreary weeks passed. Parades were a farce. No one believed he would ever be called on to handle a bomb or a Lewis gun again. There was nothing to do. Our minds and our hearts were empty. We pretended to be delicately shocked by the Armistice riots in London, 'the blasted civvies'. Our papers told us that the evangelists of the new world were stumping England with their holy doctrines of 'Hang the Kaiser', and 'Squeeze Germany until the pips squeak'. The voting papers which this honest ministry sent us arrived a week after the election had taken place. Perhaps the rest of the army were equally well served. I can conceive no other explanation of the return of the Coalition. In the meantime strenuous football was played, more to kill boredom than from pleasure in the game. Officers who had or could borrow a horse cantered about the empty downs. Money availed little those who had it; there was nothing to spend it on. A few wounded friends rejoined,

Gwinnell, Danny, Adler, and the Uncle, with the pierced elbow held painfully together by leather straps. Men began to ask unanswerable questions about demobilization.

At last it was given out that we were not going to Germany but to somewhere in Belgium. In preparation we moved, a two days' march, to a village beyond Le Quesnoy. Wargnies-le-Grand had known soldiers before; Froissart records its burning by the soldiers of Duke John of Normandy. The problem of tranquillizing six hundred men in whom only one desire flamed, to get home, was seriously taken in hand. Gwinnell and others began to initiate some into Rugby football. Uncle started to build a concert troupe. Some of us ran energetically across country. A brigade hare drive took place, over a triangle of tangled fields; '*Dress*: clean fatigue. *Weapons*: entrenching tool handles. . . . All prisoners and dead become the property of the slayer.' The higher command, at a loss, recommended education as a sedative. Here, too, under fierce protests we demobilized our first man, a miner with fourteen weeks' service. 'How the devil do you expect the men to behave when they see these brutes getting away?' I growled down the telephone at the staff captain.

At last the six days' march into Belgium began. The divisional commander offered a cup for the battalion which appeared the best and had the fewest men drop out. An elaborate ritual was laid down for this affair, with severe restrictions on the number to be employed on baggage guard. The offer pulled us together. The battalion marched like archangels. The thrill of marching had not perished. The column acquires a rhythm of its own, an intrinsic life, so that each man shares the emotions of the whole. We laugh at the same sights on the road; the same comments fly from mouth to mouth; we sing the same song; when the drums break into *Ragging thro' the rye*, our step automatically lightens.

Looking back at those firm ranks as they marched into billets, to the Fusiliers' march, I found that this body of men had become so much part of me that its disintegration would tear away something I cared for more dearly than I could have believed. I was it, and it was I.

My love is of a birth as rare
As 'tis for object strange and high:
It was begotten by Despair
Upon Impossibility.

On the fourth day we tramped steadily through pouring rain the eighteen miles from Maubeuge to Binche. One man fell out exhausted; and then, seeing a general approaching, flung himself in despair into the ranks of a field battery and clung to a gun. On the doors of our billet at Binche there hung a wooden shield with the Bavarian argent and azure chequers, a bow of crêpe knotted at the top, and the words, 'Deutschland Kaput', written in a wavering hand. On the next day, a morning of piercing wind, another game weakling was carried upright the last two miles into billets by determined companions. On the next afternoon, we reached the end of our journey, Ransart, a few miles north of Charleroi; and a day later we knew we had, by sheer effort of will, won the cup. It was five days to Christmas.

The festivity was prepared with a dreadful thoroughness. In previous years our opportunities had been slight. This was to be a true celebration. Uncle was busy rehearsing the concert party, and each evening laid our brains under contribution to provide lyrics to the tune of 'Really, now, would you believe it?' The quartermaster disclosed a cache of S.R.D. flagons, the spoil of heaven knows what raid or economies. On Christmas Day the headquarter company's dinner was a lavish affair, lasting, with some speeches, and much taking of wine, until late afternoon. Then Smith and I staggered out to pay our respects to the companies. Each provided us with some large and potent decoction in which to drink their healths, and each had subtly mixed their brewages of different ingredients. Night had fallen by the time we came to the stable where our ancient friends the transport, to our protesting horror, stood us each a half-bottle of champagne. As we reeled back brokenly to the concert-hall, we confided our forebodings to each other. We were not misled. Pandemonium was already awake, maddened by the popular air of *Poor old Mike.* Various parts of the pit broke out into rival choruses, to which discreet Belgian families, our guests, joined their own versions. The gallery teemed with cheering men. At the back lay a small bar where punch was being served. It became a matter of diplomacy for the colonel to attend. I lingered in the gallery for a short time. Our number with those topical and allusive verses was second on the programme. A roar of cheering greeted the appearance of Gwinnell and Adler on the platform. It was prolonged. It never stopped. The two gallant performers were visibly hard at work, but no voice could outroar that tempest. At last, they gave in, and joining hands, performed an elegant saraband before leaving the stage. In the bar, Smith was standing over a dixie of rum punch, a pint mug in his hand. Man after man came up, with a 'Good luck, sir,' 'Gawd bless yer, guv'nor'; and *with each he had a drink.* At a subsequent reckoning of this feat, we computed that in the course of two hours he must have swallowed fifty or sixty pints of the mixture. Friar John of the Funnels himself would have gaped at the spectacle. But even the most heroic prowess has its limits. At 9 p.m., the colonel was put to bed.

Notwithstanding, the flow of soul ran on until past midnight. I have a faint recollection of putting the Uncle under arrest, bursting into a flood of tears on his shoulder, and being led sobbing to bed by Gwinnell, who alone with the R.S.M. had preserved his virtue. We faced breakfast at 8.45, and refusing to flinch, swallowed it. But there was no orderly room. The bald eye of the R.S.M. regarded the world indulgently.

We were now implored to get on with education: but we possessed no teachers and our pupils shied away from learning for its own sake. The French classes lingered for a little, but as soon as a man found he had enough of 'the bat' to be able to tackle a girl on level terms, he preferred another teacher. Our one success was a major from the field ambulance, who translated to a round-eyed audience the doctrines of Dr Marie Stopes. A repetition of these lectures was requested several times.

In January we were in the flood of demobilization. A whole new technical language had to be mastered; we talked of pivotals, Watford details, and guarantee letter men. A hundred curious forms arrived from England and lists of unknown trades. 'Not a paddler, you ass, a puddler.' A recruiting poster for the regular army was displayed outside orderly room amidst derisive comments. Still, two of our six hundred did 're-engage'. One, a red-headed twinkling boy. 'D'you think I'll get to India, sir? I've dreamed to see that country.' Indeed, I hope he has, and is not disappointed. The other was one of our originals from my first platoon, a transport man. 'What do you want to stay on for, Hockley? You're married, got a family.' 'Well, sir, do you think there's anyone else in England, who'll keep my missus and kids *and* pay me a quid a week's pocket-money?' His vast mouth opened in a cavern of laughter. His logic was irresistible. He was re-engaged.

We opened an inquiry office in which Gwinnell and I sat each night from six to seven to answer pathetic inquiries. It was difficult to tell a man whom you had known for four years, that, since he had no job, there was no room for him in England, until wiser men had gone. 'First come, last served,' said one stalwart with the Military Medal; 'last time they get me to fight for 'em.' Ting was among the inquirers.

'Wot can I get out on, sir?' he asked Gwinnell.

'A guaranteed letter of employment, Ting. You might get it from the police.'

'Ho!' (rather doubtful) '. . . What abaht a one-man trade, sir?'

'What is it?'

'Noospapers. . . . Got a pitch outside British Museum Toob, sir. A friend of mine's been keeping it 'ot while I've been away.'

'I think you could get away on that. Get us a letter from the police.'

'Ho! . . .' Then desperately: 'Wot abaht long service, guv'nor?'

'That'll be all right, but it's the slowest of the lot, Ting.'

'Well, I think I'll wait. Thank yer, sir. Good-night.'

When this dialogue was repeated in the mess, Uncle shook his head. 'Same old game, same young beggars.' Then turning to two American M.O.'s who were lunching with us, remarked: 'You see; we're the salt of the earth; but we don't tell anyone about it.' Our guests looked at him with the blankness of incomprehension.

We were melting fast. In two months we should be down to cadre strength. We should be dispersed into an unfriendly world, Smith back at business, Whitehead sailing for Port Elizabeth, Gwinnell going east, Uncle in Chelsea. A commission for the employment of ex-service officers and men under the leadership of Sir Henry Lucy arrived at divisional headquarters. Smith, Blake and I went to hear what they were offering. I, alone of the three, needed advice and help. An elderly bilious person attended to my questions, after he had explained pathetically that this was the first holiday he had taken for four years. 'How old are you?' he asked. 'Twenty-eight! Oh, you're far too old. I'm sorry. I can do nothing. Good-morning.' Disconsolately, I rejoined Smith and Blake outside. 'My old sod,' said Blake harshly, 'told me that military distinction was a quite useless recommendation for civil life. Then I told him that I'd got a better job in London than he was ever likely to get; but that if he was going to hand out this kind of stuff to my subalterns, the sooner he cut his holiday short the better.'

We stopped in the market square. It was the day of condemnation for our horses. They were to be examined by the A.D.V.S., and those which he cast were to be sold to the Belgians. Knowing the manner in which the natives treat their animals, we were as angry at this as at every other scheme which a vile administration was putting into practice. Hallam met me with a gap-toothed grin more distended than ever. 'It's all right, sir. She's going home. Aren't you, my beauty?' Ginger took her congratulations coldly. She was quite aware of her value. Home too was the sentence for Polly and the quartermaster's Bob. Something had been saved.

Quartermasters' hair turned grey during these days. Each battalion was required to hand in the full equipment laid down, neither more nor less. And every battalion had in the past years jettisoned what it considered unnecessary and doubled its necessities. It came to a matter of bargaining. 'Who'll take two telescopes and twenty bomb buckets for half a limber and four bill-hooks?' asked A. 'I don't want telescopes; I'm two over establishment now. But I'll let you have a whole limber for eight Lewis-gun magazines and a couple of wire breakers,' B. would reply. A spare pair of mules lay on Keeble's conscience. He decided to lose them. They were ridden out six miles at midnight and left beyond a wood through which the abductors fled. At 5 a.m., they were braying outside the stables. The ruse was repeated. Back they came. In the end, the Babes in the Wood were surrendered to the Veterinary section as two strays.

The whole of our world was crumbling. Presently we

could not find a rugger fifteen; not even a soccer eleven. There were no drums to beat Retreat. Grooms, to mind the few horses we had left, became a problem, as did cooks, signallers, pioneers. Our civilization was being torn in pieces before our eyes. England was said to be a country fit only for profiteers to live in. ἔστι δε ὀυ πρὸς Λακεδαιμονίους ἡμῖν ὁ ἀγων. Many of us were growing bitter. We had no longer the desire to go back. It was an island we did not know. Isn't there a fairy tale about two countries held together by a hair, and when that broke, they fled apart? England had vanished over the horizon of the mind. I did not want to see it. In February, we were offered the opportunity of volunteering for the Army of Occupation. We debated the prospects. We were by now too fast wedged in our narrow life, and the country viewed from our rut was not propitious. Eight of us elected to go up. On 1st March, we shook hands with Smith, with Whitehead, with George Knappett, who was to take over from me, with R.S.M. Armour. They stood on the steps of the mess and grinned, English fashion. We grinned back. It was the end.

With two hundred unreleasable boys, we marched down to Charleroi and boarded the familiar horsetrucks. We journeyed all through that night, past Namur, Huy, Liège. I woke from a fogged sleep. The train was standing still. I drew back the door and peered out. There was a damp platform and the name HERBESTAHL, the frontier station of Germany. Beyond, a dark grey morning, windless with a hint of drizzle, colourless trees and hedges, and no sound but the steam from the engine. The train jerked into movement. We passed over into Germany. No trumpets sounded.